An Unlikely Prisoner

Sean Turnell is Honorary Professor of Economics at Macquarie University. In 2009 he published an influential book on Myanmar's financial system, *Fiery Dragons*, which made him an internationally recognised expert on the subject and one of Aung San Suu Kyi's most trusted advisers. He was arrested in Myanmar in 2021 following a military coup and imprisoned for 650 days.

Sean lives in Sydney with his wife, Ha Vu, who campaigned tirelessly for his release.

An Unlikely Prisoner

SEAN TURNELL

VIKING
an imprint of
PENGUIN BOOKS

VIKING

UK | USA | Canada | Ireland | Australia
India | New Zealand | South Africa | China

Viking is part of the Penguin Random House group of companies whose addresses can be found at global.penguinrandomhouse.com

First published by Viking in 2023

Copyright © Sean Turnell 2023

The moral right of the author has been asserted.

All rights reserved. No part of this publication may be reproduced, published, performed in public or communicated to the public in any form or by any means without prior written permission from Penguin Random House Australia Pty Ltd or its authorised licensees.

Every effort has been made to acknowledge and contact the copyright holders for permission to reproduce material contained in this book. Any copyright holders who have been inadvertently omitted from acknowledgements and credits should contact the publisher and omissions will be rectified in subsequent editions.

Excerpt from 'That Would Be Enough' (from *Hamilton*) on p. 117
Words and Music by Lin-Manuel Miranda © 2015 5000 Broadway Music (ASCAP)
All Rights Administered by WC Music Corp
All Rights Reserved
Used by Permission of Alfred Music

Text from *The Fellowship of the Ring* on p. 210 reprinted by permission of HarperCollins Publishers Ltd © 1954 J. R. R. Tolkien

Cover photography by Georgie Demertzis © Penguin Random House Australia Pty Ltd
Cover design by Christabella Designs © Penguin Random House Australia Pty Ltd
Typeset in 12/18 pt Adobe Caslon Pro by Midland Typesetters, Australia
Printed and bound in Australia by Griffin Press, an accredited
ISO AS/NZS 14001 Environmental Management Systems printer

 A catalogue record for this book is available from the National Library of Australia

ISBN 978 1 76134 292 9

penguin.com.au

We at Penguin Random House Australia acknowledge that Aboriginal and Torres Strait Islander peoples are the Traditional Custodians and the first storytellers of the lands on which we live and work. We honour Aboriginal and Torres Strait Islander peoples' continuous connection to Country, waters, skies and communities. We celebrate Aboriginal and Torres Strait Islander stories, traditions and living cultures; and we pay our respects to Elders past and present.

To my dear wife
Ha Vu
For everything

Contents

Author's Note   ix

Part 1 Coup, Captive and The Box
1   Coup and Captive   3
2   The Box   18

Part 2 From Gangbusters to Gulag
3   How Had It Come to This?   49

Part 3 Staying Sane in Insein
4   Crossing the Threshold   65
5   Friends, Saviours and the Other Side of the Bars   71
6   In the Cell, Food and Surviving Day to Day   77
7   Books and Bags   94
8   Making Contact   111
9   Prison Economics   119
10   Legal Follies   122

Part 4 Trials and Tribulations in Naypyitaw
11	Naypyitaw Nightmare	139
12	Government Behind the Wire	159
13	The BBC Wall Service	172
14	Show Trial	192
15	Judgement Day	213

Part 5 Insein, Free, Home
16	Back to Insein, Solitary and Death Row	223
17	Liberation, Homecoming and a Final Twist	244
18	The Junta Strikes Back	269

Some Final Thoughts and Acknowledgements	273
Notes	285

Author's Note

> We are vanquished, for a moment, by an unjust destiny. But the time will come, I feel sure, when our collaboration can again be made public, and again be free. Meanwhile, it is in these pages filled with your presence that, for my part, our joint work goes on.
>
> Marc Bloch

This is a story of suffering and redemption as it unfolded to a most unlikely prisoner. I was not quite the cliché of the bumbling academic before I was imprisoned in Yangon under Myanmar's military junta, but I fancy I wasn't far from it. There was, I understand, a near-uniform reaction from everyone who knew me, when they found out: 'Sean? No, no. There must be some mistake.'

I had been working from 2016 to 2021 as 'special economic consultant' to Myanmar's civilian and largely democratic government. It was a job that began in great hope, ripened in struggle and compromise, and ended in the catastrophe of a military coup. I was arrested and spent 650 days in some of Asia's most notorious jails before my dramatic release and jubilant return to Australia.

The redemptive aspect of this story is a testimony to how love, hope, compassion and fidelity can sometimes surmount even the most terrible things. This love – if I may group all of these virtues under this best of labels – came from my wife, Ha; our daughter, Phuong; my family; my friends; and countless people from all around the world who did not know me from the proverbial bar of soap. It kept me alive, and it ultimately set me free.

This book is my personal story, but in telling it I speak the story of others, too. So-called prisoner or hostage narratives do sometimes mention liberators and protectors, but if I have done what I set out to do in this book, my liberators and protectors will emerge as its heroes. As heroes, they appear in many shapes, turn up unexpectedly, and in the most unlikely and unlooked-for places.

Most of my heroes are named in this book. Some are not. Some live in these pages only under a pseudonym, which I am transparent about in every instance. But the issue highlights the deeper tragedy that flows beneath the events portrayed here, for the missing names and the aliases are all Burmese. This is not surprising. The people of Myanmar are the targets and victims of the military regime that rules over them. They are the people whose acts of compassion and simple decency bring forth terrible retribution. That they are the same people whose kindness at critical moments nevertheless kept me alive only underlines their courage. As I said in Yangon on the day following the coup – in what was probably an unwise and untimely

Facebook post – the people of Myanmar are the kindest and most courageous people I know. I am wiser now, I hope – but am pleased to reassert this judgement here, more certain than ever of its truth.

Part 1
Coup, Captive and The Box

1

Coup and Captive

Five days into the coup, they came for me.

Rising at 5 am, I checked my email as I usually did, and saw this newly arrived item in my inbox:

From: A Secret Friend
Date: 6 February 2021
To: Sean Turnell
Dear Sean,
You do not know me, but a friend of mine who works at your hotel has just told me that since 4.00 this morning military intelligence and police have taken over the hotel's security cameras. One of these is monitoring your door right now. You need to leave as soon as you can. Thank you for what you have done for our country. Please pray for us.

I had been expecting a message like this ever since the military coup in Myanmar the previous Monday, 1 February. Numerous government figures had been imprisoned, including the country's civilian leader, Daw Aung San Suu Kyi – always Daw Suu to me, 'Daw' being an honorific for older women and women of stature and 'U' the male equivalent. While I usually kept my public comments to a minimum, I could not remain completely silent. Not when I had fallen in love with Myanmar years earlier, cared about its prospects, then proceeded to invest nearly 30 years of my life in the place – including living there for most of the last five as Daw Suu's economic adviser. On the day of the coup, I had posted on Facebook a simple 'Myanmar will shine again, but for now I am heartbroken', with a backdrop of Yangon's iconic Shwedagon Pagoda. A day after, I thanked Facebook friends for their concerns for my safety, before writing that in Myanmar I had found the 'bravest, kindest people I know', who 'deserve so much better'. This one featured a photo of myself with Daw Suu. The photo had been taken in a peaceful moment at Sydney's Lowy Institute a few years earlier, but I felt our expressions of vague defiance seemed to match the new circumstances. The post 'went viral', the attention it drew no doubt helping to land me in hot water. My contacts in the UK, US and Australian embassies urged me to leave. There was, however, a hurdle: there were virtually no flights to be had. A small number of emergency charters had been scheduled, but these were already overbooked. I received a few vague promises that maybe one of these could be reopened for me. Nothing guaranteed. 'Yes, Professor Turnell,' said one airline representative, 'we understand you are a high-value target.'

*

Heeding the message of my Secret Friend, I swiftly packed my bag and phoned Andrea Faulkner, the Australian Ambassador, to inform her of my situation. Almost a year into the pandemic, Myanmar was experiencing a surge in COVID-19 cases and I had been quarantining at one of Yangon's nicer hotels since my return from a Christmas break in Sydney, so I set off to reception to check out. Frankly, I was not sure what I was doing beyond a fuzzy notion that before the soldiers and police got to me I might be spirited away to the Australian Embassy, where I could plan my subsequent escape.

On my way to reception, I made the first of a flurry of calls to my wife and fellow economist, Ha, in Sydney. 'Don't worry,' I told her. 'Chances are, the police are simply trying to give me a fright and hurry me on my way.' I thought to myself, though, that if frightening me was their intention, it was working.

The instant I entered the lobby, I could tell something was up. Shadowy figures lurked in odd corners and I felt a sense of menace – it had a different quality to the anxiety that had settled into my body since I'd received the message. Even so, I strode up to the check-out desk and drew out my credit card: emergency or not, the economist in me required the settlement of a debt. As I did this, the posse assembled behind me; then the goons crowded in on me from the sides. Next thing, a police officer planted himself in front of me. So close I could smell his aftershave, feel his breath, notice his starched uniform. He appeared to be the chief of the proceedings. Directing himself to the young woman at reception, he said in Burmese, 'Professor Turnell must take a seat.' They had, he explained, some questions. 'It might take a while.'

More skulkers emerged from the periphery. Within moments, the lobby was heaving with soldiers, armed police and plain-clothes types with serious expressions, dark glasses, big watches, and complicated phones. At least two dozen, I guessed.

All of this was already dramatic at this early-morning hour. But then the drama amped up. First with the arrival of Ambassador Faulkner – in the Embassy limo, and with its Australian flag flying on the bonnet. Second, via the BBC World Service – who telephoned me just as I was being escorted to one of the lobby's overstuffed armchairs. Could I speak, the producer of the *Newshour* program wanted to know. 'Most certainly,' I said. Somehow I managed to make the interview last nearly five minutes before an exasperated police officer snatched my phone away. Even this went live to air, however, and ensured – as I was to discover eventually – that for one brief shining moment, my arrest was the world's breaking-news story. Much later I would learn that this interrupted call – in which my voice gradually becomes more and more guarded – was to become a broadcast staple in reporting on me.

Back to the drama, and something of a stand-off developed. Andrea Faulkner was firm, insisting on proper process every step of the way – something that discombobulated my soon-to-be captors. Together we slowed the process down, parrying the questions of the Chief and others who chimed in with lots of our own about why I was being detained and under whose authority. They responded with furrowed brows and fraught phone calls to Naypyitaw, the country's capital. The impasse did allow for two good developments, though. First, my situation fast became news throughout the hotel, other hotels in Yangon, and then the rest of

Myanmar. In foreigner enclaves and among politically connected locals, it conveyed a valuable lesson: if Sean could be detained, so could anyone. I was deeply connected to all sorts of decision-makers, local as well as international. A trickle of departures began. Several I observed that very morning: guests threading their way uneasily through the lobby, some escorted by their embassy staff. Bound for Yangon airport, or perhaps to cars for the dash to the contested areas and the Thai border, I supposed. I had mixed feelings about this. I was pleased my predicament was helping others. On the other hand, I was the one without a seat in the lifeboat.

Minutes and then hours passed, and the struggle between Andrea and me on one side, and my expectant captors on the other, continued. The staff of the hotel kindly brought me sandwiches and – presumably having noted my terrible eating habits – French fries. But I had no appetite. Perhaps I should have made myself have more: how intensely I would come to crave these fried bits of potato.

An immigration official appeared and demanded I hand over my passport. I told him he should look inside at the official visa I had been given by the Government of Myanmar, granted for someone working alongside the country's key economic reformers. Of course, I understood that such approval from a government now largely in the cells was not much in the way of legal tender. But it was a bad moment, as anyone who has travelled will readily understand. Your passport is the one indispensable thing. Your talisman against threat. Your intersubjective validation of existence in the world of formal international process.

My phone, returned to me after the BBC imbroglio, was a source of constant sound – a symphony of pings from incoming messages. To some of these I was able to tap out a quick reply, noting the gravity of my situation while reassuring that, for now, I was physically okay at least. Ha was the major recipient of my texts and muted calls. I also spoke to my sister, Lisa Brandt, and my dad, Peter Turnell. They were worried but characteristically stalwart and ready to do whatever they could. Then my phone was taken away again, this time for good. I made a couple more calls to Ha via Andrea's phone, but soon I was banned from using this, too.

To Ha, one source of information about what was happening remained. My friend Jo Daniels, an Australian lawyer also assisting Myanmar in its reform efforts, had managed to slip into the lobby from her room upstairs. She kept up a text commentary to Ha until evacuated by some quick-acting friends from the US Embassy.

What took place next was something I had been fearing: the seizure of my computer, iPad and memory stick. I was not asked to hand them over; they were simply taken from me. When I started to object the Chief dismissed me mid-sentence: 'You will cooperate with us'. Since the coup I'd been diligently going through my devices, deleting material that I considered confidential to the government with whom I'd worked, and that I did not want to fall easily into the hands of these illegitimate and illegal usurpers. According to advice I'd obtained within hours of the coup, it was not really possible to eliminate documents on any electronic device, short of its complete physical destruction. It had been tough to absorb that information: the police, military intelligence (MI), and the thugs they worked for would use anything they could find against me. And what they couldn't find, they would make up. The seizure of my gear was a turning point in my mind. This, I knew, meant real peril.

Mostly, after that, I sat. With police officers sitting opposite and two others either side of Andrea and me, nothing but awkward small talk in broken English could really follow. Some dreadful banalities about the joys of Burmese cuisine, and why February was the ideal time to visit Myanmar. So cool and mild. More time passed, and with it went the morning and early afternoon. There was much shuffling about. At least half a dozen times I visited the bathroom. A police officer always came with me. I noticed among some of the police the embarrassed look of people who carry out orders that they know are wrong. Eventually, however, I noticed a change of tempo: the waiting was about to come to an end. The police announced that they would be taking me away for more questioning. This would be to Tamwe police station, only about a kilometre north-east of the hotel.

Before being moved I was asked to open my luggage and take out all my casual clothing, toiletries and other essentials. They were stuffed into my small wheely-bag – one of those aeroplane carry-on bags. I didn't think too much about this at the time, but in retrospect it was surely a sign that my detention in Myanmar was not going to be a brief one.

My feelings at this moment? Adrenaline-fuelled outrage and fear, coupled with an immense weariness and a sinking feeling that I was no longer in control of my fate. I tried to let none of this show, however: to make sure my hands didn't shake as I shoved my possessions into the wheely-bag.

Then a frightening realisation: I had nothing to read! Just about all of my reading material was in electronic form and inside the devices the police had confiscated. Even my emergency reserve physical book, a historical account of the Royal Navy in the Napoleonic era, was taken away. When I asked for this back I was told it was needed 'as evidence'. 'Evidence of what?' I asked. No reply. I was beyond the looking glass now.

At the last minute, Andrea grabbed a handful of newspapers on a stand in the hotel lobby and thrust them into my arms. Not all of them were recent, but it turned out that would matter little over the coming days. I would have been grateful for a cereal box to read. Stepping aside, Andrea told me the Embassy consular team would follow me to the police station. That I would not be alone.

A small crowd of police officers now surrounded me and gestured for me to move with them outside, where several police cars were waiting. I was escorted to an SUV of Chinese origin, all blue and white, with the truly surreal phrase, 'May I help you?' written on the side in English. The slogan had always struck me as ridiculous; now it seemed to mock me. Someone opened the back door, then one of the policemen shielded the top of my head – in that manner so familiar from TV cop shows – and I was bundled into the vehicle, wedged between two officers. They did not seem to be armed, but their toolbelts bulged with handcuffs, batons and other items of unknown – to me! – oppression. The SUV had an open back tray, on which two young police officers were perched. They were certainly armed. An automatic rifle each. Well-used, unmatched, and mean-looking armaments of unclear provenance but deadly purpose.

In a show of courage and compassion that is characteristic of the people of Myanmar, the hotel staff lined the driveway to wave goodbye, and to signal their discontent at what was happening. I waved back. A good many of them were in tears, I noticed. Some raised their hand in the three-finger salute from the *Hunger Games* movies – a gesture adopted by people all over Southeast Asia to express unhappiness with their rulers, and much used these days in Yangon.

For Ha back in Sydney, my silence was a giveaway.

Through that morning, we had been reassuring each other that I would not be taken into custody, that at worst I would be detained, but not for long . . . that I would be allowed to leave for the Embassy . . . I would be hurried to the airport. And, above all, 'It will be all right.'

Much whistling in the dark.

Then the silence. I did not return messages, did not talk. The analogue world proved once more it has a way of intervening in our digital order. But the silence was also eloquent in its way, since it told Ha I had been taken away.

What should she do now?

For the moment, practical things. Talking with my dad, and with Lisa. Contacting Macquarie University to try to ensure my emails were secure. The Department of Foreign Affairs (DFAT) in Canberra called: Kim Lamb and Greg Wilcox of the Consular Operations Section. They confirmed I had been taken away. No new information, nothing yet as to the 'where'.

*

The car journey to Tamwe was a short one, and although I saw protesters here and there, my faculties were too absorbed in apprehensive thought to notice much.

We arrived at the police station. A large rambling colonial-era building, it sat close behind a concrete wall in a small compound crowded in by trees. A big arched door at the front, a run-down lobby behind it, with offices running off either side. I could see cells down a dimly lit corridor. Very crowded cells. Many young people were in them, but all seemed to be in high spirits and completely uncowed by their surrounds. From what I could tell, most of the incarcerated were overwhelmingly ordinary Burmese citizens who had been arrested for protesting against the coup. They were armed with youth, the bravado that accompanies it, and that tremendous motivating spirit of being on the side of liberty and virtue.

From outside Tamwe police station came the sounds of a massive demonstration. Banging of drums as well as pots and pans, and a grand chorus of voices singing Myanmar's famous old protest songs. I knew all of these tunes from Burmese friends in Australia, from an era of activism that everyone thought and hoped had come and gone. As the protestors passed what they knew to be the police station, the volume dramatically increased.

Self-pityingly, I wondered whether they knew I was inside. It transpired later, when I met a few of these very same protestors in prison, that they did, and some of the shouted messages were indeed meant for me.

A consular officer from the Embassy arrived at the station soon after I got there and stayed with me for a while. I appreciated his presence. After ducking out briefly, he returned carrying a small roll-up mattress and a mosquito net. 'For you,' he said. The situation outside, he told me, was volatile. News of my capture was all over Yangon, and already banners bearing my Facebook photo with Daw Suu were being handed around.

In the prison office, meanwhile, all sorts of preliminaries were in play. Forms were filled out, photos taken, harassed-looking police officers marched in and out, all while a volley of agitated phone calls streamed in from what seemed to be higher authorities.

Eventually, this came to an end. It had grown dark outside. Curfew time was imminent. My consular officer departed, promising to be back at the police station the next morning.

What now for me? Well, it was time to be moved to a cell. Despite the overcrowding, one was cleared of other prisoners. In this, a pattern was set that would continue for the duration of my captivity in Myanmar. At all costs, the foreigner must not be allowed to contaminate the locals, enemies or not.

At this point too the police tried to take away my personal effects. My watch, given to me by Ha and Phuong at Christmas, my wallet. They wanted to take my wedding ring too. On this I stood my ground.

'No,' I told them. 'I made a promise to my wife never to remove this. You are not taking it.'

They were taken aback. A silence followed. The policeman in charge who had been the principal form-filler earlier shrugged.

'Okay,' he said, 'but they might take it later.' I flinched inside. Who might 'they' be?

The cell I was led to did not constitute any favour to me. It was, to put things simply and honestly, a space of such filth and decrepitude that I am reluctant to sully the pages of this book with too detailed a description of it. Primordial muck – that I suspect dated as far back as the inauguration of the building – had created a layer on which I was meant to place my mattress and to perch my mosquito net.

And then I spotted it. A rat. An enormous rat. Now, I do understand that people exaggerate the size of these creatures, and this had been an exhausting and taxing day. Nevertheless, I am certain this rat was as big as a cat. Moreover, it was unafraid. Bold even, as it sat gnawing on something unspeakable in an especially grotty corner of my cell.

I hate rats. It's a distaste I've always had, but that scene of the inhabitant of Room 101 in George Orwell's *1984* had sealed the deal. And here I was, it suddenly occurred to me. In Myanmar, the haunting location of Orwell's first brilliant novel, *Burmese Days*, and – according to most Myanmar people I know – all the rest of his novels, too.

Numbly, I settled myself as best I could. I prayed the rat would stay on his side of the bed.

Around midnight, guards banged on the door of my cell. They escorted me to an open-plan office where a whole bunch of police were bent over a desk, concentrating on an object in front of them. It was my computer! The police must have been having trouble gaining access to its files.

When I approached, the policeman who had been tapping away vacated his seat and thrust me into it.

'Password!' he barked.

My PC was open at my home screen; the lighthouse of Macquarie Uni's coat of arms was beaming at me. I hesitated.

To the best of my knowledge, I'd deleted every last link, message or file that was sensitive, and certainly all content that might land me – or those with whom I'd collaborated – in trouble. Nevertheless, I did not want Myanmar's now junta-aligned police – or anyone else – accessing stuff they had no right to. Freedom from unwarranted interference of the State, any State, was my deepest political principle, and not to be surrendered easily. Especially not to thugs like this.

'What do you want?' I asked. 'This is my private property, my private information, and you have no right to it. I am a professor of a university and I have material on my computer that is held by me in trust.' I'm not sure why I went down the professor route, but it seemed the most appropriate and perhaps least confronting avenue at that moment to make a point of resistance.

It didn't work. My antagonist was tired and under pressure, as it seemed were all the other police and hangers-on in the room.

'You must hand over your password. It is the law,' is what he came back with.

Again I hesitated, took the temperature of the room. With a gesture of resignation, I started typing a password. Hit enter. Wrong password. This was deliberate, of course, and the police around me made exasperated noises.

The officer in charge lost his temper.

'You foreigners, you think you can do what you like. But you are here. There is no-one to help you.' I let a silence linger. Then he said, 'If you do not give us the password now, you will never see your wife or family again.'

At this, I caved and typed in the right password. Up came a rush of familiar icons of a more pleasant past. The thugs were free to browse. I comforted myself with thoughts of my deletions, but I knew enough to worry.

Now the police were all smiles. 'You are fine. We will look after you. Do not worry.' My escorts led me back out.

Although the prisoners crammed into the other cells couldn't see me, when they realised someone was walking by they started singing out. Mostly words of encouragement, but they were curious, too. Who was I? How had I come to be there? Some knew immediately who I was, and I could hear the info being passed on cell by cell. Then the questions changed. How was *Amay* (mother) Suu? Had I seen her?

'Be quiet!' a guard shouted out.

We reached my cell, the gate closed, the bolts shot home.

'Go to sleep,' they said. Gruffly. I was nothing but trouble for them. Sleep, however, was elusive. Though bone weary, I was agitated beyond measure as I turned over in my mind about a million impressions, thoughts and feelings. Then there was the matter of my cellmate – the scuttling of which, in that rodent way, was enough to keep anyone awake.

In the end it didn't matter since, around 2 am, I was abruptly pulled out of my cell, put into a police minivan, and driven through Yangon's darkened and curfew-emptied streets. None of the police officers told me where I was going, but I knew Yangon well enough to realise we were headed north-west, towards the river and, tantalisingly, the airport. Ominously, Yangon's infamous Insein Prison was also in the city's north-west.

Surely not? Not yet!

Not for the moment – but my destination was somewhere at least as bad. As the van pulled up, I could see we were outside yet another colonial-era building. The sentry towers and bright lights of Insein were ahead, through the foggy dark, but this place was outside its walls. The sight of police cars parked around its enclosed grounds was an important clue: it was the headquarters of the Criminal Investigation Department (CID) of the Myanmar Police. It housed Police Special Branch as well. The first supposedly investigated major crimes; the brief of the second included the term 'national security'. *So*, I thought, *I am in the hands of both.*

A police orderly pulled me roughly out of the van and, hands on my shoulder and arm, started propelling me along. I reflected that this was the first time I had ever been physically manhandled in Myanmar. Or, indeed, anywhere. It was all a long way from my former life as a university professor – or as a trusted adviser to Myanmar's democratically elected leader.

I was steered through an old arched doorway into a large room and then into a shoebox of a room within it. *Surely they're not going to put me here*, I thought.

Then the door was locked behind me. I was alone in The Box.

2

The Box

For two months I was held in The Box.

It was about the size of a small shipping container – one of those 20-foot equivalent units – and had a concrete floor and faux wood-panelling walls. It was devoid of any furniture except for a steel chair bolted to the concrete floor in the centre of the room; there was scarcely enough room for anything else. To this chair were attached wrist and leg chains, and manacles. Though I was not immediately placed in the chair, the image was medieval. Patently designed to intimidate any poor wretch ending up here, its effect on me is hard to put into words.

No natural light could penetrate The Box – it was an isolated 'room within a room'. In addition to its single door, The Box had one small slit window, through which the police could view their captive inside. Light was supplied by three spotlights that were – deliberately – left on 24 hours a day.

A fan inset high in one of the walls distributed some air from outside, but at all times The Box was hot, stuffy and extraordinarily claustrophobic. Matters got even worse during Yangon's frequent electricity blackouts: there were usually four to five a day. The fan stopped, and The Box became insufferable. Matters got worse still, however, if the blackout lasted beyond a few minutes. A diesel generator would then kick in. This supplied The Box with light and air, but in a piece of fantastically poor design, the generator that served The Box was placed immediately below the air inlet for the fan. This meant that when the generator started up, The Box would fill with diesel fumes. I had to put my face close to the floor just to be able to breathe.

My captors controlled every aspect of my life. When I ate, when I slept, when I awoke, who I would talk to (no-one but them). I was not allowed outside, so I never felt the sun on my face. The only time I was allowed out of The Box was to go to the toilet – this entailed banging on the door and waiting to be escorted to the grossly unsanitary bathroom – plus once a day for a shower.

While I was given food in The Box, its nutritional value might be judged by the fact that I lost 10 kilos – nearly 20 per cent of my body weight – during that eight-week period. Going into The Box I was not overweight, but when I emerged from it, I was rake thin and gaunt looking. My cheeks were sunken, my skin rough and sallow and, to quote a fellow detainee, I looked as though I had 'just emerged from a concentration camp'. I was often sick – sometimes from the food, sometimes as a bodily response to ever-present anxiety. At the end of that period, my body was in a more-or-less permanent state of 'fight or flight'. To a certain extent it still is.

Getting to sleep in The Box was, at first, near impossible. The blackouts invariably took place during the day, when electricity demand was high, so the lights in The Box blazed serenely through the night. I had my mattress to sleep on, but a pillow brought – somehow – from the hotel was taken away. Stretching out my body was a constant challenge in that limited space because the immovable steel chair occupied most of it. The only option was to huddle around it, being careful not to become caught up in the chains that dangled from it. Their clanking was a monstrous sound that mocked any efforts to pretend to be somewhere else.

I was completely isolated in The Box and, for the first week or so, not even the Australian Embassy knew precisely where I was. Initial efforts by the Embassy to find out my location were rebuffed; then staff found themselves dealing with obfuscation and misdirection.

Meanwhile, I was given no details of any possible 'legal' action against me, or even the reasons for my detention. At no point did my captors and interrogators, who visited often, identify themselves – they didn't so much as reveal the branch of Myanmar's security organs to which they belonged, let alone their own names. My hunch was that they were a mix of CID and Special Branch police officers, but I was near certain MI people were among them, too. Whoever they were, from the outset it was obvious to me that all of this was little more than a military state–organised kidnapping: in other words, I was a hostage in a bigger play.

While in The Box, I soon became disorientated with respect to time. Without natural light, often it was hard to know whether it was day or night. All of this was exacerbated by the unpredictable habits of my interrogators, who could arrive at any hour and rouse me brusquely from what was already a poor sleep.

One way I learned to tell when it was night was by the sounds of Yangon. The banging of pots and pans in its evening protests expressed an almost joyous defiance. To my horror, this morphed into the sounds of gunshots and explosions: in this way I bore witness to the decision by the military to turn on the citizens it ostensibly had a duty to protect. After this, more harrowing still, came new sounds – the screams of fellow prisoners being tortured in rooms close enough for me to hear them.

It is no accident that I am exposed to this, I told myself.

All this was ahead of me on that first full day in The Box. Left alone to stew in my anxiety, with nothing to read, nothing to divert my mind, I calmed myself by doing what all sentient beings do when placed in confinement: I paced. Back and forth, around and around. Clockwise, anti-clockwise. Touch each wall. Count steps. Eight steps from one end of The Box to the other.

No-one came to see me. I continued to have no exact idea of where I was, who was holding me, what they wanted. No food, no water. The indications were not good as to how I might be treated, and how long all this might last.

My thoughts kept turning to my actions of the past week. Had I been too complacent? Had I acted quickly enough, desperately enough? Why didn't I give my computer and other devices to the Ambassador as I sat beside her in the hotel lobby? All these things stirred in my head: fodder variously for recrimination, self-justification, and ultimately, to a certain extent, understanding – accurate or otherwise – that there was next to nothing I could have done to avoid the fate bestowed on me.

Out of the blue came a bustle of activity: that first day at least, I knew it was evening when this happened. The (four!) bolts on the door were drawn back, unleashing a suite of sharp noises, and a uniformed policeman stepped in to hand me a bowl of instant noodles. A minute later, half a dozen people came through the door: more uniformed police, a young guy in a black *taikpon* and *longyi* (the former a collarless jacket worn in the way of a suit jacket, the latter the long wraparound sarong-like skirt worn by men in Myanmar), and a pair of MI and/or police Special Branch/CID officers dressed in casual Western clothes.

The MI/CID types took charge and began putting questions to me. Initially, their manner was relatively friendly. Then the questions started to get decidedly random and odd. Absurd, rapid-fire, barked out in loud voices, obviously designed to disorientate and intimidate me.

It turned out that the young guy in the *taikpon* and *longyi* was an interpreter. He seemed nice, sympathetic to me, and he reminded me of the young researchers I had worked with in the former government. My instincts on this were spot-on. 'My name is Police Captain Kyaw San Han,' he declared. Dropping the formal tone at a moment the interrogators seemed preoccupied, he went on to tell me he had been a student at Flinders University in Australia, a recipient of an Australian Award Scholarship, and had graduated in 2019. At the time of my arrest he'd been studying for a police exam, he told me, and had been suddenly called in to translate for me on this first night. He'd been shocked to see me.

Kyaw San Han had already been unusually frank, but as the interrogators left for a break he lingered enough to give some valuable advice: 'Keep your answers brief, *Saya* (Professor). Don't overcomplicate things. These guys don't know anything, but they'll get suspicious the more complex you make things. I understand that you are trying to make them understand, but don't. Keep things short and simple.' I heard him out, didn't push back, but I was not yet savvy enough to take it up fully. To my cost. In my defence, in this wilderness of mirrors that I had entered, I didn't yet understand that logic and reason were not my friends. At this point of low trust in everything around me, I did not know that in Kyaw San Han I had a genuine friend, brave and true.

This first interrogation round lasted until about midnight, by which time I was exhausted. The thin mattress was brought in and I was told to sleep.

Before leaving, my interrogators promised to come back. And they did, again and again over the weeks ahead. On and off, in a totally arbitrary fashion; arriving in the middle of the night was a favourite tactic.

After a few days my interpreter was changed. No longer Kyaw San Han, but a tall and overweight police officer who told me he had learned English in Singapore. At first he did not even pretend to be friendly, renewing the threat made to me in Tamwe police station that, 'Sean, only through your full cooperation with us will you be able to see your wife and family again.' Because of his mixed role as interrogator and interpreter I called him, in my own mind at least, the 'Terroter'.

In every interrogation, I was seated in the steel chair with its chains and manacles. For some I was chained up; other times they did not bother. There was no discernible pattern to this; all seemed to depend upon the whimsy of whichever officer was taking the lead on any given occasion.

Always there were at least two inquisitors in these sessions, including the Terroter. They would sit at a folding table that they brought in. One would take notes; the other would intermittently get up and move around behind me. I wouldn't be able to see this roaming inquisitor, especially if I was chained up, but I could sense him. It was all about intimidation, keeping me off balance.

If present, the third interrogator only occasionally chipped in. Sometimes he also took notes or spoke into a phone. Otherwise he simply wandered around, eerily echoing my own pacing around The Box when they weren't there. That third interrogator was often a small, compact guy who wore a leather jacket and carried multiple mobile phones – never fewer than three. Unimaginatively, I assigned him the label 'Leather Jacket'.

Over time, my interrogators honed their questions to try to get me to implicate Daw Suu or other Myanmar colleagues. To make it seem as if Daw Suu and the others had provided me with confidential information inappropriately, even had been acting under my (foreign) influence. Wise to this, I steered clear of what were their fairly obvious verbal traps. What did surprise me was the ignorance of my captors and the extent of their xenophobia. For instance, they brought up the International Monetary Fund (IMF): it was controlled by the well-known American financier George Soros, they declared – and I had been collaborating with the IMF to 'take over Myanmar'. I pushed back on this and, adopting my idea of a patient yet professorial tone, went on to talk about the circumstances that led to the creation of the IMF and the World Bank at Bretton Woods in 1944 – a subject that had been at the centre of my PhD, written a hundred years ago. In short, I let my ego control my response – but I should have saved my breath because nothing I said appeared to have the slightest bit of impact on them, especially Leather Jacket. Even though the sharpest questions and comments came from him, so did the most closed-minded observations about the world outside Myanmar. My sense was that he had been dosing up on the Kool Aid of the junta's message since long, long ago. It seemed to have excised his ability to have an exchange of ideas.

In any case, my answers did little to stop the lengthy monologues that my interrogators routinely indulged in. And they broadened their range of topics, treating me to soliloquies about Israel, the World Bank, the United Nations, the International Criminal Court, the vices of global capitalism, and the enemies of Myanmar everywhere. George Soros was a particular obsession, though. 'You know George Soros, you have met George Soros.' Given that they could easily google this, and I knew there were pictures online, I had no choice but to confirm what they wanted to hear. 'Yes, I know Mr Soros. I even went to his wedding. But I am not here working for Mr Soros.'

At every opportunity, I was anxious to stress my long acquaintance with Myanmar, my prominent role as a historian of the country, and the work I had done with Myanmar colleagues to help the country reintegrate into the world. I told them I could get the Embassy to give them a copy of my book on Myanmar's monetary history.

Of course, I knew that they knew who I was and I knew, too, that in much of my writings – easily accessible online – I had been especially blunt with respect to the military's awful record of ruling Myanmar. Past military regimes in Myanmar had done terrible damage to the country, and their economic record was almost unmatched anywhere for its incompetence, corruption and venality. My academic work down the years had fleshed that out in considerable detail: none of this was a secret.

My heart sank when my interrogators told me they were using Russian software to access the hard drive of my computer, even though I had expected they would do something like this. As I mentioned, it wasn't that I had anything nefarious to hide, but I knew I had material highly critical of the people my captors in The Box were now working for. One of the documents taken off my computer and presented to me now by Leather Jacket, for instance, was a memorandum I wrote for Daw Suu in 2019 on ways we could use our knowledge of Myanmar's financial system to sanction members of Myanmar's military who had engaged in genocidal actions against Rohingya in Rakhine State. I had placed a 'Confidential' watermark on this memo. It stood out, and so caught the eye of Leather Jacket.

'How did you get this?' he demanded. I looked at him, and realised that he had not noticed my name on it as author. Nor, I fancied, had he or the Terroter read it.

'I wrote it,' I replied.

He was only momentarily fazed by this. Leaning in towards me, he shouted, 'It doesn't matter! You shouldn't have had it, and you shouldn't have read it.'

Of course, I also had a fear that my captors might 'plant' incriminating documents and other things on my devices. I was not dealing with people wedded to the rule of impersonal law, proper procedures, or the rights of the individual. When I asked Leather Jacket on what legal basis I was detained and demanded to see a lawyer, I got nowhere. 'No lawyers for you,' was his only reply.

Whether it was some kind of 'good cop, bad cop' strategy, who could say, but the Terroter suddenly became friendly to me. Attempting to reassure, he said: 'Don't worry, Sean. This will last for a few weeks. You're not the target of our investigation. Once we're finished, you'll be released in a month or two.' At that stage, 'a month or two' sounded like a long time – way too long – and I despaired.

The Terroter started to disclose things of a personal nature to me, telling me about the stresses of his job, the long work hours, and his kidney complaints. As I grew to know the man, I developed some empathy for him. I must confess that I also grew to loathe him. Probably unfairly, I thought his education and exposure to the world made him more knowingly complicit in the actions – including this very interrogation of me – of this illegal and brutal regime he served.

Psychological maltreatment and poor conditions were the principal methods exerted by my interrogators, but every now and then they would resort to physical abuse too. It was nothing compared to that routinely dished out to my Myanmar friends, but it was shocking and terrible to me. Mostly it came in isolated moments, but two incidents stood out.

One was an open-palm slap to the side of my head – after I truthfully answered a question on the economic record of past military regimes. The blow was delivered by one of the younger, unidentified officers, whom I took to be military intelligence (MI). It was not delivered with force, but it created a percussion that hurt my ear and caused a wave of dizziness and a feeling that I was going to fall over. Luckily, perhaps, I happened to be chained to the metal chair that day.

On another occasion when I was being questioned in the chair, an interrogator – likewise MI, I presumed – walked around behind me. I sensed him come close, and then felt a searing heat at the back of my neck. I flinched and tried to look around. The interrogator seated before me put his hand up in a gesture that ordered his roaming colleague to stop. I heard the clicking-off of a cigarette lighter, and as he came back into view in front of me, saw him push a lighter into his pocket. After the interrogation I passed my fingers through the hair at the back of my neck where he had held the flame: it was singed.

In detention odd things would come to mind: certain details would matter to me that I would turn over and analyse, dwell on for swathes of time. For instance, I drew tremendous comfort from the fact that I had been arrested *after* all of my Myanmar colleagues. Why? Well, simply because it allowed no suspicion to fall on me as being an instigator of others' arrests. As someone who 'gave people up'. When you have lost all other status, or anything really to maintain self-esteem, the respect of fellow inmates and allies was everything.

Unbidden thoughts and mind-numbing boredom were problems that I applied myself to solving. I had few ways to divert my mind from the horror around me. All my reading material had been taken away with my electronic devices at the time of my arrest. The newspapers Andrea had grabbed for me that day, I now knew off by heart, and I despaired of reading them again.

Perhaps they'd let me have my Royal Navy book, I thought. It was the one physical piece of English literature that had been in my possession. My captors were bound to have stored all my things nearby, so it had to be somewhere within my physical proximity. When I put in a request to have it, alas, back came the objection that it was safely secured as evidence of my crimes. I could not resist asking my Terroter whether the junta still feared the return of perfidious *Albion* sailing up the Yangon River. Or, perhaps, as noted men of letters, Min Aung Hlaing and his pals simply disapproved of my taste in sensationalist historical literature. That earned me a dirty look from both Leather Jacket and the Terroter.

In place of the external psychological comfort of reading, I came to invent my own diversions. Most basic of all was simply to pace up and down the cell – much in the way I had done on that very first day in The Box, but now more systematically. It was oddly comforting when combined with counting. Given that it took eight steps to walk from one end of The Box to the other, making 1250 crossings of my cell gave me my 10,000-step healthy daily step count. If I did 1500 laps – well, clearly then I was on my way to self-improvement.

As near featureless as The Box was, I found in it various imperfections, chips and scratches in its walls and floor and these became prompts for thoughts and stories in which I could seek refuge. From red, black and white paint splashes on the concrete floor, for instance, I conjured the image of a Manchester United player kicking a goal. From another set of scratches I visualised a Dr Seuss character. I could see no green eggs and ham, though, Sean I am.

To try and stay sharp and keep random panic at bay, I played various memory games. Most useful were efforts to come up with all 50 US states (I got them all out after about a dozen goes – Idaho was the last one to come to mind!), US presidents in chronological order (for a long time I got stuck, as one does, at James K. Polk), and Australian prime ministers (I got all of them!). As well, I reflected a good deal about what we had been trying to do in Myanmar. I started composing sentences for this very book: in so many ways, it is the one positive product of The Box!

In spite of all of this, however, suicidal thoughts were with me every day. I'm not sure how close I came to enacting any, since The Box provided nothing practical to assist me. Putting it bluntly, there was nothing upon which I could cut myself, and nothing that would support my weight in order to hang myself. I pondered 'suicide by police' – provoking my captors enough that they would shoot me. Even this option I rejected – after concluding that I would only end up getting a beating or being humiliated in some way. They held all the cards, and I was completely vulnerable to their whim and caprice. 'To be or not to be?' was not a question I could answer.

After a while, I focused on simply enduring. As well as the games, the pacing and counting, I drew upon my narrative memory. Of good times past, but anything really. Before my detention I'd had concerns about what seemed to be my increasingly poor memory and, I guess like most 57-year-olds, had begun to worry about early-onset dementia or worse. But as I started the process of recall, I became astonished at how much I'd managed to store in my mental attic and how much became accessible. Like most crowded attics, it was largely rubbish, but even the trash was a diversion from the terrors of my situation.

This will horrify any reader who has ever fought to ward off slumber during university lectures, but I even tried to recall the classes on economics I used to deliver at Macquarie. Further, I found myself deriving the income expenditure model, turning it into IS–LM (investment-saving and liquidity preference–money supply), and then into an Aggregate Demand/Aggregate Supply framework. Too much? I promise it's the last time I'll mention it.

In The Box, I was desperately lonely but I also craved being left alone. Nothing was more jolting to my psyche than the sound of footsteps outside and those bolts on the door being drawn back. Solitude, routine were comforts.

Occasionally, I would hear a TV in the police officers' mess room that was adjacent to The Box. Apart from action movies of various types and origins, the viewers seemed to mostly watch the English Premier League. If it was a match played by one of the big teams, a crowd would gather, their cheers and jeers keeping me awake. In some ways, that was a soothing clamour.

One day I heard my name mentioned on this TV. The officers had turned the sound up to listen. The tame State broadcaster was telling a story. About Daw Suu's foreign economic adviser, who had tried to escape with secret intelligence to use against the State. Luckily, thanks to the brave efforts of Myanmar's soldiers, he had been captured. Caught red-handed. After this, I noticed that some of the younger police looked at me with more apparent respect. A spy!

Quite early on, I decided to only use English in my interactions with the police and everyone else I encountered in The Box. English, to my captors, was the language of modernity, prosperity, and freedom – a notion some of them must have hated. The trauma seemed to have rendered useless what little fluency I had in Burmese anyway – though I was quite capable of understanding most of what I heard on TV, for example, not that I let on. Forcing my interlocutors to use English to order me around was my way of grabbing back some leverage. In most other respects, I had completely lost all power. I'm not especially proud of this strategy, but in prison, anything you can use to tip the scales somewhat in your favour is eagerly grasped.

For Ha back home, the wait for updates on my status stretched on agonisingly. Hours into days, the days into a week. Former political prisoners in Myanmar told Ha that the new junta were unlikely to physically harm me, and would deport me soon. Probably, they told her, 'they will keep Sean ten days or so.' A report from the Israeli Embassy but sourced to Mossad seemed to back this up. At the time Ha was horrified. Ten days sounded like ten years.

Meanwhile, as a consequence of my disrupted interview with the BBC, media interest kept building. In the days that followed my arrest, Ha and the rest of the family, but especially my sister Lisa, became inundated with requests for comment. DFAT was likewise swamped and advised Ha, my dad and Lisa to issue a family statement.

This statement, written in English and Burmese and put out via DFAT and on Facebook, extolled my virtues as a dedicated family man. A practical economist, anxious to apply my expertise and experience to a good cause. It explained that no 'cause' for me was more important than Myanmar, a country I had fallen in love with, and worked to assist for over two decades. The family welcomed 'the calls by the Australian Government, other governments and by Sean's many friends around the world seeking his immediate release'. The statement concluded by saying that Ha and the family 'would not be making further public comment given the complex and sensitive situation in Myanmar'.

In these early days of my incarceration, Ha coped as best she could. These were terrible and strange circumstances, for which she was wholly unprepared. Panic attacks came and went, sleep was difficult. Time differences exacerbated everything. Ha woke up throughout the night at every ping of her phone. More often than not these heralded incoming texts from anxious friends around the world, hoping to get information, rather than anyone able to give it.

Ha could have stepped back at this juncture. Left things up to 'the authorities', to friends 'in the know' about Myanmar, or even subcontracted the efforts to get me out to professional hired help. None of these options would have been an unreasonable response. Ha had not grown up within the culture of Australian foreign affairs or Australia's legal system, let alone Myanmar's. But she did not step back, then or later.

A prime factor in Ha's ability to keep going was the love and strength of our daughter Phuong, now on the verge of turning twenty and becoming a person of fortitude and savvy about the world. Another emerging pillar was the support of an old friend of mine, Janelle Saffin. A former Australian federal MP and (in 2021), a member of the New South Wales parliament, Janelle has friends and influence in high places that she leverages in good causes. Janelle was an influential figure in the manoeuvrings that led to Timor Leste's independence and had been involved in Myanmar's democracy movement for decades. She is also a lawyer by training, and one of just a few in the world who knew anything about how Myanmar's legal system really worked.

Upon my arrest, Janelle was introduced to Ha by Michael Marett-Crosby, my closest colleague in my Myanmar work and someone for whom the expression *éminence grise* might have been invented. Thereafter Janelle was with Ha all the way: as counsellor, strategist, advocate and on many occasions a friendly shoulder to cry on. In their very first conversation Janelle told Ha she was in, to do 'whatever it takes'.

A team formed around Ha – one that operated from many parts of the globe. News came through that I was being held by CID, the Criminal Investigation Department. That they found this out, however, was courtesy not of any official notification, but thanks to the indefatigable work of American economist Curtis Slover.

Over the years, Curtis and I had worked together on a number of projects aimed at getting more capital into the hands of Myanmar's poor farmers, and most recently on a scheme encouraging and protecting savings in microfinance firms. Curtis had run microfinance and other grassroots financial institutions all around the world, from Afghanistan to Somalia, Syria to Sudan. He'd started out with the Peace Corps in the Philippines, and had been in Myanmar from 2014. Libertarian in philosophy and politics, Curtis was one of the most original thinkers on the Myanmar development scene, and combined intellectual acuity with conspicuous kinetic energy.

On the morning I was detained, I had been due to have coffee with Curtis. When the email arrived warning of my impending arrest, I'd phoned my friend to say, 'Danger! Stay away!' Immediately, Curtis reached out to Ha, which was no mean feat as he did not have her phone number, only her publicly available email address at Macquarie University, where she is a lecturer in economics. Since the internet was being intermittently blocked in Myanmar, Curtis got through to Ha via his wife, Jill, back in Madison, Wisconsin.

After he and Ha put their heads together, Curtis set off to Tamwe police station the next day, where he was told I had been moved to Insein Prison. He was the first person to know this, and passed on the information to Ha, who in turn passed it on to DFAT and the Australian Embassy. Meanwhile Curtis charged on, getting confirmation from a young prison officer at Insein's guard house that I was being held at CID headquarters, just outside the prison walls. A more senior officer arrived soon after to officially deny it. His wink told Curtis otherwise.

From that moment, and for the next year and a half, Curtis acted as man on the ground in Myanmar for Ha and the team. Essentially he did everything that involved face-to-face contact with the Myanmar police and prison authorities. At no time did he have diplomatic protection or anything like it. This, as well as the fact he was so openly my advocate and contact, placed him at immense risk of arrest himself. It did not deter him in these first days, nor ever.

The junta kept the Embassy away from me for the best part of that first week in The Box. Refusing to adhere to proper diplomatic conventions, the junta denied all requests for personal consular access. Eventually – citing COVID concerns – they agreed to a Zoom call but stipulated conditions.

None of this was known to me on 11 February, when I was escorted from The Box. During the short walk – the destination turned out to be a nearby room – I felt tremendous apprehension. Then I stepped inside to find that a camera and tripod had been set up. A single chair faced the camera. About a dozen people were in this improvised 'studio' – some on computers, some there as scribes to take verbatim notes, some taking pictures, some on phones.

Having been given no indication about what was going on, when I saw the set-up, all I could think of were those confession videos used by the Islamic State regime and other hideous outfits. At the sight of Ambassador Andrea and some of the Embassy team on the screen at the far end of the room, I exhaled: I wasn't about to be beheaded after all.

Seeing Andrea at that moment gave my spirits an extraordinary lift. Although I had known I was not going to be abandoned by the nation of my birth, there was nothing like seeing the proof of it with my own eyes. I felt as if reason and rationality, along with compassion and sympathy, had suddenly arrived in this dungeon of wretched absurdity I found myself in.

Before proceedings began, a police officer told us all that every word we said would be translated and subject to scrutiny by the Ministry of Home Affairs. He also told us we would have 20 minutes, no more. Andrea nodded, then started by asking me where I thought I was.

'Somewhere near the Insein prison complex, and in a building just outside of the jail walls,' I replied. Later in the call, Andrea addressed the police surrounding me and tried to pry from them precisely where I was.

That elicited a curt reply: 'No-one in the room is authorised to answer questions.'

Kindly, professionally, she questioned me about my health, what my physical conditions were like, whether I was receiving food, was I being mistreated.

I had questions for Andrea, too. 'On a scale from one to three – one being least and three being most – how confident are you that I will be allowed to leave soon?' Andrea told me she did not have an answer to this.

'Everyone at the Embassy is working towards your immediate release,' she said. She added that nothing was clear but described all the diplomatic activity that was swelling behind me. I had expected something, of course, but I was taken aback as to what seemed its extent.

'Have any other foreigners been detained?' I asked. Andrea shook her head. 'Have you heard anything of the whereabouts and safety of my Myanmar colleagues?' Again, her answer was in the negative.

Unquestionably, the biggest boost I received that day flowed from the messages Andrea was able to pass on from Ha, Phuong, my family and friends. Ha's positivity was reflected in her message, which was characteristically bold, optimistic, solicitous of my health and wellbeing, and more than a little funny. Underneath all of this would be immense anguish – I was keenly aware of this – and her determination not to burden me by betraying any hint of it.

In this first message, Ha subtly laid down some codenames for people she was collaborating with – individuals whose identity needed to be protected. Bear in mind that she was assuming I might soon be free. She provided me with some fun in her choices: Cuthbert, the Jedi Master, the Good Politician, and so on.

Ha had asked the Embassy to take a photo of me during the call, which they did. When Andrea showed it to me, I was struck by how upbeat I looked.

In response to my anxious enquiries, Andrea was able to convey that Ha, Phuong, my dad, Lisa and all the family were safe and well, albeit distraught over my situation. She told me a consular officer had been assigned to Ha, so she had '24-hour' access to DFAT on anything.

Before we wrapped up, I quizzed Andrea about recent world events. When it comes to current affairs, but in particular international news, I have long had a terrible case of FOMO (fear of missing out). It would have come as no surprise to Ha and my friends then that I was particularly interested in what was going on with Donald Trump – 'Has his second impeachment trial concluded?' (it had!), developments with COVID in Australia, and whether the Grand Prix season had started (yes to that too!).

The call ended and I was returned to The Box.

Above, I used the word 'determination' in relation to Ha. Here is a taste of what I mean.

Ha was in touch with prominent Myanmar legal, business and civil society leaders throughout my time in The Box. Alas I cannot name them here, for fear that even now they be punished for their kind and courageous efforts in assisting her.

One interesting outreach, daring in its chutzpah and that need not be kept secret, was Ha's open letter to Daw Kyu Kyu Hla, wife of junta leader Min Aung Hlaing. This letter was sent (as well as posted on Ha's Facebook page) on 22 February, 16 days into my detention:

> I am writing this personal note to you, Daw Kyu Kyu Hla, from one wife to another wife. I plead you to speak to your husband to let my husband return home to my family in Australia.

In publicity terms, the letter had quite an impact. Later, I was impressed to hear how it gained traction on social media and was picked up by the mainstream press in many countries. The *Australian* newspaper even used it as the basis for an editorial (leader) titled, 'Ha Vu's Plea Should be Heeded'; it concluded that 'Daw Kyu Kyu Hla should respond quickly to Dr Ha Vu's plea.' Needless to say perhaps, this did not happen.

Then there were Ha's efforts to highlight the obligations of the Myanmar regime under the Vienna Convention on Consular Relations, which required governments to give consular access to foreign prisoners. She began writing to the International Committee of the Red Cross asking them to help secure my release on humanitarian grounds. She pushed for a 'care package' to be sent, for a photo to be taken so that she could see I was well, and even urged that I be allowed a Kindle or an iPad – these were still the early, more optimistic times.

There was a lot of correspondence with DFAT. Ha started prodding them to redouble their efforts to obtain consular access. My sister Lisa likewise swung into action, sending multiple letters on behalf of both herself and my dad – seeking more action, noting the more vigorous actions being done by other countries for their citizens, requesting more information on what was being done, and how I was.

Ha established bonds of trust and affection with the team of people she engaged with in DFAT. She got to know them by name; they bestowed on her the affectionate abbreviation 'NOK' (next-of-kin). Nevertheless – and I guess this can only be expected in the course of such difficult and intense of experiences – tensions emerged once in a while.

Usually, this centred on information. Within the very first month of my detention, Ha lay down her expectations, telling DFAT that she must be 'kept in the loop' at all times, notified before anyone else of developments in my case, and certainly before the media. Lisa backed up Ha's demands, sending DFAT a letter around the same time that she had been horrified to hear in a radio broadcast that Australia had made a policy change towards Myanmar without mentioning it to Ha.

Ha established early and direct contact with Australia's Foreign Minister – initially Senator Marise Payne (in the Coalition government headed by Scott Morrison), then Senator Penny Wong (in the Labor government of Anthony Albanese that took office in May 2022).

Another initiative Ha tried out in these early days was to ask DFAT to push for me to be moved into house arrest, rather than being held in a prison. This was not an uninformed thought, but one based on the experience of two Australian business consultants in Myanmar, Christa Avery and Matthew O'Kane. They were detained under house arrest soon after the coup, then allowed to leave the country in early April 2021. On her release, Christa Avery herself voiced support for Ha's suggestion, telling the press that she hoped that 'even if Sean cannot be released very soon, he can, at least, be moved to house arrest for his physical, mental and emotional wellbeing'. Avery and O'Kane even offered their house as a location for my detention, should the junta agree. DFAT pushed back, saying it wouldn't work. Ha responded in turn, 'How do you know if you don't try?'

These and other occasional slips aside, for the most part there was an extraordinary degree of harmony and cooperation between DFAT and my NOK.

One of the most promising of the early attempts to secure my release, long before any charges were laid, came via the efforts of the Australian Government to initiate a dialogue between Myanmar's Deputy Commander-in-Chief, Vice Senior General Soe Win, and the Vice Chief of the Australian Defence Force,

Vice Admiral David Johnston. Ever since I'd known anything about Myanmar, the conventional wisdom had been that in its interactions with other countries, Myanmar's military responded more positively to military officers than anyone else. So, this contact – which began in the form of a phone call a little over two weeks after my arrest – seemed a good strategy.

According to the transcript of the call provided to Ha (selectively paraphrased below, with permission), David Johnston:

- requested my immediate release, and consular access in the meantime
- sought urgent confirmation of my current location and safety
- said if Myanmar authorities were able to deliver me to the safety of the Australian Embassy, the Australian Government would ensure my immediate departure from Myanmar
- said I was an eminent economist who had dedicated his considerable expertise to the benefit of Myanmar
- said my release would be in the best interests of both our countries and
- noted my ongoing detention risked damaging Myanmar's international reputation, as a large number of nations, regional organisations and businesses were carefully watching my case.

This was all pretty forthright stuff but it ran into the brick wall that was Soe Win's response. He claimed ignorance of my circumstances, including that he was not aware of where I was. But, he said, my situation was 'good enough'.

*

An Unlikely Prisoner

After about a month of daily interrogation, my questioners abruptly stopped visiting. About three weeks passed, then all of a sudden a whole bunch of people turned up at The Box one morning. A dozen or so burst in and I could see several others milling about in the corridor. The Terroter was among the arrivals, yet for some reason the interpreting work that day was not done by him, but by a young woman who said she was from Myanmar's Ministry of Foreign Affairs (MOFA). Wherever she was from, she was nice to me: later that day, when she departed, she even left me a small book, a condensed biography of Mark Twain. Only one thing I didn't like about her was that she constantly exhorted me to 'stay strong'.

What did 'stay strong' mean? Was I meant to be defiant? Was I supposed to make a noise or be stolid and quiet? Or did it simply mean, to use a more recent buzzword, to be vaguely 'resilient'? Maybe it just meant to eat whatever green vegetables I was given. How I grew to hate that phrase. As well I knew, I was being too harsh. What should she say? What can anyone say to someone in front of them in chains?

As it turned out, my MOFA lady was there for a reason, as it was the morning of the day the junta had decided to place me under something called 'formal investigation'. This was a kind of prelude to being charged.

From The Box, this entourage accompanied me to a small room nearby in which a laptop computer was set up, with its screen open to a Zoom page. I was asked to take a seat in front of the screen, on which the face of a man appeared. The man looked at me impassively: I was told he was a judge. Dressed in a conspicuously formal black *taikpon*, he had on his head a

Gaung Baung – the headdress worn on formal occasions by men in Myanmar, and de rigueur for officials in the country's courts.

Police, interrogators and myriad unknown others crowded in around me. Then the judge spoke. When he paused, the MOFA lady relayed the message that I was under investigation for various crimes in Myanmar, including some sort of breach of the country's Official Secrets Act. Confusingly, there was a hitch with the Zoom link – it was lost at least three times in all – but I gathered from my interpreter, who seemed slightly dazed, that I was being given some sort of formal notification. After 20 or so minutes, the judge got me to state my name and that of my father; he had no questions.

The screen went blank.

Oh, that's it, I thought. None the wiser, I was returned to The Box.

It emerged that this disorganised spectacle was a turning point. What it signalled was that my period of informal detention by the police was now over and that I had entered a period of remand.

Of most immediate importance was that this meant I was to be moved. The first I knew of this, however, was later that afternoon, when roughly the same entourage returned to The Box. I was ordered to gather my pathetic bundles of possessions. Then I was fingerprinted and photographed in the manner of TV dramas.

The Terroter stepped closer for one last exchange. Towards the end, he said, 'I have been protecting you all along, Sean.' He added that he had frequently rendered my answers less potent when he'd translated them for prosecutors. Finally, he repeated his assurance that within a month or two I would be released.

An Unlikely Prisoner

The first part of what he said, I knew to be complete bullshit. The second? Well, I hoped that this most untrustworthy man might be saying something truthful after all.

This day had been full of uncertainty. At its conclusion, one thing was crystal clear: my destination. There was only one place I could be moved to: Insein.

Part 2

From Gangbusters to Gulag

3

How Had It Come to This?

… foundational to all … is a recognition of the economic dividends yielded from being a democracy. An end in itself and, as such, needing no other justification, it is the case that being a democracy brings the application to Myanmar of the most powerful engine of economic growth known to human history. A system based on individual rights and freedoms, democracy and its accompanying institutions aligns incentives, allows spontaneous solutions to problems, promotes technological advancement and the delivery of public services according to demand, and expands choice and opportunity. In short, democracy and a focus on individual rights and the rule of law are simultaneously the ends of policy, and the vehicles through which Myanmar may escape poverty and achieve the prosperity our people deserve.

Sean Turnell
Contribution in the 'Myanmar Economic Resilience and Reform Plan', Government of the Union of Myanmar, 27 January 2021

Why was I in Myanmar in the first place?

A reasonable question for an Australian guy born and raised in the western suburbs of Sydney, but one to which I think I had an okay answer. It was all about economics. Indeed, so much of my life had been about economics. History had been my first love, but economics at its best is a subject that contains not only the wisdom of the ages, but a set of tools to make the world a better place. And the economy of Myanmar had been my burning passion over the last nearly 30 years. Moved and inspired by the country's tragedies and possibilities, and keen also to help out Myanmar friends I had made at university, from the early 1990s I increasingly worked alongside Myanmar's democracy movement in an attempt to analyse what was going on in the country, and how things might be turned around. Getting Myanmar's economy right was not a sufficient condition for this, but it seemed to me a necessary one.

In 2016 I became Daw Aung San Suu Kyi's economic adviser shortly after she took up office as State Counsellor, effectively the leader, of Myanmar's newly elected democratic government until the coup in 2021. In this period, as well as Daw Suu, I worked alongside all of Myanmar's economy-related ministers, senior economic officials, as well as reformers more broadly within Myanmar's National League for Democracy (NLD) and beyond. I also functioned as an unofficial emissary between the reformist elements in this government and the wider economic 'community' – the World Bank, International Monetary Fund, Asian Development Bank, and so on. Except for much of 2020, when I was stranded in Australia because of COVID, I spent all of the period of the NLD Government living and working in Myanmar's purpose-built capital city of Naypyitaw.

To me, my job was about the best there could be. As an economist, it was a rare opportunity to experience firsthand the conversion of the best theory into policy practice. As a student of history, it placed me in a front-row seat for what promised to be one of the great stories of the early 21st century – as one of Asia's poorest and most troubled countries attempted to become the last and best of its 'tigers'. It was the capstone of decades of my own work on Myanmar, and an opportunity to give something back to a country and a people I had grown to love.

It was in the context of my Myanmar work that I first came to the attention of Daw Suu. Initially, this was via a series of broadcasts on Myanmar's economy I did for the BBC Burmese Service, to which she surreptitiously listened while under house arrest in the early 2000s. Later, she read some of my writings on Myanmar's economy, including my 2009 book on Myanmar's monetary and financial history, *Fiery Dragons*. It was after reading this book that she was later to tell CNN's Christiane Amanpour that I was her 'favourite economist'. Following her release from house arrest in 2010 – for what all her supporters assumed would be the final time – I first met Daw Suu in person. We established an instant rapport, and soon after I joined her and the rest of her economic team in crafting a broad outline of what economic reform might look like under a future democratic government. Famously, such a government did come into place after the NLD's landslide election win in November 2015, in the wake of which Daw Suu asked whether I might come to Myanmar full-time to take up an unofficial but central role in the reform process. I jumped at the chance and, after getting the support of my university – Macquarie University in Sydney – as well as the Australian Government, within a few months I was in Naypyitaw.

In the intervening months, I undertook something of a 'deep dive' into the role and history of foreign advisers in transition countries such as Myanmar's. The track record was a mixed one and there were many pitfalls to avoid – moral as well as intellectual. The more I read, the more I was determined to try to follow in the footsteps of someone like Albert Winsemius in Singapore rather than a 'Chicago Boy' in Chile, a János Kornai in Eastern Europe or a Heinz Arndt in Indonesia. I found the reflections of Albert Hirschman, both with respect to his specific roles in Latin America and upon the issues more broadly, especially valuable. The lessons I took from Hirschman: listen, be humble, but bring the best that economics has to offer. Likewise valuable were the recollections of Louis Walinsky, an American economist who, in the 1950s, occupied a similar role to that I was about to take up, albeit in his case for Myanmar's first post-independence prime minister, U Nu. Little did I realise then that my job would end the same way Walinsky's did in 1962 – amid a military coup and a proliferation of uniformed men and tanks on the streets.

The scope of my job in Myanmar was extraordinarily broad and flexible. The only specific instruction I ever received from Daw Suu was to never second-guess what she wanted to hear but to always tell the truth as I understood it. I trust I was always faithful to this injunction. Daw Suu was – and is – a most perceptive person. Her economics were not cutting-edge perhaps but they were sound and much more liberal than might be supposed. Above all, she had a knack for knowing what would work in the Myanmar context and what would not.

My daily activities were every bit as broad and varied as my overall 'riding instructions'. Routinely, I would meet with Daw Suu every couple of weeks or so, with other meetings on demand as issues came up. Routine meetings were invariably held at her residence in Naypyitaw – the house assigned to her and befitting her simultaneous roles as Myanmar's Foreign Minister and State Counsellor. To these meetings, we would both bring a set of agenda items that we would methodically work through, but there was always time left over to discuss broader economic trends, international issues, as well as any matters arising out of the various memoranda and policy papers I would have sent her in the meantime.

These routine meetings were accompanied by Burmese food – usually the latest offerings of Myanmar's growing cohort of culinary entrepreneurs, keen to gain the State Counsellor's imprimatur on what they hoped would be Myanmar's latest export success. In this role, I was a most willing international guinea pig.

My meetings with other ministers and officials, foreign diplomats, businesspeople, and development professionals were even more frequent, but just as positive. This was especially the case in the early years of the NLD Government when, for anyone interested in development issues, Myanmar was very much the place to be. Almost regardless of the interlocutor, there was a feeling in the air that we were part of something bigger than ourselves. That we were creating something new, something good, something special. The last and best of the Asian tigers for sure.

Inevitably, not everything about my job was so positive. Of particular concern to me was the trope in political and media circles that I had some sort of executive function in Myanmar, even that I was the power behind the scenes of the country's economy, the person pulling all the strings. At first this was vaguely flattering and even funny, as when then visiting British Foreign Secretary, Boris Johnson, came bounding up to me at a British Embassy party in Yangon to declare he was 'delighted to meet the man responsible for Myanmar's economy going gangbusters'. *Goodness!* I didn't know how to respond to this. Myanmar's economy was not really going gangbusters at the time, and it would hardly have been down to me if it was.

Boris's attention was soon diverted otherwise, but the issue itself did not go away. Soon it was absorbed into a bigger conspiracy theory that Myanmar was in the grip of a sinister foreign cohort – led by George Soros – that aimed at undermining Myanmar's sovereignty and returning the country to colonial rule. The implausibility of the theory did little to put a dampener on the enthusiasm that some held for it, not least among Myanmar's security services and others hostile to the country's nascent democracy.

The backdrop to this troubling urban mythmaking was the xenophobia, ethnic chauvinism, and religious bigotry that unfortunately has a grip on parts of Myanmar society, to the detriment of the country's ethnic minorities. Soon I would find myself targeted, too: the subject of lurid and fanciful headlines. But for the time being, I want to talk about the years before my arrest, when I was among those who believed change was possible in Myanmar. The country's problems were tragic and chronic, but not unique nor incapable of solution. What's more, I believed change was well under way.

The government I joined in 2016 had a mountain of tasks ahead of it, and an even taller mountain of expectations that it could not hope but to disappoint. So it proved. However, on the economic front, the NLD Government was vigorous in implementing and establishing some key policies and institutions, as well as demonstrating that a democracy provided a safe pair of hands for development.

That it was so successful in these ways was overwhelmingly due to the strength of the local team. Intellectually, it was led by a small cohort of 'deputies', most prominently the Deputy Minister of Planning and Finance, U Winston Set Aung, and the Deputy Governor of the Central Bank of Myanmar, U Bo Bo Nge, and is testament to the quality and coherence of their economic vision. This vision centred upon the economic virtues of democracy itself, as well as such virtues as the rule of law, secure property rights, sound monetary and fiscal policies, a market-determined exchange rate, elevated spending on health and education, adherence to core labour and environmental standards and, above all perhaps, openness to foreign trade and investment. Within this broad frame of liberal democratic capitalism, however, pragmatism ruled. Traces of the Washington Consensus were apparent, but arguably no more so than policies yielded from the successes of the tigers. Meanwhile, the NLD's broader concerns for social justice permeated all, even if in implementation some of this went missing.

I assisted in the development of policy in these areas and helped my Myanmar colleagues bring them together in a series of 'plans' announced during the tenure of the NLD Government. I wore several other hats.

The NLD Government suffered from an inability to communicate their often highly impressive actions. In contradiction to the usual problem, they could walk the walk, but not talk the talk.

Assisting in communication was thus also often my job. An ability to talk becomes second nature after you have lectured first-year economics students for 20-plus years, so I regularly found myself acting as something of an intermediary for Myanmar's economic team. My role was mostly international in focus – explaining Myanmar to the multilateral financial institutions, the governments of other countries, foreign investors, international NGOs, and so on – and vice versa. Sometimes I gave domestic talks with the idea of rendering understandable the arcane and jargon-filled world of economic reform. Most notable in this regard was an annual talk I gave on Myanmar's economy that was sponsored by my alma mater, Macquarie University. This would routinely attract about 1000 or so people. One year it was held at the Novotel Yangon, drew nearly 2000 people, and caused traffic chaos.

The showman in me, never too far away, loved this gig.

Another role I undertook in Myanmar – one of my most rewarding there – was serving as the Director of Research at the Myanmar Development Institute (MDI). A semi-government think tank located in Naypyitaw, MDI was created with funding from South Korea and modelled on that country's storied Korea Development Institute. The purpose of MDI was to conduct research and inform policy, and to equip its primarily young (Myanmar) researchers with all that they needed to be the policy-makers of tomorrow. To all of these ends we produced a biannual journal called the *Myanmar Economic Bulletin*, of which I was the editor and the MDI researchers the principal writers. They were extraordinary young people, and it is one of the greatest honours of my life to have worked alongside them. With them in mind, before the coup I even dared to be optimistic about Myanmar's future.

Not the least of the many achievements we hoped for MDI was to see it become an institution that made the likes of me obsolete. Homegrown economists are always preferred over imported ones, and MDI was a fantastic place to nurture them.

Following the coup I met a number of my MDI colleagues in Insein and Naypyitaw prisons. They remained awesomely impressive in this new and terrible situation – brave, resourceful, irrepressible. They personify all that I love in Myanmar, and their fate makes me cry.

Apart from a largely self-appointed role of being a constant advocate for ever more economic freedoms, my original contributions were focused on Myanmar's monetary and financial sector. Not that I saw this as a limitation. My decades of work in Myanmar had convinced me that the country's dysfunctional, crisis-prone and criminally oriented banking system was central to the country's broader political-economy miasma. Further, I believed that reform in this area – as opposed to reform just about anywhere else – could start turning things around. In the words of fashionable-once-more American founding father Alexander Hamilton, "Tis by introducing order into our finances . . . not by gaining battles, that we are finally to gain our object.'

Economic reform is resisted everywhere by vested interests whose economic rents are threatened by greater openness and competition. In Myanmar, this opposition took a particularly colourful form in a group of local oligarchs known throughout Myanmar as the 'cronies'. But the deadliest opponent of economic reform always remained the military. They would end reform completely with their coup of 2021, but throughout the NLD era the military constantly blocked reform initiatives, as well as constituting a hovering menace to the liberalisation project more generally. Infamously granted an array of 'special economic powers' and privileges under Myanmar's 2008 Constitution, the *sit-tat* (the Burmese name for the armed forces) had total control of the ministries of Defence, Home and Border Affairs, while two giant military companies (Myanmar Economic Holdings Limited and Myanmar Economic Corporation) dominated whole sectors of the economy.

Myanmar's military also had complete discretion over their own budget. This in a country with little in the way of genuine external threats but overwhelming spending needs in education, health, and basic infrastructure, resulted in a chronic misallocation of resources. It was also the foundation of what I call the 'original sin' of macroeconomic policymaking in Myanmar: excessive state – ergo, military – spending funded by the highly destructive expedient of printing money.

As it turned out, though, the worst damage to the reform program of the NLD era came via the genocidal atrocities being committed by Myanmar's military in the country's Rakhine State and other places. These brutalities, coupled with the government's own missteps in responding to them, severely undermined international support for the economic reforms that, in my estimation, provided one of the few plausible avenues to the emergence of something better.

Financial sector reform united the cronies and military in opposition. While this told us we were right to focus on the sector, it created powerful enemies for Myanmar's reformers – enemies who would exact their revenge later.

Fixing Myanmar's banks was a nearly impossible task and was incomplete when the coup occurred. At the time the NLD took office in 2016, scarcely a bank in Myanmar would have been solvent had proper accounting standards been applied. Most banks were little more than corporate cashboxes for the crony conglomerates within which they sat, and often did little more than facilitate money-laundering, tax avoidance and influence-peddling. Some were barely disguised Ponzi schemes. The worst were simply fronts for the financing of the narcotics trade, human trafficking, and other criminal activity.

In light of this, and understanding that a banking crisis would unravel the entire reform process, the NLD's reformers boldly took on the banks. This entailed actually applying proper financial regulations. They did exist but for years had been just a façade. Most problematic for many of the banks was the implementation of 'fit and proper person' tests for bank owners and managers. These, alongside the NLD Government's embrace of the Anti-Money Laundering/Counter Terrorism Financing standards of the Financial Action Task Force – the global anti-money laundering agency – put many bank principals in Myanmar under the spotlight. And made them very angry.

By 2020, continued foot-dragging by the banks coincided with growing problems of non-performing loans (that is, loans that were in doubt of being repaid). A cohort of some of the biggest and most badly run banks agitated for a government bailout. Matters came to a head. Key bank reformers in the government insisted that adherence to proper practices was due now, and not some forever distant 'later'.

Worried about a collapse of the banking sector, and of growing links between the banks and elements in Myanmar's military complicit in financial crime, we persuaded Daw Suu to participate in 'track two', or back-channel, negotiations with some bank owners. I was also involved in informal but direct approaches to the banks. Some were open to these efforts, and a new reform momentum started to gain traction. Others dug in, and sought to undermine the reforms further, including by threatening some of the key reformers. One bank executive told me that his message for the NLD Government was, 'If we go down, you'll all go down with us.'

Down, down, down we went. The military coup of 1 February 2021 came two months after a general election in Myanmar that delivered the NLD a resounding victory, increasing the already large share of seats it had claimed in the election win of 2015. Immediately, I turned my attention to the packed agenda of a second term of NLD Government. There was so much to do.

When it came – just two days before the sitting of the new parliament – the coup took most people by surprise. I was shocked by it. Like many others, I had been reading and watching with growing alarm the efforts of the Myanmar military to undermine the legitimacy of the November 2020 elections, and with even more alarm the extent to which they were taking comfort from the similar campaign then being waged by Donald Trump in the United States. None of these efforts had struck me as being existential, however. Despite the rumours, I had no inkling at all they would end in a coup.

As I mentioned earlier, I was in Yangon on that Monday morning the coup was launched. I had been due in Naypyitaw the day before the tanks rolled, but my return was put back a few days at the advice of Daw Suu and her staff. They did not, in my judgement, expect a coup, though they were worried about 'rogue soldiers on the road to Naypyitaw who might harass someone known to be close to her', to quote what a staff member said to me.

Straightaway, I got in touch with some Myanmar friends who had contacts in the military. When I asked them about reports of unusual numbers of troops in the capital, they told me the soldiers were there for the opening ceremony of the parliament. Nothing to worry about.

Nothing at all.

Part 3

Staying Sane in Insein

4

Crossing the Threshold

Insein Prison is as mad and bad as its name sounds.

Built in the late 19th century by the British colonial regime that then ruled Myanmar, its frontage was designed to intimidate all who glimpsed it. It seemed to project a warning: 'Defy authority, and this is where you will rot.' The message worked for the British Empire. Successive regimes built on that promise, ratcheting up the use of terror accordingly.

And now I was arriving at this dreadful place. Me. A 57-year-old professor of economics from Sydney, Australia, who had never even received a traffic ticket. A person who had spent just about his whole life in the halls of the academy. A person whose idea of uncomfortable confrontation was telling a student their essay was not really that good. A person utterly, terribly, out of his depth.

Because I was handcuffed, I had to be helped out of the minivan that had brought me from The Box. My stuff, packed in pitiful plastic bags and my small carry-on case, was set down beside me. My phalanx assembled: CID officers, MI guys in their dark glasses, my sympathetic female interpreter, plus prison guards who had emerged from Insein itself. A bureaucratic pause of greetings, forms and procedures haggled around me.

I knew that in a minute or two I would be forced to enter this ghastly place and it would be one of those moments in life that you can never erase. I was sweating profusely. It was hot. Very hot. Sticky, humid. As might be expected, I was apprehensive of what was ahead, yet also oddly detached from everything, too. I was conscious of this combination – that one part of my brain was observing my situation from afar, while another was grappling with how I was conducting myself. How I behaved now was going to be remembered. By my captors, by other arriving prisoners – several were watching me with undisguised fascination: 'Who is this guy? It's Daw Suu's economist!' – and, not least, by my inner soul.

In front of me was the forbidding gatehouse and at its centre an enormous old and gnarled wooden door. The door was the exact sort you see in castles in fantasy films and fairytales. Were it not painted bright red, I would have fancied it for the Black Gate of Mordor, the portal to the grim world it hid. The door's surface bore layer upon layer of paint and was pitted with the knocks and grooves of a century of use. So big was the door that, just like in the movies, there was a smaller door within it that allowed the passage of objects of human size.

We were a high-priority delivery and so while there was much bustling about, there was a distinct sense of urgency and tension, too. I heard the jangling of keys, locks opening and the drawing back of heavy bolts – sounds so clichéd they almost parodied the moment. The small door opened, and I was hustled inside.

It did not extend all the way to the ground, though, so I had to lift my legs high to step over its bottom lip. Among the prisoners waiting outside, I'd noticed that a few were wearing leg-irons and I thought of them as I struggled through.

On the other side of the door, and with my whole entourage of captors hurrying in behind me, I found myself in a vaulted space. This ended in another massive door. I was between the inner and outer doors of the guard house, a space that doubled as the receiving area for new prisoners. Rickety old wooden desks and battered filing cabinets lined the walls and provided office space of a sort. Greetings were exchanged, and papers handed over. Lots of paper. Stamps and ink pads appeared and much banging ensued. I was photographed. From the front, both sides, from the back, with my bags, and without. Sensing the notoriety of the occasion, quite a few of the police took selfies with me. How could I refuse, or even not smile?

Despite the noise swirling all around me, I noticed that my shouted name was rendered into Burmese as 'Shaun Tunna'. From then on, it was written thus whenever my name was directly translated from jail documents into English. As was the case in The Box, my father's name was constantly required on documents, too. Only occasionally was my wife's name asked for, but without fail 'Dr Ha Vu' was replaced with 'Mrs Tunna'. Mrs Tunna was unimpressed when I told her later.

A couple of minutes into all of this, a khaki-uniformed prison officer adorned with lots of braid and ribbons strode towards me. 'Professor Turnell' – mind you, this was my interpreter's rendition – 'my name is Kyaw Tun Oo [changed here out of caution], and I am the Superintendent of Insein Prison. My men are now going to take you to Ward Four. We will treat you properly during your stay. I'm sure you will not be here long. Please be patient as we complete your documentation.'

Well, okay, I thought. It wasn't exactly the patter of a concierge, but it seemed unthreatening enough. At the end of this short welcome, the Superintendent gestured to one of the guards to undo my handcuffs. While they did so, four or five prison guards went through my belongings. As I'd been nearly two months in their 'care' already, I didn't expect them to find anything problematic. But they did: my belt. As he took it away, the Superintendent explained, in what I took to be a friendly and even jovial tone, 'This is just so you don't hang yourself.' I don't remember laughing.

Lots of backslapping between my captors from The Box and my new ones from Insein seemed to indicate that the handover was done. I was now, for who knew how long, an inmate of this most notorious prison. Just then another senior officer approached to tell me my prison number, and that I would need to remember it. I repeated it – once out loud, and at least once more to myself. I would be asked many times in the months ahead for this number. To the endless annoyance of my captors, I didn't remember it once.

Now the inner door could be opened. I was propelled through another little door-within-the-door. From the dim light of the guard house, I emerged into open air, and the novelty of this after weeks in The Box did not escape me. It was about 3 pm. The sun blazed from above and reflected off the whitewashed walls that marked out what appeared to be a thoroughfare leading to the centre of the prison, and the colossal watchtower that dominated the scene ahead of me.

An Unlikely Prisoner

The watchtower was the core of Insein physically, but it was also literally pivotal to its design. Inspired by the writings of British philosopher and social reformer Jeremy Bentham and his idea of the panopticon, Insein Prison was laid out in the pattern of a giant wagon-wheel. The watchtower was the centre of the wheel and the hub from which lines of prison cells – as well as long, communal prison buildings – extended like spokes. Or pizza slices. In theory, every cell, every yard, every part of the prison, could be observed from the tower, which to my mind loomed over everything like Sauron's lair in *The Lord of the Rings*, complete with its binocular-equipped guards performing a version of the great unblinking eye.

With their manacles, truncheons and oversized sets of keys clanking all the way, my cavalcade of guards and police walked me up to this eye before we doubled back into one of the pizza slices known as Ward 4. It consisted of a row of about 20 cells in a single-storey concrete bunker–like structure. Each cell was fronted by a door made up of rusty old (but, I fancied, still immensely strong) iron bars. Ward 4 must have been one of the original late-19th century parts of the prison: its physical condition might be best described as constituting, in real-estate parlance, a renovator's delight. The cells were a grimy white, the paint flaky and covered here and there with mould, while the barred doors were painted red in the bits not covered in rust – matching the Great Door to the prison itself. Through these doors, the cells were completely open to the elements. Straightaway, I did a mental inventory of those elements: the oppressive heat and humidity of Yangon with the approaching summer, and then the damp and decay of the monsoon. *What about the fauna of Yangon – the rats, mosquitoes and other insects?* While I hadn't expected a picnic, registering this threw me: *How am I going to do this?*

The only other source of natural light into the cells, aside from the light through the barred doors, came from a small window high up on the rear wall. This too was a simple affair of iron bars, without glass. Not only were the cells dim, damp and uninviting caves, they were also of decidedly modest dimensions: about 2 by 3 metres (8 by 10 feet), I estimated.

Fearfully scanning them as we moved further into Ward 4, I wondered which of these was assigned to me.

5

Friends, Saviours and the Other Side of the Bars

It is painful to recall my feelings of mounting horror as I took in my new physical environment.

I tried to steel myself, to repress them, worried I was about to spiral into a psychological pit. I surely would have done, were it not for an intervention: suddenly and overwhelming, prisoners surged towards me in welcome. Ignoring my uniformed escorts – who thankfully stepped back, their work done now that they had got me to my cell – they formed quite a crowd. From it emerged a friendly and – to me – absurdly young prisoner in a bright orange T-shirt with Daw Suu's face blazoned upon it.

'Sean, you are safe now. You are with us.'

These words were balm. Soon I would become acquainted with the person who spoke them: Paing Ye Thu, a remarkable man in his early 20s. He was an emerging leader within the NLD and a confidant already of Daw Suu on youth affairs. A resident of Yangon, Paing Ye Thu was early to express his opposition to the military coup and in organising peaceful protests against it.

For all of this he was also an early arrest, and was charged and convicted under the junta's newly invented Section 505 of the Myanmar Penal Code, which outlawed free speech and more or less any peaceful action against the regime. As his greeting to me might suggest, he was a jovial character with an indomitable spirit and an infectious smile.

Paing Ye Thu having broken the ice, so to speak, the other young political prisoners came up to me, too. There was lots of '*Mingalabar, Saya* Sean' (Hello, Professor Sean) as well as handshakes, fist bumps and shy hugs. They all seemed pleased to see me, but assuredly no more than I was pleased to see them.

Of course, my new friends were full of questions as to what had happened to me in my two-month disappearance. They knew precisely who I was. What's more, they told me they had been expecting me. They were curious as to whether I had news of The Lady, and were full of apologies for how I had been treated. On the latter, I reassured them that they had absolutely nothing to apologise for: 'You're all fighting the bastards, and that's why you're here!' I told them.

I loved my new friends from the get-go. They redeemed what could have been the worst day of my entire life. Echoing what Paing Ye Thu said, they all vowed they would stand for no ill-treatment of me. And to be my 'protector avengers' – their label!

About 20 minutes went by, with me answering their questions and they answering my anxious enquiries about what to expect in this awful place. What were the prison guards and other officials doing while all this was going on? The truth is I do not remember, and I don't think I noticed on the day.

Seemingly, they melted away. Of course, the prison officials would run my life for much of the next 21 months, but for the moment they disappeared from my thoughts for the first time since my capture.

Soon my protector avengers went about more practical ways of expressing their friendship: by making habitable the cell that was apparently mine. It was Number 14, and thus the fourteenth in the line of cells of Ward 4 that extended from near the base of the watchtower to the circular perimeter of the jail. Earlier that day, the cell's most recent occupants – two prisoners – had been hastily moved out and taken off to another ward altogether. Apart from cleaning the cell, my new friends constructed for me a wooden platform that would serve as a bed. They also scrounged up other things I would need: a cup, a plate, a bucket, a 'shower' scoop, a spoon – no knives or forks allowed, though they could be made – and numerous other basic accoutrements of survival.

Standing a little back from the others at first, but soon to join the joyful melee, was the man who more than anyone was to keep me safe and sound in Insein. Khin Maung Shwe was about 40. On the shorter side of average height, he was well-built and muscular in the way of someone primed and experienced in taking care of himself. Dressed like most of the others in a *longyi*, what made him stand out from everyone around him was his beard. Khin Maung Shwe was Muslim. This fact explained the discrimination he had experienced all his life in Myanmar, and the extra suspicion and fear with which he was viewed by the prison guards. Lest it be thought otherwise, I must add that this prejudice was not shared by his fellow political prisoners, who always called him, as I did, too, by his preferred Islamic name of Jacoob. Jacoob's faith was central to his identity, the basis of his moral beliefs and actions, the core of his resilience.

Among those who cleaned out my cell, I noticed Jacoob took on all the worst stuff. Not least, he tackled cleaning the indescribably awful squat toilet, a task that did not appear to have been attended to since its installation – maybe a hundred years earlier.

'No, no, no, mate,' I told him. 'I can do this. This is not for you to do. I am in this with you all, and I don't want or expect special treatment. We are all together.'

But he was adamant. His extraordinary generosity to me – which he did not acknowledge – was simply a function of his deepest convictions, political as well as religious.

'Helping you, Sean, helps The Lady, and my country,' he said. 'In this, I believe I am following God's will.' Not a forgettable sentiment, and one not easily dismissed.

Although buoyed in my spirits by these unexpectedly wonderful encounters, as I tried to sleep on that first night in Insein – not easy as fluorescent lights were never switched off at night – a tide of cognitive dissonance and anger rose in my mind; its ebb and flow would be a permanent fixture. No matter how many positive or meaningful interactions I had with fellow prisoners, nothing would change a basic legal fact: I should not have been there in the first place. I was not charged with anything, and at this point even the idea that I was on remand was still not settled. Being imprisoned as I was in the regular jail of Insein was contrary to law and even the stated practice of Myanmar's Prisons Department.

Of course, this was a minor matter when weighed against the wholesale collapse of anything passing for law and justice in Myanmar. Nonetheless, that such treatment of a high-profile foreigner took place was illustrative of a central fact, then and later: when it came to human rights of any form, for anyone, Myanmar's military leaders simply did not care.

Back in Australia, Ha, Phuong, my dad and Lisa were cranking up their campaign to get me released, and to ensure I was not forgotten – not least by my own government in Australia. This effort would grow into a vast hydra over the weeks, months and year ahead.

From the outset, they grappled with the dilemma of how, when, and how much to engage the media. As newcomers to what is sometimes called 'hostage diplomacy', they had to weigh up the pros and cons of using the megaphone of publicity on the one hand and 'quiet diplomacy' on the other. As is her wont, Ha steered a path straight down the middle, using the media when she thought she needed to, remaining silent when the situation suggested discretion might be best.

An example of this was publicising my health history. Ha revealed that I had experienced a dehydration/stress-induced seizure a few years earlier. When my dad was diagnosed with prostate cancer early in my imprisonment, she also ensured that information made its way into news reports. Her thinking was that this might prompt the junta to take better care of me, while applying pressure on the Australian Government to go the extra distance, too.

This might sound surprising, but in situations such as mine, the media is often best employed as a vehicle for 'encouraging' a prisoner's home country government rather than the imprisoning one. The latter are often regimes impervious to public pressure: Myanmar's junta certainly belongs to this category. Democratic governments such as Australia's, however, are usually much more responsive to stories of their citizens in distress overseas.

I was certainly one of these.

6

In the Cell, Food and Surviving Day to Day

All too soon, I became utterly familiar with my minuscule cell.

My new friends had cleaned it from top to bottom and done their best to equip it. I hesitate to refer to it as my home. Open to the elements as already described, it offered no protection from uncomfortable heat and moisture, not to mention an array of insects and rodents that would make their way into my cell at some point and, every once in a while, all at once. Too dim by day, too bright by night, I can't say I fully adjusted to or ever felt safe in my cell.

It really did feel like an animal pen. Even though I never wavered in my belief that I had done the very opposite of anything wrong, occupying this site of shame and humiliation was a daily hurt, a battle against degradation. As someone who had struggled to achieve a certain level of esteem and respect, who had worked hard to achieve the highest education qualifications available and as someone who regarded himself as a responsible and reflective global citizen – the idea of being locked up in a cage was beyond shocking. Within this place, few basic liberties were permitted, most activities of daily life were prescribed, all my actions open to scrutiny. Always frightened, always vulnerable.

Discernible beneath layers of white paint inside the cell was the graffiti of past occupants. Much of it I could not decipher, but among it were poems of loss and longing, declarations of innocence, words of religious and philosophical wisdom, and occasional scatological references. Notches were numerous, in the familiar groups of five, counting down or up the days. All in all it was a virtual archaeology of silent vertical screaming. For reasons impossible to intuit, embedded in the concrete wall near the doorway was a small thumbnail portrait of Spiderman, by persons unknown.

In Insein, as elsewhere, I was always the sole occupant of my cell. Those surrounding me housed two or even three prisoners apiece – the latter, tightly! To be honest, I liked the solitude. But even if I hadn't, it would not have made any difference. The junta leaders were most anxious this pesky foreigner did not pollute the minds of anyone from Myanmar, even those they regarded as their enemies.

The nervousness with which the jail authorities approached almost everything to do with me was brought home soon after my transfer to Insein. Another political prisoner – an elderly and venerable NLD campaigner – invited me to have tea with him in his cell one morning. He was of that generation of relatively elite Burmese who had grown up with English as a default second language, so we were able to range far and wide in our conversation. That said, we never touched on any topic that was controversial – the walls, and everything else in the place, had ears.

For the better part of the visit, the two of us compared notes about Sydney landmarks that he recalled from a visit in the 1970s. A couple of hours after our meeting, however, the prison authorities showed their claws by evicting my host from his cell. Half a dozen guards bundled up his belongings and moved these, and him, to another ward.

Being locked inside our cells was the default status of prisoners in Insein. For two periods a day we were allowed outside to exercise – from 7 am to about 9 am, and then again from about 2 pm to 4 pm. Actual times depended upon the ward concerned, and the whim of the guards in charge. We could not wander far – only within the prison 'yard' of the ward. In the case of Ward 4, this was a small area comprising little more than the five-metre strip that ran between the front of the cells and the wall opposite. This space was crowded with large water troughs and other things, but provided some walking space at least. There was no shade, and sometimes I had to trade off the desperate desire to walk with the cost of severe sunburn.

The most common collective punishment of prisoners was to cancel the exercise and keep us locked up in our cells. This practice was also followed whenever a VIP visited. There seemed to be an awful lot of them, including that especially useless cohort of junta-appointed members of Myanmar's National Human Rights Commission. The associated lockdowns seemed a weekly occurrence.

The troughs outside and opposite the cells were primarily for the washing needs of prisoners. We would scoop water out of the troughs with buckets – if, say, we wanted to wash our cells or launder our clothes – or with shower scoops or bowls to dunk one's self under. That operation, according to taste, would take place as soon as the cell doors opened early in the morning or approaching lock-up time at dusk. It was all outside, but Burmese are a modest people, even if segregated by gender, and most prisoners were highly adept at showering with a dynamically repositioning *longyi* in place throughout. For those of us less adept, it was a matter of not caring.

During the frequent blackouts, the absence of functioning pumps would cause water levels in the troughs to decline rapidly. Then we were forced to bathe in stagnant and increasingly smelly water. Since it was so hot, more or less all the time, not bathing daily was something I could never contemplate.

Another opportunity to move around was when food was delivered. This happened twice a day: in the early morning and in the evening before we were locked in our cells for the night. The food arrived in three oversized buckets, borne by fellow prisoners – forced labourers. One bucket contained boiled rice. This was usually of very poor quality, over- or undercooked, and invariably containing teeth-breaking small stones and other impurities. The second was a watery lentil soup. It was by far the most nutritious item on offer, but depending on the water-to-legume ratio, was often insufficient to satisfy either hunger or good health. The third and final bucket contained a 'meat' item of some sort. By the time the latter reached the prisoners, however, its contents had been stripped clean of any nutritional value – the bounty sold off, allegedly – leaving little more than bone, gristle and an oily residue.

An Unlikely Prisoner

On arrival of the buckets, we would line up to take a scoop of one or more out of them. A large ladle was usually sitting inside each bucket. Sometimes it would slip below the surface of the soup in Bucket 2, leading to many a hygienically challenged hand-retrieval operation. Some people would eat straightaway; there were those who would fashion from these basics something better; others still preferred to take the food to their cell to eat behind closed doors. I took the latter option, reading while I ate and pretending to be somewhere else. Initially I read the slim volume gifted by the nice interpreter until other books started to arrive.

The food provided was not sufficient to keep body and soul together, and so most prisoners came to rely on food sent by family and friends or purchased through a system run by the guards that allowed basic items to be brought in. Through poverty or other circumstances, including the risk of becoming 'marked out' by the junta and its servants, many prisoners did not receive food or anything else from outside. I observed numerous fellow inmates wasting away on the prison-only diet.

Drinking water was a constant problem: both in quantity and quality. The same prisoner/workers who delivered the food would also bring in large water cooler–style bottles of water to be shared around that were supposedly filtered. It was often not, and rather than risk illness, a lot of prisoners sought to buy water or have it sent from outside. This worked most of the time, but it was hostage to the whim of the prison authorities, and a ready reprisal point for sins real or imagined.

The ebullient Paing Ye Thu had made it his mission to keep my spirits up. It was his habit to come along to see me as soon as the cell doors opened. Paing Ye Thu had plenty of friends and contacts in and outside of Insein, and he brought me news of what was happening in Myanmar, including sometimes what was about to happen to me, well before anyone else.

In food as well as in other things, Jacoob would help me in all sorts of ways for the six months we were prison mates. His cell was next to mine. We usually had breakfast together, often joined by Paing Ye Thu and others in the morning hours we were allowed out of our cells.

Jacoob belonged to the category of those who used the prison food as the base for his creations. He was an inventive and innovative cook, and with the most simple ingredients – which was all he could get – could turn anything into almost anything else. It was pure alchemy to me as I watched his wok magic. I say wok, but I guess it was really just a frying pan which he managed to attach to the prison's mains electricity via stray wires, a dollop of ingenuity, and some carefully distributed largesse to the appropriate prison guards. His skill was widely admired and he was often approached for help. Though he wouldn't always share his ingredients, he would lend inmates a hand to turn their dreary ration gruel into something significantly more nourishing.

On my birthday in June 2021, Jacoob, along with a group of fellow prisoners, collaborated on a task. They were without some critical ingredients, and also an oven, but managed to produce about the most wonderful birthday cake I have ever seen or eaten. Not for either the first or last time in my imprisonment, I wished I'd had a camera. Unfortunately, I often wanted

An Unlikely Prisoner

this device in order to record things less happy than a birthday cake.

Jacoob was unusual in Ward 4 in receiving almost no help from anyone outside, and he got no food parcels or any other deliveries of stuff to make his life in the prison more bearable. In order to survive and even thrive as something of a leader among the political prisoners, he had to rely on his wits to make money. His efforts centred on making up and selling packets of betel nut to prisoners and guards alike. Betel nut is a mild stimulant used widely through Southeast Asia, to which a lot of people in Myanmar are addicted. It's sold in a combination of the betel (areca) nut itself, which is wrapped in a betel leaf and slaked in lime – sometimes with tobacco added (Jacoob's variant did not usually contain tobacco). These ingredients came to Jacoob separately via various channels – from which he assembled the final product.

I don't want to give the impression that Jacoob's betel nut activities were a big or lucrative operation, or held a sway over the prison in any way. They allowed him just sufficient profits, and a modicum of respect, to survive. And then, to help others.

As well as the political prisoners who were my staunch friends and saviours, Insein held other prisoners of various types.

In Ward 4, they were mostly foreigners, there for the most part on narcotics convictions, as well as local prisoners who were prominent in some way. This will probably come as a surprise, and would have done so to me had someone suggested it before these events – but I got on famously with the narcotics traffickers. Notable amid our cohort in Ward 4 was a group of young Taiwanese men, all of whom were serving 14-year sentences after being caught in a big drug smuggling case a few years earlier. Beyond being young in years they struck me as being very naive about the ways of the world, and I found myself ready to believe they were sacrificial pawns in a game run by others, in both Taiwan and Myanmar. Admittedly, the tag of naive might be attached to me, too, in this assessment, but my interactions with these young guys reminded me much of my students back in Sydney, and even of my young relatives and friends. One of them reminded me so strongly of my nephew Timothy that I adopted this name for him. He was delighted, and it stuck. Just about everyone called this young Taiwanese guy Tim after that, if not 'Sean's nephew'.

Pawns in a bigger game, as I have noted, my Taiwanese companions seem to have at least continued to enjoy some support from their 'patrons', mostly in the form of a constant flow of goodies and creature comforts from outside. They also had plenty of money to bestow on the prison and its staff to improve their surrounds, and 'financed' the construction of cooking facilities, as well as exercise equipment in the space outside their cells. Their cells also got a makeover and, although I must be careful not to exaggerate the resultant comfort, came to be equipped with TVs, mosquito nets and other items not available to anyone else. All that said, the Taiwanese guys were extraordinarily generous to their fellow prisoners, too, and would share food and things around. On one occasion they used pineapple juice to concoct alcohol. It tasted pretty awful, and I took no more than a sip. More than the taste, I did not really fancy Insein as a place to get drunk. Or to cope with a hangover.

As is inevitable with large groups – let alone in a prison! – there were some awkward characters I had to deal with. With respect to me, however, these were mostly non-threatening – with one exception. This was Aung Win Zaw, a resident of my own Ward 4, who was in Insein because of his role as a co-conspirator in the murder of U Ko Ni in 2017. U Ko Ni had been Daw Suu's most important legal adviser. Indeed, he was the person who discovered the legal loophole in Myanmar's 2008 Constitution – which was otherwise carefully crafted to disallow Daw Suu from high office, and the presidency of Myanmar in particular – that conceded the creation of the position of State Counsellor, the office via which she was able to effectively lead the country. U Ko Ni had been murdered in broad daylight as he waited for a taxi at Yangon International Airport after returning from an official trip to Indonesia. He was holding his granddaughter in his arms as a gunman stepped up behind him and shot him in the head at point-blank range. U Ko Ni was killed instantly, and his assailants got away, at least for a time. A taxi driver who tried to pursue them was also murdered. Though the case remains murky, two of the assassins – one of whom was Aung Win Zaw – were eventually caught and received (commuted) death sentences.

From the outset, Aung Win Zaw made no secret of his distaste for me, and indicated more than once that the fate that had befallen Daw Suu's legal adviser could easily be visited upon her economic adviser, too. I kept my distance from him.

In other wards, many hundreds of prisoners were kept together in giant cells with little in the way of facilities and even less privacy. These were so-called Class C prisoners. Ordinary people, basically. They might have committed genuine criminal offences, but by the time I was in Insein, this category was overwhelmingly made up of young people, not least students, involved in protests or other activities against the junta. Mostly they were charged under the junta's previously mentioned Section 505 of the Penal Code. Some 17,000 people had been arrested by the time I had been placed in Insein.

Just as some of the Class C prisoners were shockingly young, others were shockingly elderly. Old-timers stood out. Toothless, their bodies gnarled and broken, and sometimes even with grey hair – black hair dye was ubiquitous in Myanmar, even in Insein – they were often occupied in skilled labour tasks, such as fixing the unfixable infrastructure around the jail.

The Class C prisoners were little more than slaves. Woken at 4.45 am and forced to pray and recite Buddhist mantras, they were given a meagre breakfast of a sort of rice porridge then put to work. Some of this work involved 'real' activities: Class C prisoners were widely used as servants – fetching, carrying and cleaning essentially. However, a lot of it was 'make work' of various kinds, with tasks chosen seemingly for their unpleasantness and pointlessness; for example, 'mowing' sections of grass by getting prisoners to pluck one blade of grass at a time with their fingers. Such activities took place right through the hottest parts of the day. Few prisoners had anything to protect themselves from the sun. Naturally, and pretty much regardless of the work, there were no tools to use, no protective clothing, no aids of any kind. Injuries were common.

Although strictly segregated in their own ward, I used to walk past a great many of the female prisoners of Insein during my sojourns out for phone calls and other things. As with their male counterparts, I was struck by their youth and the fact that most were pro-democracy protestors. Many were obviously middle class and educated and had the demeanour of people who were way out of their comfort zone: I knew the feeling. Yet none looked cowed. Quite a number of the women prisoners had their children with them. To me, this was a distressing sight, though I recognised that this might well have been the better of limited options.

One very positive surprise of my time in Insein was the easy acceptance I noticed within the prison population of LGBT inmates. Myanmar is a conservative society but, among the prisoners certainly, you wouldn't have known that. Instead, it seemed to me, there was a distinct understanding that a liberal spirit in this and other matters was a most articulate 'up yours' to the parody of traditionalism espoused by Min Aung Hlaing and his bigoted gang.

Earlier in this book I wrote of my experience in The Box of hearing prisoners being tortured. Torture of prisoners took place in Insein, too, then and later. Here, I was able to see its results firsthand: signs of beatings and canings in the form of bruises, welts and scars. These were typically on the victim's back but sometimes on the shin. The only treatment these wounds received was a purple powder concoction, based on a plant held by traditional medicine to ward off infection. I saw perhaps a hundred or so such marked prisoners in my time in Insein. The same prisoners seem to have been allocated particularly uncomfortable labour. Whenever I was not in my cell, I tried always to project a spirit of optimism to other prisoners, especially the Class C people I encountered outside my ward. Since I stood out rather dramatically, I would often be stared at, albeit in a friendly way. And with a certain mystification if they didn't know who I was. The prisoners who knew of my links to The Lady would grin and swap thumbs-up signals, sometimes even venturing the three-fingered salute that was a favourite gesture of resistance towards the hated junta.

Sometimes other prisoners would approach me, perhaps to urge me to speak out once I could do so, to not forget them. I have not forgotten them, and on all sorts of fora I have sought to bear witness to their suffering and the grotesque injustices meted out to them and their fellow citizens. This book is just one of the vehicles for doing this. Yet, their stories and entreaties haunt me still.

For the most part I was treated reasonably well by Insein's prison guards. A large percentage of them were barely out of their teens and – with the exception of a few who were obviously on the up, so their current role was merely a stepping stone – all were poor, ill-educated, and with few other options. Most of the guards – probably a sizeable majority – had voted for the NLD themselves in the 2020 elections (I asked), and every one of them seemed in awe of Daw Suu – an awe that rubbed off on me a little, to my benefit. Meanwhile, many of the senior prison officials had been appointed during, if not by, the NLD administration as part of a push to try to reduce at least the worst of the horrors with which the name Insein had long been associated.

I learned many important and useful things while a prisoner in Insein. But I also learned a lot of things I didn't want to know about. I came to know far too much, for instance, about the ranks of prison guards, police and military. Way too much of martial etiquette. One star, two star, three star, really big star, most humungous star . . . I got to know who among the guards was likely for promotion, who was being railroaded out. Who was up, who was down. Who was well-connected, who was not. I really didn't care. I did, however, learn to care about which guards had green campaign ribbons on their tunics. These coloured ribbons meant they were ex-military: too often a sign that the person so-decorated would be especially mean to political prisoners, or just more likely to be a bastard.

One of these, a young man whose father was a senior military officer, was regularly belligerent to me. He wore what was presumably a fake gold Rolex, and by the name 'Gold Watch' was forever known to me and – after I bestowed the label – to the others, too. One evening, he was especially harsh in ordering me into my cell long before closing time. He was taken to task by my faithful and courageous Jacoob: 'Don't you ever do that again. You have no idea who you are dealing with.' Thereafter Gold Watch was more circumspect in his dealings with me. Like some of the other guards, he was frightened of Jacoob.

On any given day and at any random time, the prison guards would raid our cells searching for contraband and bribes. Unsurprisingly, they were on the lookout for knives, even the 'homemade' ones that served as cutlery. The biggest prizes were electronic devices of any form, but the Holy Grail was mobile phones. I certainly did not have one of these, and I neither saw nor heard of any throughout my entire incarceration. Rumours abounded of their presence – and the size of the kickbacks needed to procure one.

Usually the guards found nothing at all. As this outcome was not acceptable to their superiors, they would improvise: most searches followed some kind of theme in order to appear effective. One time they targeted clothes hangers. We all had these – they were essential items to dry clothes: suitable wires or protruding nails were few and far between. All the hangers were plastic, and none remotely usable as a weapon or for repurpose as anything nefarious. Out they all went, though. At least we could enjoy the spectacle of prison officers hidden beneath a rainbow array of plastic triangles. Afterwards, however, drying clothes was even more of a hassle.

Raids were always carefully filmed, and the footage sent directly to the junta Home Affairs Minister. At no time did I have much in the way of contraband and in the end nothing was ever taken from me, apart from those wretched clothes hangers.

What was that about not having *much* contraband?

Okay, so I did have some. I had a knife. A knife created out of an aluminium lid from a can of peanuts. By bending it again and again, I managed to break it into two sharp pieces which, with a little judicious folding at one end, functioned as a handle. My knife was hard and sharp enough to cut food, as long as it was very soft. I was proud of this knife.

One other. My pen. It was only a cheap plastic biro I acquired from a fellow prisoner – the sort of instrument that, as something of a pen aficionado, I would once have rejected with a shudder.

But it was just about my most precious possession. My precious. I kept it secret. I kept it safe.

Living in Insein was tough – physically and psychologically.

Conditions were harsh and hard. Sanitary standards were especially low, even as COVID raged across Myanmar. Thanks to the sharing of food and the inadequate toilet and waste facilities, diseases were easily acquired and easily spread.

Psychologically, the cocktail of fear, anxiety and monumental boredom morphed readily into self-obsession. Every hour of the conscious day was imbued with real, exaggerated and imagined suffering. As prisoners we experienced a complete lack of agency over the most basic aspects of life, an understanding that our fate was completely beyond our control. This was especially difficult for most of us 'politicals' – highly active people, used to making decisions, used to being autonomous. Now we were at the mercy of a regime that, outside the prison walls, was going about killing people in order to remain in power: they were all about brutality, irrationality and dysfunction. And here we were, trussed up for these killers, who already identified us as enemies of their Potemkin state.

And it was hot. So hot. And there were the insects, about which it was impossible not to obsess. Ants crawling over you at night. In your food and belongings. On your utensils. Eating their way through everything. The fear you might step bare feet on a centipede or be stung by a scorpion on the toilet. The awful buzz of the mosquitos. And all of this exacerbated at night, when these creatures were drawn to cell lights that were never switched off.

How to survive all of this? How to stay sane? How not to succumb to despair?

For me, first up was simply to walk. To pace the cell as I had done in The Box, then to walk the concrete path outside. No matter how hot, no matter how sunburned I became.

Physical activity was the primary survival strategy of pretty much everyone else. As political prisoners we did not have to work, so we had loads of excess energy, frustrations and anxieties to burn off. For some others this, too, meant walking, and via this I was able to establish a warm friendship with another walker, a Malaysian prisoner named Fariz Azman.

Fariz had come to Myanmar a year or two earlier to seek out investment opportunities in renewable energy, a priority of the NLD Government. A series of entanglements with local cronies and figures in Myanmar had culminated in trumped-up drug trafficking charges, and further judicial and police corruption brought about Fariz's conviction and a 14-year sentence in Insein. Pounding a path together outside Ward 4, we became firm friends. Fariz was open about his missteps, his despair at his imprisonment and occasional inability to function, as well as the ways he was able to surmount it all – and even to be hopeful an eventual pardon would come his way. We spoke about other things – not least our experiences and ideas in common on development economics, and our interpretation of the seemingly arbitrary and erratic events around us. We shared stories of our families, and an appreciation of Grand Prix motor racing. My walks with him were pleasant ones. Fariz would be released in March 2022, by which time we were no longer held in the same facility.

Many prisoners, if they did exercise, chose activities rather more vigorous than walking. Most were way younger than me, so I didn't feel too bad in the contrast. Their activities were varied, but they included table tennis – at which Jacoob was both the most accomplished player and leading coach – and *chinlone*. The national game of Myanmar, it's a non-competitive sport in which six players use their legs and head to keep a rattan ball from touching the ground. *Chinlone* requires tremendous skill, it has always seemed to me, and much stamina.

By far the most popular physical activity among the prisoners was weightlifting. Yes, that staple of every prison movie ever made. Its appeal, even in far-off Myanmar, seemed universal. All a bit much for me, but it served its purpose. At the close of the cell doors, the weights – much of it acquired courtesy of the Taiwanese drug traffickers – had to be put under lock and key, in case they were turned into weapons.

I should note that, as enthusiastic as many of them were, none of the prisoners I saw ever 'bulked up' Schwarzenegger-style. Fit for sure, but they remained skinny Burmese guys: no-one got enough to eat to be a body builder. Our captors had no cause to fear prison riots of would-be Arnies.

7

Books and Bags

Securing my release was Ha's highest priority. Throughout the long wait for this to happen, she did her utmost to ensure my wellbeing every moment I was a captive in Myanmar.

The junta were extremely wary about opening up avenues of communications of any sort between me and the outside world, and the consistent contact Ha and I eventually had via allowed phone calls (more on this in Chapter 8) took an achingly long time to set up.

Among Ha's top concerns for me were that I had insufficient food to eat and nothing to read, plus she was fearful I would suffer from any number of new and existing health conditions. I can't say her worries on these fronts were unwarranted. Rising to the challenge, she devised a system of parcel deliveries across the distances that was astonishing in its reach and efficiency. It was the Berlin airlift and then some. Ha was able to get parcels to me via the Embassy, via Curtis. These contained food, medicines, books, and essentially anything else that I needed and was permitted to receive.

The food included not just items that could be bought in Yangon, but items Ha made at home. Ha is an excellent cook and an even better baker. She would make me cakes and cookies, allow them to cool, then immediately preserve them in vacuum-sealed bags.

Ha would send her package via courier from Sydney to DFAT in Canberra, where they would be put in the diplomatic pouch to Yangon. There Curtis would pick them up from the Australian Embassy, include them with his own and extra Embassy items – and transport them to me in the prison. My sister, Lisa, was also a part of the parcel chain, filling in for Ha every now and again and including items of comfort familiar to someone who had spent his formative years in Sydney during the 1970s and '80s. Lisa has a well-developed sense of humour, and she would draw smiley faces and funny messages on food packets and other items in her parcels. I got a huge boost the first time I saw one of these.

But the books! How did those get past the junta's gatekeeping system? Isn't the history of despotism punctuated with book bannings and/or burnings?

Only after much struggle and perseverance of a great many people is the short answer, and via all sorts of avenues and with much skulduggery along the way.

It began simply enough. Understanding intuitively my distress at having nothing to read Ha, in collaboration with Curtis, included a set of books in their first effort to deliver a parcel of food to me in Insein. Deliveries of essentials were routine for regular prisoners, but only nervously agreed for me at this point.

Ha and her team had a hell of a job convincing the authorities that books were essential. Curtis is a difficult man to deny, though. The books began to flow.

From then on, Ha would spend her weekends finding books and articles for me. Her quest was wide, deep and relentless, and reached into surely every fascinating crevice of economics, history, philosophy, travel and aviation, maritime lore, and – somewhat poignantly – spy fiction. She kept me informed with news items from the *Economist* and *Financial Times*, and entertained with the *History of Economics Review*. Once the system was established, she was assiduous in taking my specific requests and in denuding my own bookshelves at home.

In sourcing books in Myanmar, Curtis had some ready allies. These included Australia's Ambassador, Andrea Faulkner; Tom Coward, of what was then the UK's Department for International Development; and Alex Albertine and Scott Kofmehl of the US Embassy, all four of whom volunteered their entire libraries for Curtis to raid on my behalf. As time wore on, they would all buy books for me: in Yangon, Bangkok, London, New York, Sydney . . . and from Amazon.com.

Crucial to the system was Curtis's skill as the 'last mile' deliverer to the prison. Curtis is eminent and eminently eccentric among what is sometimes the grey pallor of economic development specialists, which partly explains his success at interacting with the prison guards of Insein. I suspect even now that what would become the regular flow of books to me in Insein was largely due to his efforts, and his powers of persuasion.

One of the reasons I can be near certain of this is that the formal barriers to me getting books were high. All book titles had to be submitted for approval by Home Affairs, with any that mentioned Myanmar rejected straightaway. Dissident authors, works of famous human rights campaigners, books on international politics – all were subject to immediate rejection. Problematic histories were taboo, as was anything to do with Taiwan, China, Russia, or anything critical of junta allies.

After a title was approved in principle by Myanmar's Home Affairs, a summary of it had to be written by the jail translators for the relevant senior officer of the prison (usually the Deputy Superintendent). Lastly, when it arrived, the physical book came under minute scrutiny for hidden messages, codes or insertions of contraband.

In practice, and over time, Curtis and my band of book traffickers managed to surmount many of these obstacles, and books covering all sorts of topics made their way to me. To illustrate the success of my benefactors, I might highlight that one of the books they got through to me was George Orwell's *1984*. This seminal work for freedom everywhere has special relevance in Myanmar: the longstanding and bitter joke in the country is that it is in fact Book 3 of Orwell's trilogy on the country, the other two being *Burmese Days* and *Animal Farm*.

On a number of occasions, the guards did push back on the volume of books I was getting. One told Curtis, as he delivered another stash, 'He already has a book.'

It was books more than anything that kept me going day to day. Books have always been central to my life. Now they saved my life. I am itching to describe in detail all of the books I got, and which particular intellectual and emotional niche they nourished, but that would surely stretch this book to beyond, well, even *Lord of the Rings*: yes, that was one of 'em! Restraining myself then, I might suffice to mention that among the most important were Clive James's *Cultural Amnesia* (an in-depth celebration of liberal democracy through its bravest defenders – which I read at least a dozen times), Ron Chernow's *Alexander Hamilton* (which I'd read a bunch of times before Insein – but hey, why not half a dozen more?), Robert Skidelsky's giant biography of John Maynard Keynes (another old favourite), Michael Ignatieff's splendid biography of Isaiah Berlin (a revelation), and some fiction from Ian McEwan, Simon Barnes and Daniel Silva. Eric Lomax's *The Railway Man* was probably the most relevant, considering my surrounds. If all this sounds a little highbrow, let me confess to many a trashy thriller, too. Given the purported reason for my imprisonment, I read spy variants of the latter with more than a few feelings of the absurd.

In an act of especially inspired genius, Lisa sent Curtis some of my nephews' old Famous Five paperbacks. Enid Blyton is very out of favour these days, but lashings of surreal enjoyment followed the arrival of these.

I fancy that another factor in my own survival was my ready access to the imaginary world that had accompanied me since childhood, which I had never really outgrown. Give me a quiet place, and it was a simple thing for my mind to wander into all sorts of narratives. In Insein, I would think of my heroes of youth. More recent role models had been hard to come by – many had fallen in my estimation as I'd grown in my understanding of the world.

My imaginary world was itself a function of books, of course: the books of my childhood and early teenage years. Such tomes were invariably what could be called boy's-own tales of derring-do, but my repertoire extended to classical epics. Stories of fighter pilots, gallant sailors, great explorers, sporting champions, knights errant – I'm sure the genre will be a familiar one. Within this, however, I had specialised in the sub-genre of escape stories. Mostly set in prisoner-of-war camps, mainly in the Second World War – Paul Brickhill and *The Great Escape*, *The Colditz Story*, Weary Dunlop, tales of Changi and *The Bridge on the River Kwai*, and so on. They provided good old-fashioned inspiration, and a desire to measure up – or, more relevantly perhaps, not to fall short.

In the awful real-world situation I found myself in, however, this foundational reading and the lessons I took from it created for me something of a dilemma. Should I be trying to evade or defy my captors? Did I not have a duty to do so – especially as a foreigner who may be untouchable by retribution? I would, in fact, be somewhat defiant and 'bolshie' later, but during this first period of formal detention, I did little to resist. Frankly, I felt too vulnerable to the potential loss of discretionary concessions – the phone calls, the books, the food and Embassy supplies. I was also still hopeful of release, and/or the dropping of charges. Defiance, exposure of the regime and its cruelties, would be best done when I was free, when I had the tools and the opportunities to make it count. Or, at least, this is what I told myself. I also realised quickly that the idea of any sort of escape and evasion was fanciful. I was not a British officer in Colditz, but a prominent Westerner in mainland Southeast Asia.

To say that I would have stood out like canine testicles surely understates matters.

But if a decision not to try to escape was beyond reproach, this still left other dilemmas. Of being too thankful, for instance, for routine allowances and acts by prison guards that were little more than what could minimally be expected from another human being. Certainly I 'lost it' now and again. Shouting at the injustice of everything and of Min Aung Hlaing's parentage and sexual proclivities were standard features of such rants. Some shaking of the bars. The guards looked on and said nothing.

Maybe there was an explanation for that. One thing I had gleaned from the disproportionate amount of time in my youth spent reading prisoner-of-war and assorted stories was that achieving some sort of emotional connection with the guards could be important for my survival. Not easy given the linguistic, cultural and even generational divide. One possible way in was that a high proportion of the guards – the younger ones, especially – donned English Premier League jerseys whenever they felt disposed to put aside their uniforms. I wasn't too familiar with Premier League, but I knew enough to initiate conversations about the respective virtues of Manchester United vis-à-vis City.

Even more effective in this context, however, was a strategy I learned from American war-correspondent Robert Kaplan's book *Imperial Grunts*, which Curtis brought to me. It included advice on how to survive a kidnapping. Kaplan suggested that family photo sharing was a way to promote empathy in a situation like mine, so I showed the guards photographs of Ha and Phuong. It appeared to work. Not least since, after seeing pictures of Ha, my esteem seemed to rise in the eyes of my captors.

'Really,' I could almost hear them asking, 'she's with him?'

One absence that I felt acutely, from the first moments in The Box to Day 650, was music. I am not remotely knowledgeable about music, nor do I play a single musical instrument. I never have, and I'm sure – given my complete lack of the necessary talent – I never will. Yet, music is important to me. It moves me, comforts me, inspires me. It helps me think, it helps me relax. Now I heard nothing of it. Deprived of music, I craved it.

The best I could do in the circumstances was try to whistle or sing my favourite songs, and this I did. Badly. In Insein, I gave my whistling full voice. But this may be a good time to issue a warning: I should confess that not only am I not knowledgeable about music, what I do know is probably better forgotten. I had, and I have, appalling taste. No song from the disco era of the '80s era, for instance, is beyond my whistling repertoire. ABBA? Oh, yes. Boney M? Even better. 'Love Unlimited' by Barry White? Now we're in the groove.

But I had some idiosyncratic tunes of defiance in my repertoire, too. Christopher Cross's 'Ride Like the Wind' got a guernsey, as did 'Tie a Yellow Ribbon Round the Old Oak Tree'. I could never pass up The Pretenders' 'I'll Stand by You', even though it never failed to make me tear up. Last but not least was the tune always playing in my mind when the chips were really down. At the darkest, deepest moments – as when I stepped over the threshold into Insein and, later, at my sentencing – I found myself humming the theme music from the 1969 movie *Battle of Britain*, composed by Ron Goodwin and played by the Central Band of the Royal Air Force. This probably sounds corny, and yes, it is a touch of old-fashioned jingoism – though of another country to my own! – but there you have it. With its bold fanfares and stirring symphonic flourishes, it conjured exactly the spirit I needed.

An important way that other prisoners survived was to immerse themselves in religion. In my experience, people in Myanmar are more devout than most, so a recourse to Buddhist rituals – beyond those enforced – seemed to come readily. This was facilitated and encouraged by the prison in plenty of ways, not all of them good. For instance, only religious books were permitted to be circulated among some prisoner cohorts. On Sundays, Christian services were conducted, and I could hear Catholic masses and Baptist hymns from nearby. I was forbidden to attend any of these, even though I asked to a couple of times. Because I'd grown up going to church, I thought the sights and sounds of church and its familiar rituals might have helped. For the prison authorities, however – anxious not to allow me any visibility and worried that information about my condition might leak out – this was not something they could countenance. They did not want me mingling with, or being recognised from afar, by too many other prisoners.

The potency of rumours in Insein was phenomenal. When combined with the wishful thinking that I discovered to be a characteristic of us prisoners, some truly fanciful narratives resulted. One rumour that came to be regarded as 'hard fact' – even by the most sober and mature of prisoners – was that

US aircraft carriers had been sighted off Yangon: an American invasion was imminent and the demise of the junta a foregone conclusion. I took on the self-appointed task of pouring cold water on these and similar stories of rescue by Western democracies. It was not a task I enjoyed. I wished the stories could have been true.

Another more or less constant rumour, though one I did not feel qualified to comment on, was that Insein was about to be overrun by the People's Defence Force, the sharp end of the opposition to the junta, which was emerging as a genuine threat to Myanmar's thuggish military. Believing in what you ardently wished for was so very hard to resist.

My constant wish was for something intangible and quiet: predictability. During my time in the prison, I came to fear the unexpected. I craved routine. Change was disturbing and, in my recent experience, almost always for the worse. A good day for me was one where nothing much happened.

There were tangibles I wished for, too: I lacked so many things in the cell, things that could make life more bearable. Like a clock. It might sound counterintuitive, but wasting your life away in a prison is worse when you can't see it happening on a clock face. In Insein, most days were utterly unstructured beyond the broad patterns of waking up, meals, basic functions. But when to do all of these things? How to overlay endless monotony with some feeling of direction or movement? While the answer to this came primarily via the other activities mentioned in these pages – the walking, reading, talking with other prisoners, and so on – foundational to everything was being able to plan: by knowing what time it was.

Clocks were forbidden, but that simply meant they were difficult to obtain. So, I did get one. Eventually. It came via Jacoob. But then it stopped working, so I put in a formal request for a clock to the highest levels of the prison, which I gather ended up on the desk of the Minister of Home Affairs himself.

Another item I lacked was a chair. To make do, I sat on a blanket on the concrete floor. But I was then 57, and getting off and then up from the floor was increasingly a painful and ungainly business. So I asked whether I could buy and have brought into the prison a plastic chair. The sort that all the staff had, as did many inmates. One that was cheap and had a single moulded shape that could never be refashioned as a weapon. Again, the request made its way up the chain of command, and after some months, approval for such a chair was given. But the Ministry of Home Affairs saw fit to impose a caveat. The chair must not have armrests. Why this restriction? To this day I do not know. I wanted the chair, so I agreed to the amputation. The chair duly arrived. It had armrests.

Some of the long-term prisoners, including Jacoob, had been able to purloin a television. Movies and news updates would circulate via smuggled thumb drives, otherwise the viewing fare was limited to Myanmar's dreadful State broadcasters. Whenever I could, I snuck into Jacoob's cell to watch Myanmar International Television (the outward-facing State broadcaster) and its English news. The program itself was stultifyingly dull. Stodgy, amateur production values, and stories that were as bland as could possibly be. The usual totalitarian State stuff, the most exciting moments provided by pieces celebrating Myanmar's bean and pulse exports and the dedication of new tractor factories. It was riveting.

The jail authorities were always concerned about my health. Stripped of all the blather, what they were really worried about was that I would die on them. While I was not unhealthy on arrival at Insein, that was no cause for complacency because it's well-known that quite a few apparently healthy middle-aged men drop dead – from heart attacks and other things. This was hardly a low-stress environment, diseases were rampant, health and safety standards non-existent and, if anything happened, there was not much that could be done. The jail hospital had little in the way of equipment or medicines and, apart from a couple of doctors, seemingly no trained staff. But the international scrutiny of my situation was unique, and as a consequence, so were the regular efforts to take my pulse. I mean literally take my pulse. It seemed to me throughout my imprisonment that Myanmar's military leaders were keen to treat me badly, yet dreaded what might ensue if I actually expired while in their hands.

Ha and the Embassy were worried I would get COVID, and put pressure on the prison authorities to get me vaccinated. After the rapid spread of the Delta variant in Myanmar in May 2021, Ha contacted people in Canberra with a suggestion: what if the Australian Government were to offer enough vaccines for *all* the prisoners at Insein as a way of getting the vaccine to me? Canberra demurred but around this time the authorities in Insein did take upon themselves the task of vaccinating the prisoners. In an effort to push back on what seemed to be accurate reports of prisoner ill-treatment and neglect, the junta made a great play of their distribution of the Chinese-provided Sinopharm vaccine around Myanmar's prisons. The propagandist and theatrical elements of this were on full display with respect to me: I was chosen to be the very first prisoner vaccinated, and my jab was broadcast on Myanmar television. Photographs of the procedure also appeared throughout the media.

The by-product of this for my family and friends was that at last they could see an image of me in Insein. Proof of life. In these images – which I only viewed after my release, a year and a half later – I am dressed in a blue surgical gown, with a hair net and face mask. It was what prison personnel insisted I wear whenever I was brought out of the ward. I recall being mindful I was being filmed and wanting to project resilience and defiance. Given the PPE gear I was swathed in, this rather stretched my thespian abilities.

About three weeks after receiving my Sinopharm vaccination, I caught COVID. The first of five times that I would catch the virus while imprisoned in Myanmar.

During my time in Insein and later, I was plagued by a recurring dream. I had been freed and was with family and friends back in Australia – but there was a catch: by the end of the day I had to return to the prison, and my cell. Details of location changed from one night to the next, sometimes even the cast of characters. So vivid did the dream seem to be that often I asked myself within it, *Am I dreaming?* But the narrative remained unaltered. Waking up, still in my cell, I would feel crushed.

Somewhat related to my dreams was the fact that I kept being told by other inmates that I would soon be released.

An Unlikely Prisoner

That this is what happened to foreigners. The more politically savvy the prisoner, the more likely they were to offer this assurance. Even the guards joined in, hinting at inside sources.

It did not happen.

Fellow Australian Ross Dunkley was one of the most remarkable characters I encountered in Insein. A former Walkley award-winning journalist and entrepreneur, in 2000 Ross had founded the *Myanmar Times*, which quickly became the premier independent English-language newspaper in the country. Ross was 'old school' and lived up to just about every stereotype of the Aussie newspaperman in Southeast Asia: it's highly likely he created a fair few of these stereotypes. He was, accordingly, a somewhat controversial figure well before his imprisonment in 2018. I liked Ross. He was a fantastically entertaining companion for a meal or a drink. We'd met for dinner once or twice during my time working in Myanmar, and I used to see a bit of him at various events in Yangon.

Ross was housed in a different area to me – in the hospital wing, partly because the prison was now running out of space – but he got messages through to me via prisoner intermediaries. In these he was as irrepressible as ever, urging me to 'hang in there', and telling me that the first six months or so were the worst, after which things 'got much better'. At that point still under the (mis) apprehension I might only be there for a few more weeks, I was horrified at the thought I might have to wait so long to get out.

Most significantly, and the surest indicator of Ross's big-hearted generosity, was that he sent over books for me, the first I received in Insein. They were truly a godsend. I remember they included Doris Kearns Goodwin's story of Abraham Lincoln's cabinet, *Team of Rivals*, which got me thinking about my own experiences with Daw Suu's government. I have a propensity – at times it's a distinct weakness – for becoming so absorbed in what I am reading that I am oblivious to practically everyone and everything around me. No doubt this has been to the exasperation of loved ones at times, but now this trait came in handy. I may have physically been in Insein Prison in 2021, but my mind could wander to Civil War era Gettysburg, Antietam, and the other places of the legend.

Ross was released amid a mass pardon by the junta of 23,000 prisoners in April 2021 to celebrate the Buddhist New Year. He sent another secret note as he was leaving and another bunch of books. We never did meet in person in Insein, but I felt even more isolated when this only other Australian in the prison departed (another Australian citizen would come soon as the protests escalated). Ross told Australian reporters on getting home that he feared that, given my association with Daw Suu, the junta might detain me 'for much longer'.

In contrast to my correspondence-only interactions with Ross, I met Danny Fenster a few months into my Insein stay. An American journalist – first with *Myanmar Now* and then the highly respected *Frontier* magazine – Danny was convicted of inciting unrest under the Penal Code and unlawful association under the colonial-era Unlawful Association Act, and sentenced to 11 years in prison. I briefly met Danny at the time of my COVID vaccination, but afterwards we found various surreptitious ways to swap books and *New Yorker* magazines.

After an enormous public campaign in the US and beyond, Danny was released in November 2021 following face-to-face negotiations between the former US Senator and Governor of New Mexico, Bill Richardson, and junta leader Min Aung Hlaing. I heard the news of Danny's release – by then I was in Naypyitaw – with some relief. This seemed to suggest the old ways with respect to foreign prisoners remained in place.

After the early release of Danny Fenster as well as other foreigners, notably some Japanese journalists, I became painfully aware that, in addition to my status as the first foreigner arrested after the coup, I was now the only one in custody.

Not all the foreigners in Insein enjoyed the support of their government. I'm thinking particularly of a group of Nigerians, who were incarcerated prior to the coup due to a range of financial crimes, mostly involving tampering with automatic teller machines. Many of the Nigerians had, in fact, served out their sentences but, with no money for plane tickets and a government back home unwilling to take them upon discharge from jail and deportation, they were stranded in Insein.

At times I was able to chat with these rather entertaining con men. They were a long way from home in all sorts of ways, and I couldn't help but feel sorry for them because of the hopeless position they were in.

Outside of Insein, and unconstrained by the bounds of 'official' policy-making, were the efforts of friends around the world to try to bring about my freedom.

One of the most prominent was the 'freeseanturnell.net' campaign run by seven academic/foreign policy friends: Professor David Throsby, Melissa Crouch, Charlotte Galloway, John Liljeblad, Nick Cheesman, Monique Skidmore, and Garry

Woodard. The website they established regularly updated people on my situation. Very early into my captivity, they also organised an open letter calling for my release – the 'Manifesto of 500 professors' – which was signed by academics around the world.

Leanne Ussher, an old friend and a professor in New York, coordinated what she herself described as a 'ragtag team of loyal Sean supporters'. Using network mapping of possible contacts, she ran a number of innovative campaigns, always in conjunction with Ha and Lisa. Among these campaigns were some spectacular efforts that, for various reasons, never quite made the cut. They included a plan to project my image on to the 'sails' of the Sydney Opera House, and another to distribute eggs with my portrait on them. I guess I would not have seen all this – but, wow!

8

Making Contact

For some weeks after my transfer to Insein, I had no contact with the Embassy or with Ha.

In the interim, I smuggled a message to Ha via Paing Ye Thu: yes, the same wonderful young man whose greeting to me when I first arrived at Insein had so lifted my spirits. Paing Ye Thu had received an amnesty and ahead of his release promised me he would email Ha as soon as he could. He was as good as his word.

Paing Ye Thu sent Ha a photograph of a piece of paper I had given him. On it I had written a message that was brief, to the point – its purpose was to allow Ha to realise it was genuine: 'Paing Ye Thu is a friend. Proofs: "V" and "Rock Scone". I am OK, but no contact with anyone from outside. I love you. Sean.' As I mentioned earlier, certain codenames and signals had been worked out with Ha early on; 'Rock Scone', on the other hand, was an item of Ha's baking that was a particular favourite. It could hardly have been less relevant to my present surrounds. It was ideal.

After about a month of measured formal approaches, the Embassy was able to assert my right under the agreed procedures of Myanmar's Prisons Department and I received a drought-breaking second consular call. Among many other things, they explained that four of these were to be allowed each month. Twenty minutes at a time. The Embassy was to submit a request to Myanmar's Ministry of Foreign Affairs (MOFA) at least seven days before each call. MOFA is, however, a ministry without much status in the country's military power structure and so, in practice, almost anything concerning me ended up being forwarded to the Ministry of Home Affairs – and usually the Minister himself – for approval.

Ha managed to get the Embassy and Canberra to agree that three of the four monthly calls would be exclusively between her and myself – with the Embassy providing the link – while the fourth would be shared: ten minutes with the Ambassador, ten with Ha. An unusual arrangement perhaps, but a wholly reasonable one in the mind of the formidable force that is my wife.

For me the calls entailed a good deal of logistics and palaver. Every time I set foot outside my ward – including for the weekly phone calls – I was required to don full COVID PPE gear. This was a requirement placed on all the 'political' prisoners, but rarely on others. What a charade it was. These items, dispensed once, were never changed. Further, the guards and fellow prisoners who had to attend trials and interrogations came and went from the prison without COVID-testing of any form. Luckily, the prospect of the call outweighed the nuisance factor of having to put on this stuff.

When it was almost time to go, my escort would assemble for the long walk back to the guard house, where the phone and related facilities were located. Without fail, I was accompanied by two prison guards from my ward, a senior officer of Insein – sometimes the Superintendent himself, but mostly his deputy – plus the prison doctor, a member of military intelligence, an office of police Special Branch, a representative from the Ministry of Immigration and Population, one or two regular police officers, a sound engineer to record the conversation, and an official from Home Affairs to film it all. There was also a stenographer/interpreter, invariably a fellow prisoner – nameless here, alas – and as the weeks and months wore on, the two of us would become friends.

Once there, everyone had to assume their positions in the room. I can visualise still the telephone used for these calls. A plastic unit of 1990s vintage, it was attached to the jail's phone network via copper wires crudely twisted together with a landline cable pulled out from the wall.

During the call, I had to exercise caution in what I said. For obvious reasons, there were certain topics Ha and I steered clear of. References to political developments in Myanmar had to be strictly off-limits. They could be used against me in the trial – I was accused of passing on information and being a spy, after all – or simply as an excuse to cut out the calls. Other matters we spoke of purely in our prearranged but far-from-perfect code. Sometimes, it was a flop! To compound the challenges, Myanmar's communications infrastructure is universally dreadful – although improvements had been dramatic before the coup – and this was on full display in most of my phone calls. I don't think we got through a single call without the line dropping out at least once, and sound quality was such that I had to sometimes guess what Ha was telling me. I got no 'credit' for the time lost in the dropouts, by the way. Twenty minutes was the time allocated for the whole process. No more, no less.

For the first few calls, I was a little guarded when talking about personal matters. Then, not only did I cease to care about that aspect of my privacy – 'Let them listen, they might learn something!' – but I came to view our emotional openness as a strategy in my pushback. A senior prison officer who was present for most of the calls later told me, in a rare moment of attempted human connection, that he felt inspired by the ways Ha and I routinely communicated and was trying to emulate that with his own wife. Maybe we saved a marriage.

As mentioned, in her informal dealings with DFAT, Ha now went by the nickname 'NOK' (next of kin). Somehow it suited, and it became my favoured name for her. On Ha's part, her favourite name for me was 'The Liability'. If you have watched any Jason Bourne films, you will know that every agent/assassin employed by the CIA under deep cover is referred to as 'The Asset'. Given the circumstances, calling me The Liability had a certain ironic appeal. It also had the upside of being a label that sailed completely over the heads of the Myanmar authorities listening in to our call. Speaking of which, the number of these eavesdroppers, and the lengths they went to, was extraordinary.

As soon as possible after we had hung up, the video and transcript of each call would be dispatched to Home Affairs in Naypyitaw. I'm not sure they could have learned much from them, beyond the fact that there were some relationships, some interactions between people who were immune from the corruption and cowardice that was *their* stock in trade.

The instigator of the phone calls, Ambassador Andrea Faulkner, could not have been more supportive during my imprisonment. To the extent permitted by the prison, she swung the resources of the Embassy in meeting my physical needs but also in keeping up my spirits. In an early message she was at pains to say that I had done nothing wrong. She knew I knew that, but wanted to give me her assurance and, implicitly, that of the Australian Government. I appreciated it.

As with Ha, I had to devise a coded way to describe conditions in Insein. Andrea had included in one of my book deliveries her very own copy of Robert Hughes' classic on Australia's convict past, *The Fatal Shore*. This seminal history documented at length the horrors of Australia's founding penal colony. When I told her on the fly that the conditions in which I was living were 'Norfolk Island' rather than 'what Napoleon had on St Helena', the message was not lost.

The phone calls were one avenue through which I was able to stay in touch with Ha and the outside world. Another came via the letters Ha was able to send me with the parcels of food and other essentials via Curtis and the Embassy.

While I was in Myanmar's prisons, Ha wrote over 100 letters to me. Not all of them got through – in this as in myriad other ways, we were always hostage to the whims of individual prison officials – but most did. In the letters and via the phone calls, she laboured to keep my spirits up, even as she suppressed her own fears and anxieties. She kept worries – for example, over money – away from me by taking them on herself. All the while, she was also a full-time academic and a full-time mum. It was an existence of unrelenting stress, anxiety and sheer hard work.

Ha's first language is not English. She was born in Vietnam and only came to Australia for the first time in 2005. But these letters were, in my admittedly biased opinion, a masterclass of prose devoted to love, loyalty and plain practicalities. Honesty was at the heart of them, with Ha determining from the get-go that anything less than candour would undermine my morale. In Myanmar's penal system, I lived in a world of lies, and so from her only truth would allow us to make the right decisions. We had to face realities. I could not be given false optimism, even if it might make me feel better.

Ha was open in her letters in expressing her sadness, fears, loneliness. This was from an early letter, about three months in:

> I miss your voice. I have been playing your voice messages you sent me since you left home again and again many times, some very funny, and I still laughed out loud. Please don't think too much, try to enjoy the books and articles we send you. Please endure the hardship a bit longer, we are almost there.

Knowing well the inspiration I had long taken from the story of Alexander Hamilton, who rose to become the first US Secretary of the Treasury, despite decidedly inauspicious beginnings, she quoted from the eponymous musical:

So long as you come home at the end of the day,
That would be enough.

On several occasions she declared she would come to me:

I could travel to Myanmar and be there, closer to you ...
Then I could hang out, around the prison gate, perhaps to catch a glimpse of you every now and then.

I wish I could swap positions with you ...

My father; my sister, Lisa; nephews Tim and Mitchell; and friends and colleagues from around the world also sent letters. Not all of these were passed on to me by the prison. One special item I received was a birthday card from our daughter, Phuong. A talented illustrator, she sent a card that depicted graphically just about all my interests. A cavalcade of my nonsense, expressed in the way that only a clever teenager can. It took pride of place on the wall of my cell.

My ability to reply to letters was much circumscribed. In theory I was permitted to write one letter per month, but before it could be sent it had to be cleared by censors – first in the prison itself, and then by Home Affairs in Naypyitaw. The process took months. A letter I wrote in April 2021 did not get to Ha until October.

Equally as bad as my taste in music were my efforts to compose poems of love and gratitude to Ha. I wrote a dozen or so of these. Sincere and heartfelt they most certainly were but, well, frankly they never rose beyond overwrought doggerel. Lest you suspect I exaggerate in order to slyly boast of my modesty,

Sean Turnell

I tender the stanza below as evidence. Since – tragically, you might conclude – Ha and I are both economists, and thus privy to the romantic vernacular of the profession – I decided to use the parallel meaning of the word 'bond':

> Bonds, and Bonds
> Sean Turnell, for Ha Vu

A second anniversary finds us apart
A test, a challenge, for my sure and stout heart
The debt that I owe you, my Hanoi true blue,
Hopefully, surely, is soon to come due
A Bond of Six zeros? Nine zeros? Twelve zeros? More
Certainly beyond that which Jay Powell can keep score
Infinity! Now that's the face value I want
A figure so big, best writ in small font
Love you forever my darling Ha Vu
The gilt, the sovereign, I know that is you.

As an assignment marker of long standing, I'd like to think I might get a C? For effort?

9

Prison Economics

Once an economist always an economist, I'm afraid.

As the weeks went by I started tuning in to the functioning of the internal economy of the prison. Especially when I realised that this was more or less a mirror of the economy outside. There was an official component, which didn't work very well; a functioning infrastructure, only to the extent that it was the product of the colonial era; and a black market, in which almost anything could be obtained if you had enough money to buy it.

Naturally, the black market was by far the most interesting. Curiously, though, and against my expectations, it was not so much built on contraband as on food. Mind you, I have noted already that the food provided by the jail was not nutritionally sufficient to keep body and soul together.

On the supply side of the market, the principal actors were the prison guards themselves. Who wouldn't want to supplement a base salary of only around K170,000 a month (at the time, little more than US$100; now – with the dramatic reduction in the value of Myanmar's currency, the kyat – even less than that). From talking with some of the guards, I found out that they could lift their earnings to around 1 million kyat a month by joining this black-market activity, so they were a highly motivated conduit for food and other goods from outside.

The prison guards were not the only ones to take advantage of what was, after all, literally a captive market. Suppliers (shops, traders) were able to impose steep mark-ups – around 10 per cent or so on basic food items, tens of percent on simple comforts, and up to many hundreds or even thousands of percent on actual contraband (cigarettes and alcohol mainly).

Most fascinating of all were the internal monetary arrangements in Insein. Economists have long been intrigued by the proxy currencies that circulate in jails and prisoner-of-war camps, ever since the seminal work of Richard Radford ('The Economic Organisation of a POW Camp', 1945) shone a light on how cigarettes became 'money' in POW camps in the Second World War. In Insein, cigarettes are a highly contraband item and for this reason – not to mention that people typically like to smoke them straightaway – they did not function as a currency. Instead, the most widely accepted internal money took the form of individual tea and coffee sachets.

Just like sovereign currencies outside, however, there was a distinct ordering in the value of these currencies. Most valued – the veritable Swiss francs of the system – were local brand tea and coffee 'three-in-one' sachets that conveniently brought together tea/coffee, milk substitute powder and sugar. Reflecting local taste, tea always traded at a slight premium to coffee. High in sugar, these were preferred to international, low-sugar brands.

My preferred consumption item – the simple black coffee sachet without either 'milk' or sugar – was disdained by the money dealers. The copper coins of the prison proxy currency world.

From time to time, I got an inkling that, outside the prison, Myanmar's economy was disintegrating. Mostly this came through the rapidly changing prices of goods brought in from outside, in turn a function of the collapsing exchange rate of Myanmar's kyat. Another indicator was the dramatic reduction of flights leaving Yangon airport in the months after the coup, and their near-complete cessation in May 2021. Insein was located immediately under the flight path of aircraft leaving Yangon International, so it was an ideal land-base from which to observe the ups and downs of the aviation business in Myanmar.

It goes without saying that COVID restrictions played a big part in all of this, but the coup was at the very least the icing on this especially rancid cake. The fact was that few people were allowed to leave Myanmar; even fewer wanted to come there.

10

Legal Follies

The matter of the legal case against me came into full focus a month or so into my time in Insein.

Officially, I had still not been charged with anything, but I gleaned that 'investigations' were taking place into alleged breaches of the Burma Official Secrets Act, 1923 (OSA), a colonial-era law whose purpose was to deter government servants from revealing secrets for purposes 'prejudicial to the safety of the State'. An accompanying charge under the Burma Immigration (Emergency Provisions) Act of 1947 – also of the colonial era – was likewise being prepared. The irony of the use of British colonial laws by a regime steeped in xenophobia and founded in illegality and illegitimacy did not escape me.

There were implications to ponder. The immigration case would only become relevant if the OSA charge was proven. If it was found that I had broken OSA law, the conditions of my visa would have been breached, too. One of the crimes under the Immigration Act was attempting to interfere in the internal affairs of Myanmar. Given that this was precisely what I had been hired to do, any charge under this might be reasonably assumed to be easily brought.

Ha had been able to assemble a small group of legal advisers – in addition to the wider team of supporters working for my release. Their advice was that if the police focused on 'offences' by me under the Immigration Act, it was potentially a good sign. An indication that I was not the target of any wider investigation, but someone whom the junta needed to hold and question for a bit, and then deport. In short, the legal assessment was that immigration charges would show I was simply a pawn in a bigger game. The lawyers did not put it in writing but strongly implied that this bigger game concerned Daw Suu.

The penalties for breaches of the immigration law were jail time of between six months and five years, and/or a fine of K1500 (about US$1 at the time). One might have plumped for the latter.

So what if the junta prosecuted the OSA case?

Well, my legal advisers regarded it as a non-starter. The OSA only applied to Myanmar citizens and formally appointed servants of the State. I was neither. According to my legal team:

> If the rule of law were applied, there is clearly no case to answer and the charges should be dismissed. We have tried to explain this legal argument *'informally'* to the *'authorities'* so that they could save face when this argument is raised in Court but we believe that this endeavour did not work because the 'authorities' do not really understand the legal point regarding applicability of law. **However, if this point were explained by a trusted person to the top authorities,**

> we still believe there to be a strong chance that it would result in an early release for Prof. Turnell, as the authorities still wish to be seen to be acting legitimately.

Even if I had been a Myanmar citizen or a formally appointed official, the case would still have been exceedingly weak – 'another non-charge' according to my lawyers. Their reasoning here was multifaceted, but it included that any conviction under the OSA would require evidence that what I did was for purposes 'prejudicial to the safety or interests of the State'. Once again, given that I had been appointed precisely to do otherwise, and under the instruction of 'lawful authority', the advice of the legal team at this early stage was that I would not be charged, and the case would simply be dismissed.

The maximum penalty for breaches of the OSA was 14 years' jail if the secrets involved the military or security services; three years for anything else. It was important to know what the maximum penalties were because bail was not permitted in cases where the maximum prison term exceeded seven years. In all of the legal processes that lay ahead of me, bail would never be on offer.

Between the apparent weakness of the potential cases against me and the history in Myanmar of foreign prisoners typically being released, the lawyers were optimistic that I would be freed. As the weeks of my detention kept mounting, however, a dilemma arose for them: whether to formally appoint local legal representatives for me and have them take up my case against my captors. You might assume that the answer was surely 'yes' – but in Myanmar things are never so clear cut. Formally appointing a lawyer could facilitate more timely access to information about my case and my condition, but it might also push a judge into a corner – forcing them to start proceedings and to rule that there was a case to answer. In this circumstance, according to further legal advice Ha and the supporter team obtained, 'any diplomatic efforts to get [Sean] released or any goodwill that might cause him to be released . . . would be complicated by his having been charged. Not having a lawyer would make it harder for the regime to legitimize proceedings.'

Then there was another factor – there was no guarantee of finding a lawyer who was good, available and able to communicate with me in English. One of the external lawyers advising Ha, who had decades of experience in Myanmar, told her bluntly:

> . . . most Myanmar criminal lawyers do not speak any English and those that do have either been arrested, or were unwilling to put themselves in danger by representing Prof. Turnell, and those that were willing to represent Prof. Turnell are not competent to do so.

If all of this was not decisive enough in the 'no' case for appointing a local lawyer at this point, the legal advisers also dismissed the chance of there being any long-term benefits. It was pointed out that, 'if ST is charged, ST will almost certainly be convicted and the lawyer will not be able to do anything to prevent this'.

Lawyers in Myanmar were usually barred from saying much at all at a trial, and were hardly ever allowed to argue with the judge or even a prosecutor. In Myanmar, advocates could be jailed themselves for arguing too vigorously in court.

After weighing up all this advice, Ha and the team formed the view that it was wise not to appoint a lawyer at this stage since there was nothing they could do at the moment, and such an appointment might simply make things worse. More important than the question of a local lawyer, they agreed, was finding a good interpreter. They would be the critical person in ensuring my arguments reached a judge, once the legal formalities got underway.

In the interim, it was a case of wait and see, and focus on a diplomatic solution. Was such a solution even being pursued? Yes – not that I had confirmation of this until much later – but it was making slow progress against the junta's intransigence.

This slow progress was, not surprisingly, distressing to Ha and my family and friends outside, who continued to place most of their hope for my release on a diplomatic channel. They were frustrated at this time, however, by what they perceived as a lack of initiative from the Australian Government. While Ha was grateful for the efforts of the Embassy and individual staff of DFAT, when she saw the advocacy of other countries with imprisoned citizens in Myanmar, she was less pleased with the government. In an email to DFAT, she told them that she 'did not feel that much effort was being put in by the Australian Government to secure Sean's release', and that she 'needed the Australian Government to be more creative in yielding humanitarian and COVID assistance [along the ways taken by Japan], and in pushing much harder for military to military talks'. Ha told DFAT she was 'very desperate, so I am begging the Australian Government to do something [more]'.

By April 2021 the advice from my legal advisers no longer involved formal appointments of counsel or anything complex. In the event that I was brought before a court, they counselled:

> ST just needs to say that he has done nothing wrong and that he is not guilty and to deny all charges and answer questions honestly as they are raised.

In the light of subsequent events, this last advice seems rather optimistic. Indeed, this became apparent only a few weeks later, when I received a summons for my first remand hearing. A local lawyer was now necessary.

My first formal remand hearing took place on 12 May 2021. Getting to court was, predictably, a fuss. As usual, a large cast assembled and I was placed in handcuffs – I had become used to this. When we moved off, I found myself being forcefully pushed and shoved by my police escorts. Then, as I was waiting just outside Insein's giant door, I was unexpectedly kicked in the back of the legs by a police officer, causing my knees to buckle. After regaining my balance and composure – not easy when your hands are bound – as calmly as I could, I told him his actions were 'grotesquely inappropriate'. It seems like a decidedly overrestrained response as I think about it now, but it did lead another more senior officer to remonstrate with his junior colleague. After the kicking, I was hauled up and into an open-tray truck for the short journey to the Yangon Eastern District Court.

'Court'? Well, physically it would not really answer to the name. It was little more than a large open space with a concrete floor and corrugated iron roof; chairs and benches were distributed around to create multiple spaces for 'courtrooms'. There were people everywhere: in uniform, in plain clothes, in handcuffs, some purposefully walking about, and many others seemingly just hanging around. The overall effect was chaos. This was exacerbated by a cacophony of disjointed noise, courtesy of the iron roof. Down the years, I had observed the stately decorum of Australian courts – and the procedures this day were nothing remotely like them.

My escort and I started making our way to the space allocated. It was sensory overload and I felt my chest tightening. Then something caught my attention – a shouted greeting, a familiar face: I don't recall what it was. To my delight, the Australian Ambassador Andrea Faulkner and her staff were there, beaming and waving furiously. Ahead of time, it had not been clear whether or not they would be permitted to attend. I found out much later that Andrea, Consul Wes Knight, and a number of the wonderful local staff had been there since 7.45 am; my hearing did not begin until around ten that morning. Not allowed in the court until later, they had positioned themselves to see me arrive. There seemed to be a kind of exclusion zone keeping supporters separated from inmates so they were a good ten metres back from me. I conveyed my appreciation for their support by placing my hand to my heart and making a vague bowing gesture to them.

Then I was moved on and ordered to sit on a wooden bench. I sat there alone and more than a little confused before a man came up to me and announced through the young interpreter at his side that he was my lawyer. 'My name is U Nu [not his real name],' he said, a friendly twinkle in his eye, and he explained that he had been retained by Ha through what was the oldest and most eminent Western law firm in Myanmar. U Nu exuded both warmth and gravitas, and I received a boost from meeting him. After enquiring about my health and the conditions under which I was held, he told me, 'Everything will be all right. Don't worry.' I felt myself exhale deeply.

At various junctures in the months ahead, Ha and my team – as well as me – would have disagreements with U Nu over tactics and other things, but at no time, from this first meeting and right up to the end, did I doubt either his capabilities or integrity.

Apart from an anglophone 'Mike', I never did get the full name of the young interpreter. Like U Nu, he was a source of comfort to me – at this and subsequent remand hearings. Mike was extremely savvy, had impeccable English and a sardonic manner that was like a breath of fresh air amid all the nonsense around us.

In short order, Mike was interpreting the conversation between U Nu and the judge, which was taking place through Zoom on a laptop. All up, my appearance at this first remand hearing lasted no more than about ten minutes: it was largely procedural. Through Mike, I was made to understand that this was the beginning of a series of remand hearings that would take place every two weeks: this was also the maximum period of detention allowed between remand judgments. I was informed too that 'investigations' were continuing into my role as a spy.

Also I was given access to the first 'brief summary of the facts' of the case – namely, that, 'After a search of Turnell's possessions in his bag [ASUS Vivo Laptop, iPhone11, iPad Mini, Sandisk USB and documents] when he was arrested at the Chatrium

Hotel on 6 February, it was found that he had breached section 3.1C of the OSA.' That was all I would know for months.

Proceedings were wound up and I was able to use the limited time I had with U Nu to pass on some messages to Ha. I told him to please tell her not to worry, that I 'needed to dig deep, but was digging deep'. That I was 'trying always to think of the big picture', and that my love for her kept me going. More prosaically, I added my complaint that reading material and other things were either getting through to me with lengthy delay or not at all. I did not mention, to her or anyone else, the kicking incident from a few minutes earlier.

At the end of the hearing, in a heart-warming gesture of humanity that was characteristic of her, Andrea moved towards me. I turned to approach her until I was stopped by police and prison guards. They were acting under direct order from the highest levels of Home Affairs – and from members of the junta itself – to allow no contact at all. Home Affairs had also told the Embassy that they could not speak to me – even though, under prison regulations, they had no right to impose such a ban. Later I found out that the senior prison officer present at the hearing was scolded for not being strict enough in supervising my court appearance. Over the coming months, I would appear in person at half a dozen or so remand hearings at Yangon Eastern District Court. I came to dread them. I was relatively free of physical abuse during my formal captivity in Myanmar, with the exception of these treks.

It wasn't that I was singled out particularly. The treatment of detainees while in transit for these court visits – we were, of course, legally not yet even prisoners – can only be described at a minimum as cruel indifference. Chained together via links in our handcuffs, I estimated that there were 50 or so of us pushed into a van designed to hold no more than 20. This was especially tough for the young women, few of whom were more than teenagers and they appeared traumatised. Jam-packed together like fish in a tin, the heat was tremendous. Sweat poured down our faces. Some people cried, more cursed; some vomited, some fainted. Those who fainted mostly remained upright – sometimes purely because the crush of bodies kept them from falling to the ground; other times because their companions held on to them for dear life.

On the worst of the trips, a middle-aged paraplegic man was placed on the floor of the truck. Then 40 or more of us prisoners were forced inside. As the truck lurched off, a few people fell over, right on top of him. Others, in their efforts to stay standing, accidentally trod on his arms and legs. His cries of pain melded with the cries of rage, pity and despair of those who had landed on him: victims of gravity and the swaying of the overloaded vehicle.

Ambassador Andrea and others from the Australian Embassy happened to be at the remand hearing the day of that particularly inhumane journey in the police truck: their requests to attend the hearings were frequently refused. Exceedingly angry, I pushed one police officer away as he tried to grab me by my elbow in that familiar gesture of dominance and control.

'Get your hands off me,' I yelled. 'You're bullies and cowards. You've got the wrong people on the wrong side of the prison bars. The people in the truck today are worth a million times what you are.' I got no response.

On seeing Andrea, I broke away slightly from the pack of police and said somewhat incomprehensively, 'This is just too much.'

As we were being taken back to Insein, the Embassy staff waved to me in the truck, and were able to see the crowding of the van.

That first day, U Nu had told me to try to be patient. I remember thinking, *It's been four months in one of the worst jails in Asia in a case that is clearly a monstrous injustice.* How much patience could I be expected to have left?

Not all my memories are quite as dark. On one of the return trips from a remand hearing, a young female detainee offered me a cake. She told me her mother had given her cakes that morning as she waited for her case to come up. Defaulting to Anglo-mode, I politely declined – anxious not to take food from someone surely in a worse position than me. I told this story later to Jacoob and some others. They heard me out, but then said that I should have taken the cake. That, in Myanmar society, it was always better to accept someone's offer of food or hospitality. I had known the ways of Myanmar long enough to understand this, but something about being in extremis – though weren't we all, I reflected, chiding myself – had made me brush aside this acquired wisdom. By a happy coincidence – at least, in the context of this little narrative – I ran into the girl again at the next remand hearing. Perhaps sensing something in my demeanour, again she offered a cake: presumably, once more supplied by her mum. This time I took it. She smiled. I smiled. Then I wanted to cry at the pity and humanity of it all.

*

Ha and me in happy times, just before my fateful return to Myanmar in January 2021.

The ethereal beauty of Yangon's Shwedagon Pagoda.

With Myanmar's great bank reformer, Bo Bo Nge. Bo Bo sought to get Myanmar's finances right and to fight corruption. Here we are outside the Bank of England.

Daw Aung San Suu Kyi and me at the Lowy Institute in Sydney, 2012.

The 'Panopticon' – Insein Prison. I took this picture on a routine flight out of Yangon in 2020 and remember thinking, 'God forbid that I should ever find myself there.'

The monitor via which the police could observe me in The Box. I lived in this space for nearly two months. In this photo I'm sitting in the chair of chains and manacles. The time on the monitor seems wrong – but it certainly depicts my first night. Photo sent to me by former police captain Kyaw San Han.

Police captain Kyaw San Han served as my interpreter in the early days of my arrest, and sought to protect me in The Box. His disgust at what was happening in Myanmar after the coup led him to leave the police force.

Ha vacuum-sealing a fruitcake in our kitchen – destination Insein Prison, via diplomatic pouch.

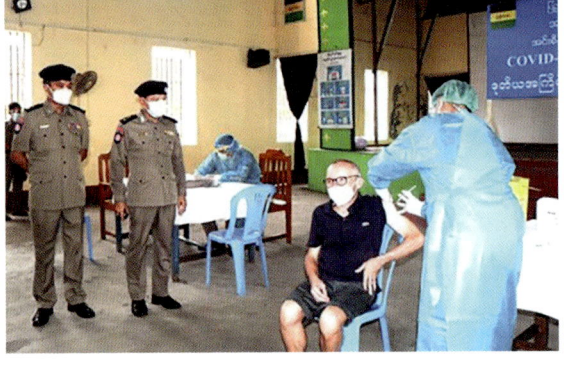

First prisoner in Myanmar to be vaccinated against COVID. Insein Prison, May 2021.

Curtis Slover. My loyal friend who came back for me. Again and again and again.

'Sean, you are safe now. You are with us.' Greetings from Paing Ye Thu to me upon my arrival at Insein Prison. He is pictured here post-imprisonment, from his camp in a liberated area in Myanmar. My irrepressible friend gives the three-fingered salute much favoured by people in Myanmar in opposition to the junta.

Jacoob – aka Khin Maung Shwe. My protector, my friend, in a characteristic defiant pose in Insein Prison. His courage and moral stature earned him the enmity of Myanmar's junta, who murdered him in Insein soon after I left his care.

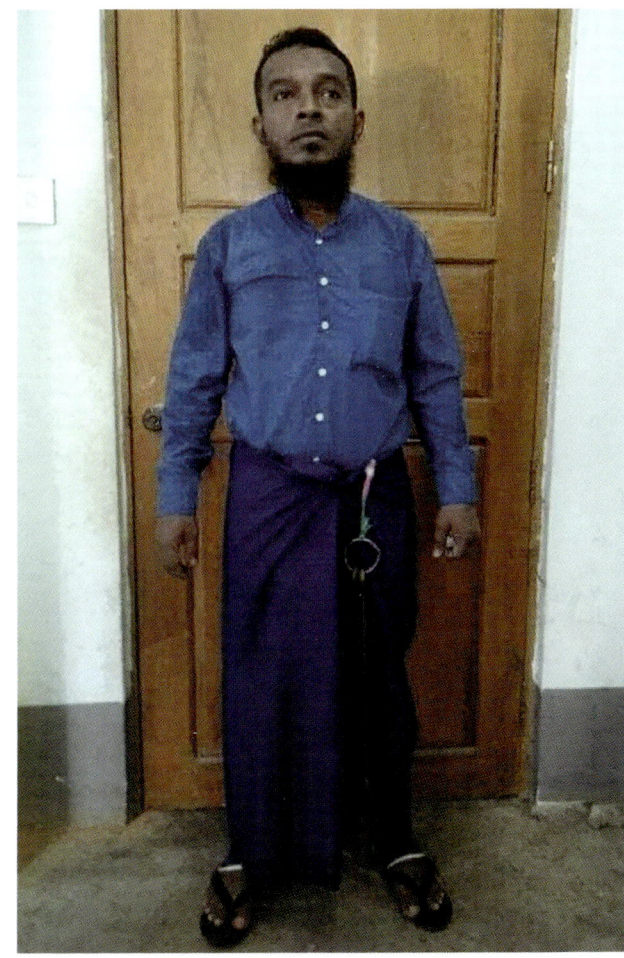

My precious elephant. Made from used coffee sachets, it was a gift from a fellow political prisoner in Naypyitaw. It was the only material thing I took away from Myanmar's prisons, and the only thing I wanted.

The moment we longed for. Reunion at Melbourne airport, 18 November 2022. Anything but awkward.

Boarding the Prime Minister's plane (aka 'The Shark') for the last leg of my return home. Less than 24 hours earlier I had been in my filthy cell in Insein, with receding hope.

Ha and me with Australian Prime Minister Anthony Albanese, and Foreign Minister Penny Wong, just days after my return home. (Mick Tsikas, AAP)

With Australian MP, dear friend and tireless supporter, Janelle Saffin. Together Ha and Janelle hatched multiple plots for my rescue.

At Windsor Castle. King Charles' concern for me, and support to Ha, was sincere and generous.

With one of the vessels of my salvation. After my experience, every Australian Embassy around the world now has them.

Home at last. Ha, Phuong and me on the couch. It seems I still had some books left.

Soon after these incidents – around July 2021 – I heard from Ha of two significant developments in my case. The first was that I was not to be charged alone.

Although given status as defendant number one, I would be joined in the OSA charges by Daw Aung San Suu Kyi in her role as State Counsellor, together with the former ministers of Planning and Finance U Soe Win (2018 and until the coup) and U Kyaw Win (2016–18), and the Deputy Minister of Planning and Finance – and aforementioned leading reformer – U Winston Set Aung. All three were in Insein, though I had had no contact with them. In alleging we collectively had breached the OSA, the junta were essentially arguing that I was the spy, and Daw Suu and the Ministers my willing agents. They were also criminalising the normal and proper processes of economic reform – a characteristically cynical act by a regime itself founded in illegality.

The other news I had from Ha was related. Daw Suu was detained in Naypyitaw and unable to leave because of other charges laid against her in the capital. Consequently, the trial would be held in Naypyitaw: the rest of us would have to be moved there.

My lawyers – and those of my co-defendants – swung into action to resist the move.

In August 2021, I was relocated from Ward 4 and all my new friends there to a secluded tree-lined 'pizza-slice' of the Insein wagon wheel devoted to 'special prisoners'. Subsequently, the definition of 'special' was stretched to include those sentenced to death. The physical environment here was much better, though the prison's claims that I had been rehoused in a 'private residence' – the description given to Ha and the Embassy – overstated matters rather dramatically. My so-called private residence was barely more than a small shack on stilts. It was one of about half a dozen structures built in the early 1990s to house prominent political prisoners, such as the politician U Win Htein. In a conversation with him later, I discovered that the little structure I was allocated had been his 'home' for nearly 15 years.

The downside? I was now effectively in solitary confinement. My shack was walled off from all the others as well as from the trees and green space of the area. Apart from monosyllabic conversations with guards over essentials I spoke to no-one. Ate with no-one. Shared thoughts, hopes and nightmares with none but myself. It was a scary, bleak existence: the isolation, worries and uncertainties about the looming trial – would the lawyers be able to prevent the move to Naypyitaw or not? – and the negative developments in my case now coming at a fast gallop. I fell into deep depression during this period.

Books and the calls with Ha more than ever kept me alive. I also nurtured the slim hope that in giving me a better physical environment via this move – did I mention the trees? – perhaps the regime was preparing me for release. While not being allowed to talk to other prisoners left me desperately lonely, I also entertained the notion that this was somehow a sign I might soon be let go. Of course, it could also have been just one more ploy to break my spirit.

Meanwhile, the Delta variant of COVID began to cut a swathe through Myanmar. The junta left people to fend for themselves, and undertook mass arrests of protesting doctors, nurses and other health professionals. The one health concession the junta did made was to declare a lengthy 'public holiday' shutdown. From mid-August to mid-September, what government there was, and much of the formal economy, ground to a halt.

For me, this had terrible repercussions. Food of any quality became non-existent. Worse was that all contact with the outside world ceased: consular calls stopped – thus I had no contact with Ha – and I received no deliveries or mail. During this hiatus, MOFA stopped responding to the Australian Embassy's requests and even stopped taking calls from them. My lawyers weighed in to say the lack of communication with me was unacceptable. Eventually the Embassy was told that their requests for contact with me had been 'escalated to a higher authority at Home Affairs, and refused'.

When channels of communication to me in the prison reopened mid-September, the tidings I received were not good. Despite the petitions of our lawyers – mine and those of my co-accused – the attendance requirements for our trial remained as originally stated by the junta. It was time to move to Naypyitaw.

Part 4
Trials and Tribulations in Naypyitaw

11

Naypyitaw Nightmare

The shift to Naypyitaw took place on 21 September 2021.

A couple of days earlier, I'd been discreetly warned that this move was imminent. My informant, a guard with whom I'd got on well and who was sympathetic – not just to me, but to the cause of democracy and freedom in Myanmar (privately, many of the guards were) – thought this a positive development.

'This is good for you, *Saya*. At last they are getting on with the trial. You'll see – they'll convict you and then deport you. You will be home by Christmas.'

Despite his optimism, and the fact I had lived there for much of the last five years so knew it quite well, the mere mention of the word 'Naypyitaw' sent a shudder down my spine.

An artificial capital city in the way of Brasilia, Putrajaya and, yes, Canberra, it sits in an especially hot and mostly dry part of the Myanmar interior. Billions had been spent – and wasted – by military leaders in building the place during the early 2000s. Why they did so is a source of speculation. Partly it seemed to be about symbolism, a xenophobic assertion of supposed Burman heartland values and so on. It was also likely the latest expression of a pattern in Myanmar's history – of dynasties marking out their rule with a change of national capital. However, and although I originally discounted the idea, it really does seem – based on my own questioning of officials while I was helping the government – that the principal reason was to create a military redoubt 'safe' from the Myanmar people.

That wasn't what put me off; I was fine with the city's eccentricities, its novelty. The prospect of living somewhere with functioning electricity and other services – during the NLD years, Naypyitaw had always been the most advanced in this regard – might once have pleased me. But no, not this time. Because now Naypyitaw was terror-central of Min Aung Hlaing's junta. Going there would push me deeper into the belly of the beast: away from the Embassy, any alternative loci of power or influence of business – foreign or domestic – away from the cosmopolitanism of the old port city of Yangon, away from the core of the resistance to the despotism, which was otherwise all-embracing.

At a more practical level, how would I get food and books? Would I get calls? Would there be anyone or any process capable of bearing witness? The sensations of fear and dread burrowed deeper in my body.

On the day of the move, I was woken up before dawn and told to quickly pack my things. There were handshakes and even some hugs from Insein's guards, but they had been given one last message to deliver and it was devastating: I had to leave all but three books behind. They promised the remainder would be sent on to the Embassy. But for the moment I had to choose. A test for

Solomon, and an excruciating one for me. Eventually, I went for Clive James and two recently arrived memoirs: Ben Bernanke's *The Courage to Act*, and Barack Obama's newbie, *A Promised Land*.

That done, I was escorted to the guard house, the grim scene of my arrival six months earlier – now more sinister-looking in the dark. There, I was joined by my three co-accused, U Soe Win, U Kyaw Win, and U Winston Set Aung. As noted, Winston was one of the prime intellectual forces behind Myanmar's reform effort. With this trio, I had worked in the great quest to reform Myanmar's economy and make the country a better place. They were three impossibly hardworking and loyal sons of Myanmar. And they should never have been in the situation they now found themselves in. I will never forget the look of dismay on the faces of these noble people as they were handcuffed for the first time.

For me this had become routine, but I still remonstrated with the police over the issue.

'Really?' I said. 'You seriously believe we are a flight risk? Shame on you. Shame on what you are doing.' As per usual, and no doubt by instruction, the police did not react beyond giving me an extra powerful shove into the waiting truck.

It was one of the trucks routinely used during those horrific remand-hearing journeys. I do not have fond memories of these vehicles. When I was shoved, I was about to start heaving myself onto the platform of truck, a metre or so above the ground, without the use of my hands. Winston and I were in our 50s, U Kyaw Win in his mid-70s and U Soe Win in his mid-80s. Our ages might be suggestive of the struggle. The shove caused me to collide with a pole in the middle of the truck-tray that was for standing prisoners to hold on to. Painstakingly, I pulled myself into a seat and was relieved to realise I had not been injured – though it had hurt.

While the adrenaline subsided in my body, I reflected that at least for this journey there was going to be plenty of room. There were only us four, our scant possessions, and our submachine gun–toting police guard: one for each of us. We settled as best we could for the roughly 320-kilometre journey. The truck rumbled to life and we soon left Insein behind.

Trussed up and guarded, I was on high alert. *How dark and quiet the streets are,* I thought as we drove through Yangon. To me, that said much. Yangon's streets are normally never like this. However, post-coup, and with curfews still in place in many parts, this old and rambunctious city was a dour and tense shadow of itself. The four of us were all eyes, though, at last able to see a world beyond bars, walls and barbed wire.

At the outskirts of the city, and at the start of the Yangon–Naypyitaw Expressway, our truck abruptly pulled to the side where a gaggle of police vehicles and a minivan were parked. These, it turned out, would take us the remainder of the way. We were helped out of the truck then transferred to the minivan. We four prisoners were kept apart, and each assigned a specific guard, to whom we were handcuffed. Mine, a young man anxious to avoid eye contact, rested his sub-machine gun on his lap, with its open barrel pressed into my knee. The concrete Yangon–Naypyitaw highway is notoriously bumpy and uneven – I hoped and prayed the gun's safety latch was on.

Before long we were moving again. Travelling in front of our van was a 4x4 crew-cab police vehicle, with four sharpshooters in helmets, bulletproof vests and balaclavas perched on its rear platform. An identical vehicle brought up the rear of our motorcade. Given that our captive cohort consisted of an octogenarian, a septuagenarian, and two PhD-wielding economic policy geeks – all of decidedly less-than-imposing physical presence – the guard and gun rollout rather smacked of overkill.

Five hours later and without anyone being shot, we were driving through the wide and empty streets of Naypyitaw (the 20-lane road in front of the parliament building is a staple of photos of the capital). This place had been my home for nearly five years in total, and I kept spotting familiar sights. Once innocuous and comforting, now they seemed brooding and sinister. It was early afternoon, and most of the buildings appeared to be dark inside.

Stories had reached us of the unprecedented electricity blackouts in Naypyitaw, and wholesale staff desertions of government ministries as basic services collapsed under the junta. Everything we saw appeared to confirm them. Sandbags, barbed wire and sentry posts marked major intersections. Roadblocks were everywhere. Shopping centres, roadside stalls and eating places looked to be half closed; the people in and around them moved about with a tentative, almost furtive air.

All such thoughts fled as we pulled up at the Naypyitaw Detention Centre (NDC). Set in a sun-blasted and desolate clearing on Myopart Road, it was not far from one of the capital's hotel districts. Yet it might have been a million miles away. Surrounded by swamps and low-lying, thick scrub, it could have been a concentration camp dropped into a jungle. Overwhelming and indescribable fear and despair fell upon the four of us.

But when we got out of the van, our mood lightened. A sense of security came over us.

The superintendent of the detention centre, you see, was ebullient.

'Welcome, welcome,' he gushed, as he backslapped, shook hands and hugged the ministers.

'Please don't worry about anything. I am sure that you being here is all just a misunderstanding that will be cleared up soon. I will do my best to make you comfortable. Please let me know if there is anything I can do to make your stay here better. Of course, we are just a detention centre, not a jail, so we may not have some of the facilities you might be used to in Insein. But life here can be quite okay.' More followed, in Burmese, in a similar vein. But even more effusively. Extra-prolonged handshakes. Smiles. Lots of gold teeth.

Then it hit me that the man could hardly stand. That the smell wafting around was not an oddly chosen aftershave but alcohol. The homemade variety. The rough stuff.

The Superintendent was drunk.

Very drunk.

Now, I had never been a believer of *in vino veritas*. In my experience, it tended to take a while for the lies of the drunk to be exposed. At the NDC on this awful September day, however, it took about 90 seconds.

That is the time it took us to nod goodbye to the Superintendent, gather our things and – prodded by yet another new set of captors – head round the corner and lay eyes on our new dwelling.

*

An Unlikely Prisoner

In front of us was a long, low bunker-like structure of ten cells. For all the world, it looked as if its builders had forgotten to place it underground. It was located in a segregated area – delineated from the rest of the NDC by whitewashed concrete walls, about three metres high, topped by barbed wire. Once inside the compound, all we could see, apart from the tennis court–sized patch of dirt in front of the cells, were the tops of other jail buildings. And, naturally, the NDC's guard house and sentry towers. The latter were set at each of the four corners of the square that marked out the prison and manned by armed guards. The guard house sat in the middle of the 'front' wall of the jail and atop it was mounted a large-calibre machine gun. That gun was the first thing I would see each morning when my cell doors opened. A life-affirming welcome to the day.

The cells of our bunker looked grim from the outside, but nothing could have prepared us for the squalor of their interiors. The floors were covered in fetid pools of mosquito-infested water – the cells leaked in the rain. The walls were filthy, and smelled of rot and mould. Although the cells in Insein were built a century earlier, these were in much worse shape than those of the old panopticon. A product of the shoddy building standards that are a hallmark of Myanmar's military regimes, the NDC cells were unlikely to fare well in a tremor: in earthquake-prone Myanmar, this was no abstract possibility.

Each cell had a squat toilet that was foul beyond belief – certainly more than I want to describe here. My cell had blood stains on the walls and around the door frame. Rough sheets of wood were placed over the damp floor to make for a bed and living space. A couple of dirty blankets were supplied by way of bedding.

The running of the NDC was in keeping with its brutalist physical infrastructure. Before entering our cells we were 'processed'. My shoes were taken away, along with paper and my precious pen. Then came the worst moment: I saw that my painstakingly chosen trio of books was being placed into my wheely-bag, which was about to be put in storage.

'No, no, no!' I said. 'You do not understand. I cannot survive without them. They are more important to me than food. Please, you must allow me my books. I will go insane. This is torture. Just kill me now if you won't allow me books.' A little histrionic, I know, but things seemed to hit an existential moment. I felt as low as could be. Lower, certainly, than at any time in my life.

My outburst did bring about an intervention – from Winston. This brave and good man. Not for the last time, he came to my assistance, speaking to our captors with his voice of sweet reason and even better temperament. Alas, this did not work. The books were wheeled away.

Once processed, we were each locked into our allocated cell. Ominously, mine was cell Number 1, and this number was emblazoned on the side of it; no other cell was so conspicuously marked.

Not allowed out that first day, we started to shout to the occupants we had noticed in the other cells. 'Who are you?'

The replies came back quickly, and from them we pieced together a sense of our new situation. The ten cells of the bunker were fully occupied – there had been a reshuffling the day before, and a doubling up of prisoners in the other cells. *All* the other prisoners (technically everyone in the jail was on remand only and not prisoners – but, the reality of life asserted otherwise – so why pretend?) were friends and colleagues from the reformist wings of the deposed NLD Government. Many ministries, departments, institutions were 'represented'.

I discovered that the cell next to me was occupied by Ye Min Oo, an extraordinary young man and rising star within the NLD; at the time of the coup, he was about to be appointed Chief Minister of Yangon. That day we struck up a friendship that would ultimately sustain us both. It started in a low-key way, with Ye Min Oo explaining that normally the detainees were allowed out for an hour or two every day, but our arrival had brought about a lockdown. He added that this compound was a sort of VIP wing of the prison for ministers of the NLD Government. Conditions were harsh, he said, but everyone was in good spirits. Our arrival had been 'much anticipated'.

For that entire first week we were locked all day in our cells, apart from being handcuffed and taken to the first court hearing. Each day I demanded, and then begged for my books. 'Or,' I said to one of the guards, 'anything I can read.' Even the ratty and unreliable state-run publication, the *Global New Light of Myanmar*, would do. Possibly the worst newspaper in the world, but at least I could derive from it a certain dark humour. Could they, would they, help me get my hands on a copy?

No. Nothing doing.

After a week that felt like a month, we were permitted time out of our cells.

Our spells in the fresh air were limited to a couple of hours each morning, and a couple more in the afternoon. Then I would walk. Through my endless walking at Naypyitaw – the survival strategy continued from The Box and from Insein – I gradually carved out distinct tracks in the dirt area in front of our cells. I had help, though. Essentially, we all engaged in vigorous walking as a primary coping mechanism. Kyaw Htay Oo, a Myanmar-born US citizen and botanist who advised Daw Suu on a range of things, including sustainable land practices, was my closest partner in stamping out a pathway.

'Mate' – he liked it when I used this phrase – 'we shall blaze a trail in the wilderness.' When, after a while, prison administrators had crops planted in this space, this didn't faze the pathfinders: we simply created a new track around the vegetables.

How familiar did this place of concrete and dirt become! I can still visualise every divot, every discoloration in the concrete, every joint between the slabs, the stained walls, the wire, the languid guard in his sentry box. I walked hundreds of laps every day of the circuit we created. This would deliver me 10,000 steps after about an hour and a half. I did the bulk of these in the morning and topped the number up in the afternoon – along with cell-pacing.

Throughout my imprisonment in Naypyitaw, by far the largest part of my life was spent entombed in my hot and dank concrete cage.

And it was hot. So hot. I know I mentioned this in the context of Insein, but the climate in Naypyitaw is especially awful. People sometimes speak of a winter and milder weather in Naypyitaw and, when I lived and worked there for the democratic government, I was one of them. But it's nonsense really. It's just damn hot, all the damn time. Even when it's raining.

And when it does rain in Naypyitaw, it rains hard: that's the default, and during the monsoon season it's particularly bad. The water would gather on the floor of our cells – that terrible pooling I described earlier, which made our first few days at the NDC such a torment, was the residue of previous rain. But while the rain is actually falling, the cells are near unliveable. Each cell was identical, and the back window, set about five metres from the ground, turned into a conduit for what I can only describe as a waterfall. Within minutes of a big downpour – literally, it is the *only* sort – everything becomes soaked. Your blankets, clothes, food, books, papers . . . everything.

When it rains at night, any thought of sleep is washed away. All you can do, all you must do, is stand up and clutch the belongings you most want to protect and hold them close. Use your body as a shield. You'll get wet, but you can dry off. Your belongings cannot, and they will be ruined.

Ironically, while we were forever having to deal with this wretched rainwater that got into everything, there was seldom enough to drink. Inadequate drinking water had been a problem in Insein, but the sheer lack of it in Naypyitaw – plus its poor quality – was a health concern.

Naypyitaw is located in the dry central plain of Myanmar and is prone to pendulum swings of weather: violent, torrential rain in the monsoon season; drought at other times. For this reason, the big troughs outside our cells that contained our water supply were often empty. Yet, there was an element of human greed operating here as well. Shockingly – according to the old hands in the compound, whose sources were impeccable – the Superintendent was in the habit of siphoning the NDC's water for an enterprise he owned on the side: a road maintenance subcontracting business. I had no way of knowing the truth or otherwise of this, but it was certainly consistent with the pattern of his behaviour.

As I adjusted to my new environment, Insein was my yardstick, and most things at the NDC were worse by comparison. Please don't think I revised my opinion about Insein and decided it wasn't that bad after all. No, not remotely. Life in Insein was nasty. Life at the NDC was unbelievably nastier. Take the food arrangements, for instance. They were the same as for Insein: food was delivered in buckets. In Naypyitaw, though, they weren't even clean. Instead, food was served from old plastic buckets that used to contain paint or cement. Paint stains and other marks reached down the sides of the buckets, while the wire handles dug into the fingers of the poor Class C prisoners who – as in Insein – had to distribute them.

An external food-buying system operated in Naypyitaw, but it offered a slim range of items – almost nothing beyond simply food – and at dramatically more exploitative prices than in Insein. The reason for that was plain: in another neat example of predatory practice, the Deputy Superintendent of the NDC owned the shop that exclusively supplied the merchandise. I have noted already the mark-ups applying in Insein. In Naypyitaw, item for item, these were more than doubled. Crony capitalism alive in the capital, and not just at the commanding heights.

Paradoxically, while the people running the NDC were taking egregious liberties, we detainees were subject to restrictions on all sorts of banal activities – in and outside of the cell. Earlier, I disclosed my singing and whistling proclivities. In Naypyitaw, one of the guards heard me humming and approached me to explain that making noise was banned. 'No songs allowed.' I was convinced he was joking – a gentle mocking, perhaps, of my profound lack of talent. No, he was serious! I complied for a couple of days, then let rip with whistling 'Boléro' as loudly as I could. The best way to deal with an edict like that was surely to ignore it.

Many of the other arbitrary restrictions were hard to work around. Once more, I was not allowed a chair. Unlike in Insein this ban lasted, and I was back to sitting on the floor, or in the drainage gutter outside the cell. I was not allowed a thermos flask. Freshly boiled water was delivered in a bucket once a day – though later, an urn was set up outside, near the gate of the compound. It would have been handy to have a thermos to keep water hot for when the cell door was closed but I had to do without. Because of this I developed a taste – even a preference – for cold coffee.

I was not allowed to wear shoes – either to 'formal' excursions outside, such as my trial hearings, or for exercise in the compound. Instead, I was forced to wear what is rendered from Burmese into English as 'slippers', but which in other places would most likely be called 'flip flops'. In Australia – oddly, now that I think about it – we call them thongs. Anyway, however labelled, in Naypyitaw I went through five pairs of them – a consequence of my walking exercise, mostly. They created calluses and other deformities to my feet, which no doubt will remain with me always.

There was a significant barrier to tackling these and other problems in Naypyitaw: walled off as we were in this political VIP compound, we had no direct way of getting requests, messages or anything else to the leadership of the jail. All requests had to go through a single guard at the gate into our compound. If he was not bothered to pass them on, nothing happened.

And for a long time the compound guard did not bother about my desperation for my books. But I wore him down. Day after day after day I badgered, cajoled, charmed, begged anew, and even threatened divine retribution. In the end, he relented and allowed for a note to be passed on. A note written with a borrowed pen on scrounged paper that laid out I would take the seizure of my books up with the Australian Embassy when, as must eventually happen, I got to talk with them.

Like magic, suddenly, my version of a new Dark Ages came to an end. The trinity of books carried from Insein was released to me and I was able to lose myself to the world of my reading material.

Which brings me to another restriction, one that remained in place, off and on during the whole of my 'tenure' in Naypyitaw. This was the ban on my Myanmar colleagues receiving anything written in English, and an aligned diktat that they only receive books on religion – in practice, exclusively Buddhist literature. The rationale for the ban was itself revealing of the junta's profound ignorance and xenophobia. This was well expressed by a very senior prisons official one day when he said to my Myanmar colleagues, 'What do you want English books for? There is nothing of value in books not written in Burmese. We are protecting you.'

*

The guards of Naypyitaw were more wary and less friendly than in Insein. Although their allegiance to the junta was doubtful, the proximity of the NDC to the generals and their informers made for a much more menacing and repressive atmosphere. As per Insein, I knew few of the guards by name, but referred to them in both my own mind and to others usually by their rank: the two-star, the one-star, the corporal. Sometimes I labelled them according to their behaviour or disposition: the friendly guy, the drunk guy, the angry guy, the lanky guy, the guy with the limp . . . and so on.

Over the months, there was a succession of guards. The lanky guy was rostered to us the most. Although less drunk than the drunk guy, he spent much of the time in our compound 'under the weather'.

The Superintendent would retire a couple of months after our arrival. His morally dubious side hustle and daytime drinking were the merest tip of a vast pyramid of ill-discipline and dysfunction that we would experience in the NDC, and which permeated the place. Another instance: the house of the Superintendent lay just beyond the wire, and he regularly hosted fellow prison officers for drunken karaoke parties. These evenings were always an ordeal for us detainees – it was impossible to block out the noise so most of us would be kept awake. These gatherings reached their nadir one night when the wife of the Superintendent took over the microphone to loudly accuse her husband of having an affair with one of the female guards. We did not lack for soap opera at least.

In another instance of melodrama, the then Deputy Superintendent – 'Two Star' – got into a fist fight with a fellow officer while my co-accused and I looked on. We were in the guard house awaiting transport to a trial hearing. You might think that witnessing such mayhem and division among our 'enemies' might have counted as a good thing. To us, however, it was a sign of a system that could not protect us – obviously not from its own deliberate malevolence, but also from its violent anarchy.

One direct confrontation I had with a prison guard remains fresh in my mind. This was early in my stay in NDC, when on one of the routine Monday inspection tours, the second-in-charge of the prison – a predecessor to the brawler above – appeared at my cell door and demanded that I kowtow to him in submission. This was something of an old tradition among captors/prisoners in Myanmar, but I had not experienced it before now. While thrown, I had the presence of mind to pretend I did not understand his demand. In what had become a well-practised gesture, I cupped my hand behind my ear to prompt him to say it again. He did so, but I then conveyed to him that I could not understand his version of Burmese. He got angry. He shouted at me. Then he directed his ire at a lowly guard looking on, stamped his boots . . . and walked away. He did not try this on again.

Every now and again, we would receive what were barely more than 'box-ticking' visits from Myanmar and ASEAN (the Association of Southeast Asian Nations) human rights officials. It had been the same at Insein. They would make a beeline for me. They would ask me to respond honestly, even as jail officials looked on. Once, I did just that: I stated that it was an outrage I was here, that the conditions were unacceptable, inhumane, and that I had heard prisoners being tortured with my own ears. The official listened. Nodded. Said I should take his word that my testimony would be passed on. As he prepared to leave, he told me how much he had enjoyed his last visit to Australia. 'A lovely country.'

'Yes,' I said. 'It is.'

Once communication links with the Embassy were re-established at the NDC, it was as though the ship had steadied after a storm – even as consular access of Embassy officials to me remained denied.

Ha's brilliant delivery system of food and other necessities continued, reconfigured for Naypyitaw. Curtis stayed on as the point man, at times driving the five-hour journey from Yangon with my parcels, other times sending them via sympathetic drivers of express buses that ran regularly between the two cities. A small band of Naypyitaw 'last mile' deliverers were recruited; actually, most volunteered. They were overwhelmingly eminent and accomplished people – brave, compassionate; largely old friends and colleagues who I tragically cannot name. They would often supplement the parcels they delivered to me. Sometimes those contributions consisted of complete meals. Homemade. On one occasion, some young researchers I had worked with somehow managed to get a pizza to me. They were brilliant kids at economics, but I realised as I shared the slices around in the prison that I'd underestimated them massively.

In my time in Naypyitaw I also received other brave instances of support from ordinary people outside the prison. Once again, I cannot give too many details here for fear of endangering people still, but an array of local businesses – some known to me from when I lived there in better days – would occasionally send food and other things. To me directly, or to all of the detainees in the NDC.

Getting back to the parcels from friends and family, the deliverers would often be the Australian Embassy staff. Consul Wes Knight usually coordinated these efforts. Sometimes it was ambassadors Andrea Faulkner and her successor, Angela Corcoran, themselves handing over the bulging tote bags to the sentries at the guard house. Periodically, the guards would become argumentative. Mumbles might be made at the volume and quality of the things headed my way: 'Shaun Tunna gets too much' and so on. Andrea, Angela, Wes and co. were made of stern stuff, however, had driven a long way, and were not to be deterred.

The immense effort all this schlepping entailed, the selection and painstaking preparation of the items . . . I appreciated every last detail. The tote bags themselves assumed special meaning. For the Embassy deliveries, these were dark blue affairs, with the Australian coat of arms emblazoned in brilliant white on the front. Parcels from Curtis arrived in bags that came from the American Club at the US Embassy. Green overall, on the front of these was a stylised bald eagle garlanded with the Stars and Stripes. I was immensely proud of these bags, and all that I associated them with. I would keep all my belongings inside them on the floor, but each evening I would push the bags to the front of the cell so that they could be seen – they could not be missed! – by the guards and other prison staff. Maybe that comes across as slightly jingoistic now, but at the time they seemed to shout for me. In my mind, those dark blue bags proclaimed: 'You don't mess with the emu and the kangaroo' – a phrase I later repeated to Australia's Prime Minister and Foreign Minister. This was not an ex-post construction. Nor was the idea of power projection encapsulated in the image of the Bald Eagle. One small step, perhaps.

Curtis's parcels invariably included a jar of peanut butter – which I had started to eat American style, like ice cream, direct from the tub. The peanut butter, like everything else, had to come in containers made either of plastic or cardboard. The prison did not accept anything in glass, anything wrapped in aluminium foil, and they rejected drinking straws. I did not understand the ban on the latter, and half wondered whether the NDC had become unexpectedly and environmentally 'woke'. Not so, I was told: it was all about the drugs we might use the straws to administer.

Without fail, the first items I pulled out were Ha's bakery delights in their vacuum-sealed bags. Nothing can convey the anticipatory euphoria of unzipping one of these to reveal the Anzac cinnamon raisin cookies or fruitcake inside. The smell of home baking, of food leavened with TLC – indeed the very specific smell of our oven and kitchen – was enough at times to remind me that, as wretched as my situation was, life still had its moments.

It's hard to express sufficiently my excitement at getting these deliveries from the Embassy, from Curtis, from home. On an expected delivery day I would be eagle-eyed at the gate of the compound. Looking for movement. Anything outside the routine. I was seven years old again, and it was Christmas morning. And then the moment would arrive. A touch of blue, a touch of green in hands clad in khaki.

Sean Turnell

On days that these deliveries didn't happen – which was often: timing in everything was arbitrary – it was like expecting a new bike from Santa and getting socks instead.

12

Government Behind the Wire

In Naypyitaw I was imprisoned alongside Myanmar's most prominent political prisoners. It's fair to say that practically all the senior leaders of Myanmar's NLD Government ended up in the same detention centre as me. Some members of this government had escaped; a smaller number were not taken into custody; but the majority of them were here.

I feel that I have something of a duty to record their names and principal role, as well as to give my account of our shared prison experience. So who were they? Across my time in the NDC they would include:

- Daw Aung San Suu Kyi, State Counsellor, Minister of Foreign Affairs.
- U Win Htein, member of the Central Executive Committee of the NLD, democracy activist and party patron.
- U Kyaw Tint Swe, Minister for the Office of the State Counsellor of Myanmar.

U Soe Win, Minister of Planning, Finance and Industry since 2018.

U Kyaw Win, Minister of Planning and Finance 2016–18.

U (Winston) Set Aung, Deputy Minister of Planning, Finance and Industry.

U Bo Bo Nge, Deputy Governor of the Central Bank of Myanmar.

U Thaung Tun, Minister of Investment and Foreign Economic Relations.

U Min Thu, Minister of the Union Government Office.

U Win Khaing, Minister of Electricity and Energy.

U Ohn Win, Minister of Natural Resources and Environmental Conservation.

U Myo Aung, Mayor of Naypyitaw.

U Kyaw Htay Oo, botanist and democracy activist. US citizen.

Why were these individuals in this prison? Above all, their prime characteristic was their seniority within the deposed government. Their charges, imprisonment, trial and convictions followed a path predetermined by this alone. There were, however, other shared characteristics I noticed while living with them in the prison. I guess the point I want to make is that all of the people I have mentioned were thoroughly cosmopolitan. All had extensive international contacts, all were highly respected beyond Myanmar. Such attributes were not esteemed by Myanmar's generals.

I knew nearly all of my fellow prisoners from my time assisting the NLD Government but, with the exception of the finance ministers and central bankers, not well. Mostly they were older than me and, I might say, far more eminent. Consequently, my relationship with them before I came to the NDC might be best described as 'respectful'. They were people of dignity, authority, and a certain gravitas.

But now, here we all were. Engaging not so much in large-scale formal policy debates but in day-to-day, cheek-by-jowl activities of survival. Sharing food, chores, and strategies for drawing clean water from the troughs. How best to dry clothes, to stay healthy, to store food, to deal with prison guards. Everyone contributed whatever they could manage. I was only too happy to assist those willing to flout the edict against reading books written in English. Anything to help cope with the frustrations of being in circumstances horribly at odds with 'life before'.

Without exception, my fellow prisoners rose to the challenge magnificently. I spent a year in this awful place, and I was struck over and again by how they held up. By the incredible camaraderie that enabled us political prisoners not merely to survive, but to push back in solidarity against our captors. In my years of association with Myanmar's democracy movement, I had long heard the stories of the extraordinary resilience of those imprisoned for their principles. Now I witnessed it, and lived among it.

In all of this, a key figure was U Win Htein, the stalwart of Myanmar's National League for Democracy party. This marvellous old man – he was over 80 when I was reunited with him in the NDC – very much set the moral tone which the rest of us then tried to live up to. He had been in the NDC since shortly after the coup, imprisoned for criticising the junta's takeover as a 'power grab'.

I had many wonderful interactions with U Win Htein during the relatively brief time we had together. He was also a generous supplier of food, clothes and new blankets to me. U Win Htein has an encyclopaedic knowledge of old movies and film scores. I must confess that we probably tortured our colleagues in recalling both – which we would do daily while we were together – and whistling and humming the latter. Loudly.

This was not the first time U Win Htein had been a political prisoner. Prior to this 2021 coup, he had been jailed for nearly 20 years by past military regimes. Yet his courage and brio remained undimmed: he challenged the prosecution and the judge in his trial to have courage and to be true to the facts and to the law. In this he was to be disappointed: unjustly and absurdly, he was found guilty of 'sedition'. Following his sentencing in October 2021, he was moved out of the NDC, which was technically not authorised to hold convicted prisoners. His parting words to me before he was transferred to Mandalay jail were 'Twenty-one years and counting, and it's all been worth it.' A last jaunty wave of his walking stick as he was led away in his wheelchair, and he was gone.

One of the 'institutions' we created while U Win Htein was still in the NDC lived on. This was the 'after-lunch seminar' we held in the afternoon opening of our cells. Seated around a drainage channel on the shady side of the cell bunker, we would discuss, debate, fulminate – over pretty well anything, really. From the profound to the profane, from high philosophy to low slapstick. All was on offer.

Sometimes this evolved into a specialist sub-seminar led by Winston and me on economics: we dubbed this the 'Barbed-Wire

University' (BWU). Supported by the books and articles supplied by Ha, under this label we would talk about the latest developments in economic theory and practice – modern monetary theory, bitcoin, and the like – and discuss how we might have applied them in Myanmar. Not to everyone's taste perhaps, but to us it was psychological as well as intellectual nourishment. Subjects such as philosophy, history, politics, aviation (when U Min Thu was involved) and even religion would get a look-in at the BWU. But economics was – appropriately, as far as Winston and I were concerned – always king.

The two of us never tired of talking policy. Beyond the BWU, Winston and I – frequently joined by Ye Min Oo – would discuss all we had done/tried to do/wished we could still do. On some days, all of our outside hours would be spent this way. Not that we didn't talk about other things, too, including the progress of our respective daughters.

Winston is a profoundly decent man who should not have been anywhere near the situation he found himself in. He helped me in countless ways, but especially psychologically. I hope I helped him. I will not go any further except to say I love this man as a brother.

Despite the bad times at the NDC, there were more good times with my fellow prisoners than I can recount on these pages, so I am singling out only a few. Another shining light among my fellow prisoners of the NDC was Kyaw Htay Oo, a Myanmar-born US citizen who was, above all, warm of heart. Besides being an adviser to Daw Suu, he was a personal friend who'd helped build her exquisite garden. Because of his US citizenship, Kyaw Htay Oo, like me, was able to receive phone calls and parcels from his embassy. The US being, well, the US, his parcels included sufficient items to fashion a passable, if cold, hamburger. Generously, he would make these up and hand them around: KHO Burgers, we called them; they were excellent.

'Get your teeth around one of these, Sean. They'll give you muscles,' he'd tell me.

Notwithstanding his citizenship, Kyaw Htay Oo had been badly beaten and tortured by military intelligence and police, and bore visible scars. He maintained his good-natured demeanour, nonetheless.

He played a prominent role in making the Christmas of 2021 stand out: it was an example of the numerous episodes of love and support I enjoyed from my fellow political prisoners. Christmas has become a 'thing' in some of Yangon's modern shopping centres and upscale hotels, but it has permeated little beyond these enclaves. When 25 December rolled around, I hadn't planned on doing anything to mark it – and couldn't really do much, anyway. But, out of nowhere, I realised that the day meant to me more than I thought. That prompted me to reflect upon Christmases past and their contrast with this one in the awful present. Sensing my melancholy, my fellow inmates, led by Kyaw Htay Oo, started singing me a carol they made up on the spot: 'Happy Christmas to You'. Since they didn't really know any Christmas songs, they followed the tune of 'Happy Birthday' and improvised the words.

What an extraordinary gesture from these wonderfully generous people. All of them were in a situation vastly worse than mine; yet, take pity on this privileged foreigner they did, then and throughout. Choked with emotion, I held my hand to my heart and thanked them. Lest they see my tears of love and gratitude, I evinced a sudden intense interest in a spot on the ground.

Like U Win Htein, Kyaw Htay Oo was convicted of his – predictably ridiculous – charges under the Penal Code, and he was moved away.

Inspired by the example of U Win Htein, Kyaw Htay Oo, and the others, at times I tried to be the one to lighten the mood. At one of our afternoon seminars, for instance, I told our government-in-the-gulag that I was going to write a book about them all.

'History will be kind to us,' I said, 'not least since I intend to write it.' Pushing it further, 'Then shall be the movie. So the big question I want to ask you right now is who do you want to play you?'

The gentle but deceptively comic U Soe Win – reflecting his 85 years – declared 'Robert Redford'. Winston 'George Clooney'. Kyaw Htay Oo 'Jackie Chan'.

I told them I wanted Brad Pitt for me. 'Apart from the uncanny resemblance, we're about the same age. But, friends, I worry Hollywood might cast Danny DeVito instead.'

In around May 2022, we were joined in our prison compound by U Bo Bo Nge, Deputy Governor of the Central Bank of Myanmar (CBM) from near the beginning of the NLD Government. Bo Bo is one of the towering figures of economic reform in Myanmar, a tyro of ideas and energy.

I had met Bo Bo a decade and a half earlier in the US, where for a while he ran a hedge fund in Connecticut. Bo Bo knew more about banking in Myanmar than anyone. I can be confident in this assessment since – and here allow me my own boasting on the matter – I wrote the book on the subject. During his time as the leading reformer at the CBM, Bo Bo sought an end to the endemic criminality and instability of Myanmar's banking sector. He was bold and decisive, and he made enemies among the corrupt old elite.

Bo Bo would be with us in Naypyitaw for less than a fortnight. The offences he was charged with were truly bizarre. Literally, they consisted of his efforts in ensuring Myanmar's foreign reserves were *safe from* corruption and mismanagement. From the NDC he was moved to Mandalay. And there, after an absurdist trial, he remains imprisoned. Bo Bo and I spent much of our week together walking and talking: we completed hundreds of laps around the compound.

On one of these laps he suddenly turned to me. 'Sean, you should not be here.' I told him he should not be either, and that one day when I got back to Australia, I would write our story. As with Winston, Bo Bo is to me a beloved brother about whom I cannot say enough good things.

Feisty and courageous and always willing to push back, my fellow political detainees persistently demanded to see the 'Jail Manual'. This publication, derived from a British colonial document, set out the rights of prisoners and detainees as determined by the Prisons Department. Since they were in breach of such provisions root and branch, the NDC declined to provide it. A practical loss, but a moral win for our team. I remember saying at the time, 'The wrong people are on the wrong side of Myanmar's prison bars.' It was one of my favourite lines. Thanks to all the things I witnessed about the workings of Myanmar's jails, I found myself saying it over and over again.

*

As you would expect, we used to discuss our respective cases – the likely sentences we might receive, bad judges, worse witnesses, poorly performing lawyers, manufactured evidence, false testimonies, and so on. Especially instructive were the experiences shared by Ye Min Oo, U Min Thu, U Myo Aung – all of whom had had levelled against them a myriad of charges that took many months to roll out. After each conviction, they would come back to the rest of us in the compound, unbowed and defiant – even though convicted, they had to stay at the NDC because of the still pending cases.

In addition to myself and my three co-accused, Minister U Kyaw Tint Swe was also charged with breaches of the Myanmar Official Secrets Act. His case was as bizarre and unjust as our own. One of the 'secret' documents he was accused of revealing, for instance, was a speech he made at the UN General Assembly. I had known U Kyaw Tint Swe for a long time, but before our joint imprisonment he had been a remote and formal figure to me. Forced together as we were, our sharing of books brought about an unlikely friendship.

A completely new friend was U Min Thu, Minister for the Union Government in the NLD Administration and an old friend of Daw Suu. I did not know him before the coup and my capture, but I developed a warm friendship with him more or less from the moment he came to occupy the cell next to me in the NDC. U Min Thu had been a commercial pilot, and he had plenty of stories from that experience to entertain us. With me, he developed a comedy routine each evening over the weather. Always concerned it would rain and that I would have to spend a sleepless night protecting my belongings, I would ask him as the cell doors were about to be closed: 'Captain Min Thu, what do your pilot eyes see in the clouds above?'

'Sean, I guarantee no rain before midnight. After that I take no responsibility.'

'No rain before midnight' became our catchphrase, our mock prognosis for the uncertainties ahead.

Rain or no rain, the writing was on the wall for all of us. No-one was walking out of court free; I knew that, however the junta decided to go about it, there would be findings against me. Once convicted, detainees officially became prisoners. From then on, whenever outside the compound they had to wear a bright blue outfit consisting of a shirt and *longyi*. Secretly, I dreaded crossing this fashion threshold.

In the meantime, as my three co-accused and I waited for a clearer idea to emerge about what our futures held, prisoners would come and go from the NDC as they were arrested and then sentenced. Sentencings triggered moments of no little distress and poignancy, but the prisoners were jubilantly defiant. Farewells were ironic and jocular. But inevitably they were unsettling for the rest of us and added to the pervasive apprehension. This place was bad, but elsewhere could be worse.

Daw Suu joined the rest of us at the NDC in July 2022. She was essentially everyone's 'co-defendant' in their cases, and with her arrival there was a sense that the trials were about to move along more decisively.

Held until now on a military base just outside Naypyitaw, at the NDC Daw Suu was housed about 100 metres from our

An Unlikely Prisoner

compound in what I would describe as a 'hut-like structure'. Maybe 'cabin' might have captured it better. Walled off from the rest of the prison, it was a small building with a single living room and bathroom off it. It had fairly large windows without blinds. It had no television or any other entertainment devices. Daw Suu was offered an air conditioner, but she told the Superintendent of NDC – a successor to the one who had greeted us, and significantly better – that she would only accept one if 'every other cell' also got one. So, she went without.

From the political prisoners' compound, we had watched the construction of her cabin without – at first – knowing what it was or what it was to be used for. The way that it was visually sealed-off from the rest of the prison suggested to us it would be used to hold her or the former President of Myanmar, U Win Myint, similarly illegally deposed and imprisoned. The latter, despite endless rumours to the contrary, never did appear at the NDC.

Daw Suu could not be seen by other prisoners in her cabin, and the jail authorities did everything they could to hide her away from us. As she was transported to and from her trial hearings – in her case, this was four days each week – the rest of the NDC was essentially shut down, and prisoners locked in their cells. A black SUV with shaded windows would pull up to her cabin, and with her inside, drive out to the court.

To the vexation of prison officials, however, Myanmar's political prisoners – especially the young ones – were nothing if not inventive, and they would figure out all sorts of ways of signalling that they were with Daw Suu. One night, scores of prisoners in one of the main wards started singing an old NLD song extremely loudly. They were subsequently roughed up by the guards. On another occasion, a small group of prisoners passed by the newly constructed 'courthouse' – just outside the jail proper but still within the grounds of the NDC – and began chorusing, 'Long live Mother Suu' at the tops of their voices. They were brutally silenced and then charged with sedition, though the charges were later dropped.

Where could such charges begin and end when so many prisoners were in jail more or less simply because of their proximity or identification with The Lady? Arguably – if not probably – I was one of these myself. But there were countless others – again, primarily young people – whose offences were scarcely more than showing support for Daw Suu on social media. One of these included Daw Suu's female bodyguard, Cherry Htet, who simply posted on Facebook, 'We miss you, *Amay* (mother).' For this she was given a five-year jail sentence.

The young political prisoners mounted a succession of collective protests that drew strength from their numbers. One of these, enacted throughout all of Myanmar's jails and beyond, was the 'silent strike'. As its name implies, this action was the very simple – but innovative! – idea that prisoners would stay silent all day, regardless of anything going on around them, any instruction issued, any questions asked. An especially powerful derivative of passive resistance, it infuriated the NDC's guards when it was tried out in December 2021, then replicated a number of other times later.

Meanwhile, acutely aware of the deprivations she endured – cut off from the kind of fellowship that sustained us in the compound, denied even books – we political prisoners racked our brains trying to know how we too could support Daw Suu.

An Unlikely Prisoner

By means that best remain unexplained, I was able to pass on some of my own books to her. Later, she was 'allowed' to receive some of Myanmar's junta-friendly newspapers, the only ones still published.

I shall leave the discussions I had with Daw Suu until Chapter 14, where I detail our shared trial. For the moment, I'm concerned to stress that the living conditions provided to Myanmar's former leader – and genuinely beloved icon for the overwhelming majority of people in the country – were hard and uncomfortable. Her treatment in this and in other ways was petty and vindictive.

13

The BBC Wall Service

Without attempting to, I formed a picture of the workings of the wider NDC. One of the more distressing discoveries was the large number of young political prisoners there – including many I had known from my time at Myanmar Development Institute and elsewhere. Myanmar's best and brightest. The ones who knew me were shocked to see me in Naypyitaw, but pleased in that way of discovering someone who the world might listen to, and who might help tell your story.

Story had power.

As in Insein, 'news' was always being circulated at the NDC. In our political prisoners' compound, it spread fast via what we labelled the 'BBC *Wall* Service', and each story was assigned a credibility rating, dependent on source and the plausibility of what was being said. It was essential to try to filter out the rumours. They were a constant, although the ones in the compound were nowhere near as wild as some of the ones in Insein, thanks to the age and experience of my fellow captives. Nevertheless, even among such people – on my part, also – wishful thinking was never too far away.

One news item that seemed implausible initially was Russia's invasion of Ukraine in late February 2022. This was especially worrying. Coupled with the coup that had landed us here in the prison, it suggested a world on the brink. But what did it portend for Myanmar? Presciently, I think, to a person we all thought the attention paid to Myanmar would rapidly diminish in the wake of this global news.

Eerily, about a month after the invasion, the junta celebrated 'army day', and we had to endure the spectacle of military aircraft practising flyovers. At least a couple of times, it seemed to me, some Russian-built Mi-35 'Hind' attack helicopters made an especially low flyover of the prison. To make a point perhaps, of who had the deadly toys, and who was in charge. On one occasion I stood in the middle of our compound and extended the middle finger to these intruders. 'Yo, way to go, Sean' was the response of Kyaw Htay Oo.

Through the Wall Service, every single person in the compound – economist or not – avidly followed the ongoing story of Myanmar's economic collapse. Any sense of schadenfreude for the clowns now ruining the show was difficult to enjoy, however, given that it was the people of Myanmar who were suffering. The World Bank's estimate that Myanmar's GDP had fallen 18 per cent in the year following the coup – a number leaked to us by a guard, later confirmed to me by Ha – made us angry, as did the halving in value of the kyat as the suppressed monetary and banking crisis rippled below the false institutional foundations.

I hated Min Aung Hlaing for the disaster he was weaving. And for his cruelty, his transparent sense of entitlement, for his profound ignorance of the world. I hated him for what he was doing to me, and what he was putting my family and friends through. I exalted in anecdotes about his faults, and was delighted to hear from fellow prisoners who had known him for decades that, as an army cadet, he been called 'Kyaung Chee' (Cat Shit). He was infamous for bullying younger cadets, and for displaying an arrogance and self-regard that far exceeded any justification for either.

The news item that had everyone's undivided attention was the progress of the two main pro-Democracy groups, the National Unity Government – an alternative, legitimate governing body that included representatives from ethnic minority groups and elected members of the previous parliament – and the previously mentioned People's Defence Force – a decentralised network of armed resistance groups that was highly proactive in its opposition to the junta.

As the protests and resistance to Myanmar's military regime continued to step up, the NDC began to get more crowded. In our compound, prisoners were moved about, and two people to a cell became the norm – with the exception of yours truly: the junta's fear of my contagious classical liberal views ran deep. Other prominent political prisoners were moved out of our compound altogether and into the Class C prisoner areas.

The management and guards of the facility seemed much exercised by the question of how they would fit everybody coming through. It was a problem that lasted some months for them, but then around mid-2022, it eased. Not because the junta had stopped arresting people, I hasten to add. Simply, detainees were by now being sentenced, after which they were transferred to prisons all over the country.

Our captors seemed to remain on edge, however. One morning a strange noise reached our ears. Boot camp sounds. Drilling, marching up and down. Physical training. The raspy shouts of a sergeant major. Voices rang out in unison, high-pitched. What was happening was plain, and an illustration of the collapsing dystopia of the junta's world: the wives, girlfriends and even daughters of the prison guards were being trained in order to form a militia. All too believably pointless and stupid, we thought. My Myanmar colleagues spoke to some senior prison officers about it. Not one of them was happy.

The unhappiness of the guards and other staff was constantly apparent. The drunkenness, the ill-discipline, the corruption – all part and parcel of it. It was also apparent in the desertions. At one period, it did not seem a week went by without a guard failing to turn up to work: then there would be reliable intelligence they had gone AWOL, leaving Myanmar for the border regions.

The aforementioned electricity blackouts – which had rarely occurred in Naypyitaw prior to the coup but were now a daily occurrence – certainly did not make life at the NDC easy. Most troubling was that they made the lengthy periods we were locked up in the cells more of a torment. You couldn't read, and additional time engaged in quiet contemplation was one outside-the-wires luxury we really did not want more of.

Sometimes we had extra hours in our cells for other reasons. Thingyan – the Buddhist festival of water, which in Myanmar is as big as Christmas and New Year are in Western countries – was one example. In Insein, it had been celebrated among the general prison population with rock music and much throwing around of water: symbolically, this washes away the previous year's misfortunes and sins. In Naypyitaw, there was nothing festive to mark the occasion; quite the opposite. Many of the guards were given leave and, to save labour, we prisoners were locked in our cells for an extra hour or two.

Sometimes, the hunger for distraction during long stints in our cells was fed in unexpected ways. Our compound in the NDC was frequented by cats. I am not a 'cat person', but I warmed to these creatures. Firstly, they kept down the rat population – *those* four-legged visitors were not remotely endearing. Secondly, they provided considerable amusement.

The favourite of pretty much all of us was a young female cat, barely beyond a kitten, that my colleagues called Thamee, which translates roughly as 'daughter' in Burmese. She was playful, would leap all over the place, and was adept at charming food out of practically everyone. She disappeared one day, and never returned. Nobody said anything, but the world seemed that little bit bleaker with her gone. Another cat died while giving birth. The noise the poor creature made in its pain and distress came following our evening lock-up in the cells. We heard it all night.

A significant proportion of the time on our hands went into trying to remain healthy. The lack of medical care, of even the most basic kind, is endemic in Myanmar's prisons. The NDC

An Unlikely Prisoner

was no exception to this. There was a doctor, a young 'three star' officer who had begun his career in the military. I was wary of him. I wondered, *Why would someone with seemingly a lot of options pursue such a career?* It was put to me that quite a number of doctors joined the Prisons Department precisely to get away from the military. Dr Three Star plummeted in my estimation early on: when I appealed to him to let me have my books, he showed not one scintilla of sympathy.

'You are alive, you have food,' he said. 'What do you need books for?'

However much I disliked him, I had to be careful not to get him offside. Although he had few medications to dispense himself, if ever I needed any drugs to be supplied to me from outside, his approval would be required.

An especially revealing episode of the lack of care we received in the NDC came about when a fellow political prisoner fell into one of the drains that encircled the cell block and broke his leg. Seeing his lower leg swivelling at right angles from where it should be, we called for the doctor. After examining my colleague's obviously broken leg, the doctor declared that he didn't have the 'forms' needed, and thus could not help. Perhaps he was away from medical school the day the Hippocratic oath was discussed? One of the other prisoners, a doctor – that is, a real and compassionate one; before the coup, he had been a leading reformer of Myanmar's health services – demanded that the prison doctor render assistance, appealing to him as a fellow professional and shaming the prison doctor into relenting. It then came to light that the NDC had no stretchers, so my friend was carried away to hospital in the back of a car while lying on an old wooden door. It was the prisoners who found that door.

Earlier, I revealed that I had COVID five times during my imprisonment in Myanmar. In total, I spent 13 months in Naypyitaw and I had all my COVID episodes there. Across these same months, I received China's Sinopharm and Sinovac vaccines four times. Was my case an articulate demonstration of the (in)effectiveness of these drugs perhaps, and how a rogue Myanmar was being increasingly taken to the cleaners by one of their few powerful friends?

Months dragged by. Despite weekly court attendance, the painfully drawn-out legal proceedings seemed to get nowhere; the biggest battles occurred between my ears. As in Insein, I ceaselessly reviewed my conduct as a prisoner. Questioned whether cooperation was getting me anywhere. Then again, was it appropriate? Harmful to my sense of self, even? Yet, the calculations relevant in Insein worked here, too, but with an added complication. Should my actions displease my captors, 'payback' could be visited upon my colleagues, and – worst case scenario – my co-accused. So, once more, for the most part I did what I had to do and complied.

However, on occasion – and these occasions became more frequent over time – I completely lost it. Meltdowns of expletive-laden rants that disparaged the parenthood of my captors, their standard of hygiene and listed other personal defects. The morning after a particularly loud outburst – which took place late

An Unlikely Prisoner

at night, while alone in my cell – some of the prisoners gently took me aside.

'Are you all right, Sean?' they asked, and explained they were worried I might be having a breakdown.

'I'm fine,' I assured them. 'I just needed to clear the air, Australian style. Shouting is a kind of safety valve, if you like, always within limits.'

Nevertheless, six months or so after arriving in the NDC, and after other prominent prisoners had requested such assistance for themselves, I was asked by the prison authorities whether I wanted to see a psychologist. My initial thought was 'under no circumstances'. Wasn't this a favourite ploy of the Soviets against their dissidents? After a while, though, and not least to just get out of the camp, I decided to go along with it. I could always stop, I reasoned.

In the end I went to three sessions with the psych.

On the way to the first session, I was glad I had taken up the offer, simply because getting to the appointment gave me a chance to see more of Naypyitaw. A city that I can only describe as 'under occupation', yet the people I encountered remained undaunted. As I moved around the hospital where the psychologist's office was located I would get thumbs-up signs, winks and grins, and – when my heavily armed guards were looking the other way – the three-fingered salute.

The psychologist I saw was a young, quietly spoken woman who sometimes gave off an impression she was not entirely comfortable with the situation either of us was in.

She threw a 'curveball' question at me in our first session.

'Are you happy?' she asked.

'No,' I replied. 'I and my colleagues are the victims of a monstrous injustice. I am not even remotely happy. Indeed, I think if I was, we really would have something to worry about, and I really would need psychiatric help.' She just nodded and faintly smiled.

I was given some drugs, though, medications that were meant to dampen mood swings. I did not want to take these since I regarded any mood swings I might have suffered from as being an entirely reasonable response to the situation I was in. Medicating against them seemed perverse. However, I did find these pills most useful as sleeping tablets. There had been no let-up of the vivid dreams that plagued me and made sleep difficult to achieve. If anything, they had worsened over time. The same one I'd had in Insein happened night after night: there'd be my release, meeting with friends and family in Australia, then the sting that – before sundown – I would have to return to my cell in Naypyitaw.

Ha, my unfailingly loving coach and inspirer-in-chief, was understanding about my meltdowns when I told her of them in one of our calls. In a letter soon after, this is how she expressed her support:

> ... you are entitled to rant, shout, and shout F here F there. In fact, you *should* do so to get things out of your system every now and then. In addition to smashing dishes, I sometimes bang the bathroom door. Someone suggested that I should try boxing, and I thought it was a good idea. So I googled 'boxing workout at home' and punched the air. Of course, it's nothing compared to hitting some object.

But it still helps somehow. So you could try it too. Should I send you some boxing gloves and a punching bag???

Her letter continued:

This journey might last longer than we ever wanted. But I am also sure that the day of our reunion WILL come. In the meantime, I am accepting and enduring. I know you are too. That would be enough. Please promise me to stay healthy, eat as much as you can to have physical strength, cry out loud from time to time to let things out of your system, and think about our future. In return, I promise you the same thing.

This might be a good opportunity to confess that Ha and I did not talk exclusively about *feelings*. We were wife and husband, but we were economists after all. So we continued to discuss cryptocurrencies, stablecoins, modern monetary theory, the merits of quantitative easing and fiscal consolidation. Totally relatable, I'm sure.

Our humour had not deserted us, either. In one letter Ha asked me whether I was 'top dog' yet. This reference to the Australian prison drama *Wentworth* – and the idea that the roughest, toughest and most cunning prisoner would rise to the top – would have gone well over the heads of the censors but it hit its mark: You might be thinking, *Seriously . . . prison jokes?* To me it highlighted the absurd incongruity of my situation and that crying or laughing were the only sincere responses to it. The latter response was more constructive than the former, though, so that's the way we went.

Words, both spoken and written, carried so much weight. Although Ha and I were used to long periods living apart, being separated from her and Phuong like this was excruciating. This had hit me hard in the lead-up to our wedding anniversary in November. Prior to my detention, Ha and I had never been apart on this day, no matter what was going on in our busy lives. From jail, I couldn't order flowers or undertake any of those tokens of love we take as commonplace.

However, I could still write terrible but sincere poetry, and read the result to Ha over the phone:

Assailed in the ways of the Epics
And even as the darkness gathers around us still
Yet our sacred bond, forged ten years ago this day, grows ever stronger
Unbroken, Undaunted, Unbounded
Happy anniversary, my darling Ha
My mate, my love, my life.

One of the ways I felt Ha's love was the pragmatism and thoughtfulness of her ongoing supply of books throughout my time in Naypyitaw. That supply chain became a well-oiled machine, a manuscript-delivery version of Toyota's fabled 'just in time' inventory system, albeit – in my mind, at least – to far more important effect. She also kept up, and expanded, the supply of news articles to me.

Not content to simply provide time-worn favourites, Ha also tried to diversify the topic portfolio of articles she selected – based upon an acute understanding of my wide-ranging and, admittedly, eccentric tastes and interests. One especially inspired selection was a series of articles she obtained from the *International Journal of Maritime History*. I would sit in my cell reading of Barbary pirates, explorations in the southern seas, and ships-of-the-line.

Books remained the central pillar of my survival strategy, but in Naypyitaw they also formed the central element of my fight-back. Burmese people were denied access to English books from outside, as I have noted – and also that I passed on my literature to my fellow prisoners. Aggressively, deliberately so. It was a little act of subversion. A small chink in the information-suppression armour.

I don't know whether it could be called subversion, but had the censors better English, a book I received that had a powerful effect in helping me get through my entire prison experience would have been unlikely to reach me. In one of our calls, Ha said she had been contacted by someone she described as simply 'Kylie from Melbourne', who had been a tremendous source of comfort to her. It took me a day or two before I clicked as to who this was. On our next call, I asked Ha to send me Kylie's book.

It was *The Uncaged Sky*, the memoir of Kylie Moore-Gilbert on her more than two-year captivity in Iran. An Australian academic and a long-term researcher of Iranian languages, culture and history, like me Kylie had been accused of being a spy; an absurd collection of lies was assembled in 'evidence' against her. I had known of Kylie's case before my arrest, and remembered seeing her extraordinary return to Australia not long before my fateful journey to Myanmar in 2021. Kylie's book included all sorts of practical suggestions on survival in the psychological as well as physical realms – and on different ways one's captors could be confronted.

As I pored over the book, I paid attention to the strategies Kylie had employed that I thought might be replicable by me. One of the most confronting was the idea of a hunger strike. I thought about this over and over in the months ahead, and even prepared myself to mount one on a number of occasions. In the end, I did not go down this path. Ha's baking was simply too tempting.

In April 2022, Australian Ambassador Andrea Faulkner's term came to an end. It had already been extended – not least, I think, to allow continuity for me. By then, Australia had decided to downgrade its diplomatic representation in Myanmar – following the pattern set by the UK, Germany, South Korea and a growing number of other countries, in response to the coup. In the place of a new ambassador, a chargé d'affaires was appointed. In practice, the difference was subtle as the appointee, Angela Corcoran, had been Ambassador to Cambodia and held ambassadorial rank. Appointed I believe – both now and at the time – because of her experience in 'difficult' countries in Southeast Asia transitioning to . . . well, somewhere.

From my perspective, there was some change in style but not in substance: the support the Embassy provided to me was as strong as ever. Angela was of that decidedly no-nonsense variety of Australian with whom I was well familiar, especially in its female manifestation. She was funny, too, but tough when warranted – particularly when dealing with the absurdities the junta would regularly serve up. I felt I knew her even from the brief snatches of phone conversations that were our only contact.

As was the case with foreign legations, the Australian Embassy had to obtain approval from the Ministry of Foreign Affairs – and, in reality, the Ministry of Home Affairs – merely to set foot in Naypyitaw. This was often not forthcoming for any purpose, let alone to visit me. No consular access was allowed at any time during my stay in Naypyitaw. Consular staff delivering packages to me were kept well away from vehicles taking prisoners to and fro.

In February 2022, the one-year anniversary of the coup and my arrest had prompted a flurry of activity about my ongoing detention. In Australia, the Foreign Minister, Marise Payne, issued a statement demanding my release, and for Myanmar's military to halt its violence against civilians and return to the democratic path.

Ha also released a statement that was picked up by the press – and found its way to me in Naypyitaw:

> It has been a year, and in our wildest dream ... we never ever thought we would face this kind of challenge ...
>
> I am grateful for the support from so many people, some have been amazing, and I don't know how I would cope without them ...
>
> I wish the trial would proceed ... so that Sean can return home.

Friends also actively marked the anniversary by submitting a formal petition to the Australian parliament that called for:

… the House [to] insist that the charges against Professor Turnell be withdrawn or the trial closed; that for the remainder of his detention he receive weekly visits by Australian officials, be able to meet freely with his lawyers, and have an interpreter in court.

And, as something extra:

We seek the appointment of a prominent person as special envoy dedicated to working exclusively on getting Professor Turnell released, with the authority and resources necessary to succeed.

In fact, the idea of an envoy had occurred to Ha and Janelle Saffin a while earlier. The person they had in mind – and who the petitioners had in mind, too – was former Australian Prime Minister Kevin Rudd. At that time the President and CEO of the Asia Society, Rudd was up for the gig. He wrote to the Myanmar Ambassador in Australia that he had been pleased to see the release of US citizen Danny Fenster following the representations of former Governor Bill Richardson. Rudd noted he had been asked by my family to undertake a similar role for me and was 'happy to facilitate this by travelling to Yangon or Naypyitaw to make such representations if needed'.

I did not hear of this initiative at the time. The junta did not take Rudd up on his offer. I remain grateful to him nevertheless.

Ha and the team had had no reluctance seeking out regional and world leaders for help. The strongest response came from Australia's traditional allies, the UK and the US. Multiple branches of these two governments mobilised in my support, and they applied pressure to Myanmar's junta in numerous ways. US Secretary of State Antony Blinken called for my release (as well as that of US journalist Danny Fenster) in the wake of Australia–US ministerial meetings in September 2021, and again in February 2022 during a meeting of the 'Quad', the semi-formal security alliance comprising Australia, the United States, India and Japan.

The US Embassy in Yangon was a bedrock of assistance, both openly and clandestinely, with Alex Albertine leading the way. In Washington, especially helpful was the Republican Minority Leader in the US Senate, and long-time supporter of democracy activists in Myanmar, Senator Mitch McConnell, and his present and former staff. Among the latter included his Chief of Staff, Robert Karam, and Paul Grove. Paul was (and is) the Clerk of the United States Senate Committee on Appropriations and, in this role, was once described to me as 'the most powerful man in the world that no-one has ever heard of'. Robert and Paul stayed in touch with Ha from Day 1 all the way through to Day 650.

The UK was not far behind in its advocacy for my release, and in seeking to alleviate the circumstances of my detention. The UK Embassy in Yangon – led by the head of the economics team, Tom Coward – was a tremendous supplier of books to me in the prison. Notable too was (the then) Prince Charles, who was an early and persistent supporter of Ha's efforts and those of others in the Myanmar cause. One did not have to be an ardent Australian monarchist to appreciate his kindness to us.

My indefatigable Ha urged the Australian Government to engage ASEAN, and contacted then Foreign Minister Marise Payne directly on this front: 'I know she is busy and travelling. But a ten-minute call via Signal or WhatsApp is all I ask for.' She also approached the Vietnamese Ambassador to Australia, and the Vietnamese Prime Minister, asking for their help. Before an ASEAN Summit in April 2021 she wrote to the Vietnamese Prime Minister imploring him to urge the Myanmar regime to allow her to contact me, and then to secure my release. Help from Vietnam was forthcoming, and the Vietnamese Government made a number of approaches to Myanmar's junta to suggest my release might be in the best interests of everyone.

Around the same time as the February 2022 milestone, I found out via the BBC Wall Service that Hun Sen, the Prime Minister of Cambodia – and the current chair of the ASEAN grouping of which Myanmar was a part – was calling for my release at the behest of the Australian Government. A few days later, further excitement: Hun Sen declared a deal, and announced that I *had been* released. He even started assigning the congratulations, saying that the release 'is indeed the senior general's credit, but at least I also contributed as the rotating chair of ASEAN.'

Setting aside the fact that I was still there in the NDC, surely this was the moment I'd been waiting for? Fellow prisoners and some of the guards came up to congratulate me. I desperately tried to keep my feelings in check. Too many times, too tantalisingly close.

Then silence.

And, on 7 February 2022, Hun Sen issued a statement.

He had 'received the wrong information'. He 'would like to ask for understanding for this unintentional mistake'.

Ouch.

That evening, I read *Alexander Hamilton* with extra intensity.

The days, weeks and months stretched slowly in Naypyitaw. I tried to stay poised and positive, but there were more than a few days when I wondered how much longer I could survive. The NDC was an unhealthy and dangerous place, and Myanmar seemed to be spiralling into civil war. How to prepare for what might come? How to avoid becoming a hostage – as if I wasn't already hostage enough – should the junta be cornered and in a last desperate shootout?

Other days my thoughts were not so dramatic, and my mind wallowed in mindless self-pity as well as (well-founded) depression. In these episodes I would reach the insight that I would survive, no matter how bad things got. That my mind and body would not allow any self-determined ending. Understanding this made me feel worse since it meant that, beyond my control, it was possible there would be no end, no floor to the potential suffering I might face. I would endure, but in an un-waking nightmare.

I remember quite a few conversations when I said to both of Australia's mission chiefs that I felt defeated. I told one of them – Angela, I think – that I identified myself with the World War I German warship the *Emden*, as vanquished by HMAS *Sydney* and depicted in the well-known painting by Arthur Burgess, *Emden beached and done for*. I'd had a copy of this on my wall as a kid, and I pictured it often now.

Things that I might previously have regarded as minor inconveniences became day-to-day impediments that weighed me down. A screw in my glasses started to prise loose. Immense distress. I had proved I could survive a lot of things, but I could *not* survive without my glasses. Apart from anything else – and there was much else! – the valiant campaign over books was meaningless without my glasses. How to get new ones here? And customised for a special type of eye affliction? Going the extra mile yet again, the Embassy tried to organise for a pair to be made in Yangon with a prescription sent from Australia. Alas the shop in Myanmar could not do it. So I held on. Nursing my glasses to go the distance. One fragile thread away.

Dental problems were also an issue, as I guess is commonplace for people of my age group. Indeed, when I set off on my COVID-delayed return to Myanmar in January 2021 I'd had a 'twinge' in one of my teeth that I knew would have to be dealt with. In keeping with my cowardly approach to such matters, I'd delayed doing anything about it.

'I'll go to the dentist on my next trip back to Australia,' I'd told Ha.

Unnervingly, my dental situation brought to mind the epic tooth extraction scene in the Tom Hanks movie *Cast Away*: the character had also put off going to the dentist. The pain he endures and what he ends up going through is terrible: has there ever been anything other than a *horrible* dental scene in movies? My pain intensified; the more my tooth throbbed and my face swelled, the more my thoughts turned to that movie. But I didn't have any ice-skates to take matters into my own hands.

In the brutal aesthetic and mean environment of the NDC, my toothache was the cherry on top of my misery cake. I let Ha know, I let the Embassy know. Thankfully, and although dental procedures were not available to me, antibiotics in this low-compliance regulatory environment were. So was codeine. Relief was at hand. The underlying issue could be postponed. Again.

Highlighting health issues – both mine and my dad's – remained a priority in the advocacy of Ha and others: it wasn't spin, it was my reality. As well as my tooth problems, I lived with the risk of seizure: no explanation had been identified after the episode I had experienced a couple of years back. The tests revealed only that exhaustion and dehydration had played a role – two maladies that were hardly unfamiliar to me in the circumstances I found myself in now.

With this being the case, I had to constantly impress upon the Embassy that I was '*not* all right' – and to avoid saying 'I'm good' in response to the familiar polite greeting that prefaced my phone calls.

14

Show Trial

My trial had commenced on 23 September 2021, two days after our arrival in Naypyitaw. It then dragged on for over a year. The proceedings were, not unexpectedly, a parade of nonsense. A façade of fidelity to truth and justice, a Potemkin village to proper process.

Bizarre happenings started on Day 1. The Australian Embassy had applied to Myanmar's Foreign Affairs ministry for permission to attend the court; they would do so for every subsequent court appearance, too. Permission was initially granted, but when the Ambassador and Political Officer turned up at court, police refused to accept MOFA's letter of approval so Australia's representatives resorted to hovering in the vicinity. Thereafter the Embassy was routinely refused attendance in any form. On a number of occasions, however, both Ambassadors Andrea Faulkner and Angela Corcoran maintained something of a vigil nearby.

An Unlikely Prisoner

There was no mystery as to the outcome: having been charged, a guilty verdict was all we could anticipate. That said, there were some surprises along the way.

The first of these was location. After the experience in Insein, I did not expect The Hague, but I was surprised that the courthouse was such a makeshift affair. Naypyitaw had court buildings, but for reasons still unknown to me, our trial was held in the highly residential Dekkhina Thiri District, in what had been the home of a former senior official in the Naypyitaw local government. Cosmetic changes had been made to kit out one of the rooms as a court, but the whole effect was monumentally unconvincing. Consequently, the physical setting functioned nicely as a metaphor for the absurd process taking place within it.

For the first six months, when the court was located at Dekkhina Thiri, U Soe Win, U Kyaw Win, Winston and I would leave the prison at around 9 am for the 10 am start. The trip, which took about 20 minutes, was a micro version of our journey from Insein to Naypyitaw – all of us in a minivan, with machine gun–toting police SUVs fore and aft. Our convoy would always drive at high speed, and usually through red lights. Stopping was clearly regarded as a security risk in the fraught and tense environment of the capital: even from the van this was apparent to us. As before, the streets of Naypyitaw were crowded with roadblocks, gun emplacements, and lots of barbed wire.

In characteristic Myanmar-junta fashion, our prison-to-court transfer arrangements were a mix of the needlessly brutal, the petty, and the incompetent. We had to wear handcuffs and were forbidden to talk to each other. But there were always stuff-ups. One day I went to sit in my assigned seat only to find it had a loaded pistol placed on it. It says something of my mindset at that time that I did not touch it, for fear this was a trap that would get me shot: 'He went for the pistol!' In the event, I casually pointed it out to its likely police-owner, helpfully suggesting he may have forgotten where he left it.

When the trial was getting underway, Daw Suu was still being held at the military base and would arrive before us at the court. Should we ever be ahead of schedule, our motorcade would slow to allow her to arrive first. They did not like the idea of us mingling with her for too long.

That first court appearance was also the first time I had seen Daw Suu in person for nearly 18 months – my COVID stranding in Australia, as well as the coup and imprisonment, both factoring here. She looked to be the same person I had always known. Slightly thinner perhaps, which is saying something – she has always been particularly slim – but as strong, calm and serene as ever. Now officially a convict – the first case against her had already been concluded – she was forced to wear the female prison clothing, a dark brown *htamein* (a skirt-like garment, the female version of the male *longyi*) and a cream-coloured Burmese blouse called an *eingyi*.

Hoping we would get a chance to speak, I had been mulling over what to say to her at this decidedly surreal reunion. My typical greeting upon seeing old friends in these circumstances was a variant of, 'It's good to see you again, but I just wish it wasn't here.' That didn't strike the right note but I couldn't think of anything better, so I decided to play it by ear. Possibly a mistake, since all I came up with in the brief window of opportunity that presented itself was, 'The Force is still with us.'

Now, in my defence, I must stress Daw Suu and I were both (not uncritical, and sometimes mocking) fans of the *Star Wars* movies; references had featured in our conversations in recent years. So, my comment was not completely random, and it did rather match the absurdity of the situation. It also reflected something of the broad relationship between us – my Australian nationality somehow allowed me an informality with Myanmar's leader that, in my observation, was rare. Six months into our trial, around the time Daw Suu was transferred to the detention centre in Naypyitaw where the rest of us were, the treks to Dekkina Thiri ceased and the hearings were switched to a similarly makeshift building inside the NDC. Yet another converted dwelling – this had once been the NDC's 'guest house' – it was no better than its predecessor in the sense of being hot, stuffy and with intermittent electricity. In both courts, a typical trial day was interrupted multiple times as the lights failed, and the scribes had no power for their computers. One of the upsides of the trial relocation to the NDC was that the long drive to the court was no longer necessary. This allowed the rest of us time to talk with Daw Suu. CCTV cameras were everywhere in both of the buildings that pretended to be a court. The rooms where we met with Daw Suu and our lawyers were the only ones without cameras, but we proceeded on the assumption that they were likely 'bugged'.

Up to this point, she had no-one to talk to in English. This – coupled with the fact that, via Ha, I was one of Daw Suu's few conduits to events in the outside world, on top of being an old and trusted friend – meant that I probably spoke more to her than anyone else.

Talk about our legal case was minimal: at most we acknowledged a shared understanding as to the essential nonsense of it all, and the inevitable 'fix' with respect to the verdict and sentence.

The trial proceedings were scheduled to take place once a week, every week. Illnesses – of defendants and the judge – brought about some significant delays, but every Thursday was nominally trial day. Both of my charges were heard together. In the Official Secrets Act (OSA) case I was joined in the court by my co-defendants, while for the immigration case I was tried alone. Because the immigration case relied on the OSA outcome to prove I had broken Myanmar law – and therefore breached my visa conditions – I had a hearing on this charge only once in a while.

Presiding over the trials was Judge U Ye Lwin. He had a reputation as a pro-junta hardliner who was anxious to do the military's bidding; this had been apparent even before the coup. U Ye Lwin was the judge who, in 2019, presided over the infamous Reuters case in which two journalists – Wa Lone and Kyaw Soe Oo – were sentenced to seven years' jail for alleged breaches of the Official Secrets Act (yes, the same old law!). The case was a travesty, and the journalists were ultimately released by pardon, but not before serving 500 days in prison. Closer to home, U Ye Lwin was also the judge who sentenced U Win Htein to 20 years. None of this was remotely hopeful.

The prosecution lawyers were two ill-at-ease young men. From the outset, I noticed that they avoided looking at Daw Suu directly; this was how they were for the duration of the trial.

An Unlikely Prisoner

I imagined – wrongly or rightly; I cannot know – that their participation in this charade, their role in this hounding of Mother Suu, might have been a source of shame to them. What did they tell themselves about the job they were doing while, as the old song goes, alone in their bed? What story did they plan to tell their children?

But while they were obviously in awe of Daw Suu throughout, the prosecuting team projected ill-concealed hostility to me. No doubt they bought into the idea that I was a perfidious foreigner interfering in Myanmar affairs. Then again, maybe they were astute enough to realise that one day I would write an account of what a kangaroo court they had participated in.

A small taste of negative media portrayal was coming my way, too. Unbeknown to me, this first hearing would be widely reported in the press – in Myanmar but also in Australia and elsewhere. In one of these reports I was singled out as looking 'frail'. While I probably wasn't at my best, given that I was flanked by people in their 70s and 80s, it was not a good look.

My main lawyer remained U Nu, who would drive up from Yangon to Naypyitaw every Wednesday night to attend. A junior lawyer assisted him in the court. Behind U Nu and his team was the legal team put together by Ha and Janelle Saffin. They received court transcripts and descriptions from U Nu and, after briefing Ha, would prepare strategy week by week.

The first few trial dates were dominated by procedure, which included the efforts of my lawyers and others to have the cases simply dismissed. They held to their fundamental belief that the trial itself was unlawful, all the way to the end. While impeccable according to every lawyer consulted by my team, the Australian

Government and every assessment of it, this line of argument was dismissed, and the trial went ahead.

A very important objective of the first session of my trial was to get approval for an interpreter. We had a splendid one lined up. Unfortunately, she was so good – not just in terms of translating Burmese into English, but in her understanding of legal procedure in Myanmar, too – that the judge rejected her straightaway. We appealed, but to no avail. We asked to have another interpreter appointed, but this person, too, was rejected.

Then the judge himself appointed an interpreter, an academic from the University of Mandalay with a specialisation in English literature. She was a nice person, and in this sense I came to appreciate her. She was, however, far from what I needed in that court. The head of my out-of-country legal team reported back to Ha, 'Her knowledge of legal terminology is very low.'

My concern was what she might be asked to reveal to the police or military intelligence with respect to our conversations. To protect her – even more than myself – I tried not to engage on substantive issues. Obviously, this rather missed the point of having an interpreter. It also meant that I had tremendous difficulty knowing at any point in time what was going on in the court. Or where my case, where my life, was going.

About a month into the proceedings, we were asked to plead guilty or not guilty to the charges against us, much in the manner of the movies and in television. In a loud, bold and I hoped confident voice, I declared 'not guilty' to both charges. I was also asked at this time to state my religion – as if this was integral to my identity. I said Christian, which I was certainly brought up as, and I guess which reasonably described my world view. But that answer was about meeting an expectation in the Myanmar context. To describe that I had metaphysical doubts would probably not have been helpful to my case. *A debate for another time*, I thought!

The five of us accused sat at the back of the court behind a flimsy-looking portable railing put in place to make a 'dock'. Even though I was Defendant 1 and Daw Suu Defendant 2 – surely the first and only time in my life I would have such precedence! – we were always placed as far apart as possible: me at one end of the dock, she at the other. Again, that concern of foreign pollution, and English whispers.

Next to me sat Winston, then U Soe Win, and U Kyaw Win. Throughout the trial – that is, for the entire 13 months it sat – we had to wear full PPE gear of gown, face mask and hairnet. Since we were not convicted prisoners, we were not required to wear the blue prison clothes, but the PPE gear was all blue in colour – a deliberate selection, in my view, to maximise our psychological discomfort.

Daw Suu was not required to wear a gown or hairnet, but wore a face mask the entire time, along with everyone else in the court. Seated next to Daw Suu – on her right – was a young policewoman who never left her side.

Once we had all entered our pleas, the case itself could begin. This included the complete enunciation of the charges, presentation of physical evidence that was deemed to support it – namely documents allegedly stored on my electronic devices – and a series of prosecution witnesses testifying against me. The prosecution strategy was essentially to set out a narrative that I was guilty under section 3(1)(c) of the Myanmar Official Secrets Act of, in the words of the charge sheet, 'obtaining, collecting, recording, publishing via a secret code, and using passwords, sketches, plans, models, articles or notes or documents affecting the safety, interests of the State for a purpose prejudicial to the safety or interests of the State'.

The electronic devices and other items noted on the charge sheet as having been seized from me were: (1) a white Asus Vivobook laptop and charger, (2) a silver iPad and charger, (3) a black and red SanDisk memory stick, (4) a black iPhone 11, (5) a blue notebook labelled 2021 Diary, (6) a black notebook and documents, and (7) a reading book called *The Line Upon a Wind*. From all of this the police produced an 'extraction report' alleging my electronic devices were storehouses of secret documents, kept for transmission to Myanmar's 'enemies'.

My co-accused, meanwhile, were alleged to have aided and abetted my espionage or, in the case of Daw Suu, been indifferent to it. They were charged, accordingly, under section 3(1)(c)(9) of the OSA.

Perhaps this sounds reasonable so far? Well, maybe if I didn't know the truth, I might have been convinced myself. Maybe I had been an Australian version of James Bond, but just didn't know it?

In the next phase of the trial, the prosecution entered the twilight zone, destroying their credibility with obvious lies, fake documents, and bizarre presentations that highlighted the Kafkaesque nature of the judicial system that prevails in Myanmar under the junta.

Bear in mind that all of this played out in slow motion, week by week across nearly 13 months. Tedious it would be to write about it in strict chronological order in a 'he said, she said' way, and even more tedious it would be, dare I say, to read. So, let me present a highlights package:

First in the low-credibility stakes were the witnesses. Nine were called against me, though six of them stated that they had simply been present at my arrest at the Chatrium Hotel, that I was who I said I was, had a valid visa to be in Myanmar, and that I had had in my possession the devices mentioned. These witnesses were regular police as well as some grassroots officials from Tamwe Township, where the hotel was located. Confusingly, some of them were quite sympathetic to me: one even gave me a wink as he quit the stand.

The three remaining witnesses were all police – two Special Branch, one a computer expert – and they required more engagement from my legal team. The two Special Branch officers claimed to have met me, spoken to me, questioned me.

There was only one problem.

Until these men appeared before me in this courthouse, I had never laid eyes on them. They were certainly not my interrogators from The Box, who at no stage appeared at the trial. I had not seen these officers in Insein. I had not seen them in the NDC. Nevertheless, according to the prosecution I had made elaborate confessions to these witnesses-who-never-were.

Under questioning from U Nu, however, the officers were to make some confessions of their own. Asked whether they had spoken to me through an interpreter, they replied they had not. 'We spoke to Sean directly,' they said.

'Do you speak English?' asked U Nu.

'No,' they replied.

As I've mentioned, I had never answered any question put by anyone in Burmese in the entire time of my detention. Someone was telling porkies. And they were big ones. Not only were the answers entirely made up, but the questions that elicited them were dodgy too. The whole testimony of these two officers was nothing short of a fairly elaborate, but not at all original or interesting, fantasy.

The final witness – the alleged computer expert – had been involved in the extraction of documents from my electronic devices. I have no doubt he was a computer expert. As I have noted, as soon as the coup took place, I had carefully and deliberately deleted all my files to keep my work out of the hands of Myanmar's criminal coup leaders. The resurrection of those files would have required a level of competence.

But what was scandalous was the meaning this police officer assigned to the documents. They were, he said, secrets of the Myanmar State, and stolen by me in order to transmit to foreign authorities – he alluded to the United States, the United Kingdom, the IMF and the World Bank, as well as Australia – for purposes harmful to Myanmar.

In an echo of the previous witnesses, his testimony contained one fundamental flaw. None of the documents was secret. Oh yes, a few had 'Top Secret' written upon them: these ones were projected on a screen put up in the courtroom. Open-and-shut case, then?

Well, no. And here comes a tip to my Myanmar police accuser. If you're going to manufacture evidence on an electronic document – say, for example, inserting 'Top Secret' as a header – be careful to ensure that time stamps reading 'document modified' do not appear in the evidence being presented to a court. And yet, there were such stamps – for everyone to see. On all of the documents marked Top Secret. The dates? All between September and October 2021. Where was I in September to October 2021? Really awkward for the prosecutors this. I was in Insein. And then the NDC. Good alibis, you'd think.

Other problems with the documents that supposedly proved my guilt were more absurd than inept evidence tampering. One document, for instance, was about the memorandum on possible measures I had recommended against Myanmar military officers who were involved in human rights abuses against the Rohingya in Rakhine State. The document had 'Confidential' written across it. The court was told – just as the questioner in The Box had presumed – that the memo had been acquired by me from the Myanmar Government in some nefarious way. Again as noted earlier, the document was originated by me. I wrote the memorandum. I put 'Confidential' on it. I thought I'd clarified this in The Box. Yet, here it was. Again.

Then there were all the other documents from my computer, not individually presented to the court, but held up as 'evidence' of some sort. Most were work-related drafts, academic papers, articles I had written for MDI and essays of my students back in Sydney. Many were entirely public documents, downloaded from the internet – World Bank, IMF and ADB reports, news articles – the flotsam and jetsam of the busy economic adviser. And, may I say, to most people, every bit as dull, unsexy and un-secret as all of that sounds.

Sins of omission added to my sense of deep injustice being perpetrated.

The letter of invitation to me from the Myanmar Government – a request for my services in the role of adviser to them, and obviously a key document in my defence – was declared 'inadmissible'. Also declared inadmissible – although once more, a fair observer might have regarded it as profoundly relevant – was my contract with Australia's Department of Foreign Affairs and Trade, within which was clearly specified all of my work activities: the very activities that the prosecutors alleged were both secret and unlawful.

Under cross-examination in the early hearings, U Nu extracted a number of unintentional confessions out of the prosecution witnesses. These included an effective admission from the police officer listed as the official complainant of the whole case that the OSA 'did not apply to Professor Turnell'. Another officer admitted that, of the 67 pieces of evidence produced and submitted, 'None . . . showed anything prejudicial to the safety or interests of the State of Myanmar, and only three of which were marked as being "secret"'. Of course, even these three were falsely labelled, as noted.

In a despatch to Ha on the prosecution case, my offshore legal team concluded:

> In fact, much of the 'evidence' consists of photos of Prof. Turnell and others, travel plans and publicly available information. Hence, if the rule of law were applied, there should be no case to answer . . .

*

An important hearing date was 9 June 2022, when judge U Ye Lwin determined that I and the others had a case to answer. He did not address *at all* the arguments put forward by our legal teams. This was widely reported in the Australian and international press. It led to the issuing of a statement from Australia's new Foreign Minister, Penny Wong, that the Australian Government 'rejects . . . this court ruling'.

In July 2022, only a couple of months before the trial was meant to end, U Ye Lwin was replaced as judge. He was allegedly ill, and had missed several weeks because of reported surgery. The replacement judge was U Win Tint from the Pyinmana District Court. Compared to his predecessor, he seemed far less interested in the proceedings, and even less concerned to pretend that this was all a proper legal process. Many times I witnessed him 'nodding off'; often he seemed to be, as we say in Australia, 'tired and emotional' (i.e. drunk). The trial meandered on!

The postponement of proceedings caused by the illness of U Ye Lwin was the latest in a succession of delays in our trial. We lost nearly two months to COVID shutdowns, and further weeks for electricity shortages and for illnesses among my co-accused. Daw Suu missed several weeks on account of food poisoning and other maladies, U Kyaw Win had surgery, and U Soe Win was absent for several months for surgery and chemotherapy – although he signed a release allowing the trial to proceed without his physical presence.

Throughout the trial the treatment of U Soe Win provoked considerable anger in me. This gentle 85-year-old man is loved by just about everyone who comes across him. The principal behind Deloitte's agency in Myanmar, and thus someone of financial standing and knowledge, he had to be cajoled into taking the post of Finance Minister by Daw Suu. Hankering for a quiet retirement and the opportunity to engage fully in family life, U Soe Win took on this ministerial role out of nothing but a sense of profound duty. He is a key driver of reform and a courageous, decades-long human rights advocate, and should have been accorded nothing but deep gratitude and respect. From time to time he got a modicum of this from the guards, but from the authorities, police and the junta more broadly, he was treated most shabbily. The charges against him were absurd. He was not even in office when I was first appointed and, although I treasured my meetings with him, I saw him just once or twice a year. He should not have been there in the NDC. U Soe Win's limited mobility made life in the cell, and in moving about the prison, incredibly difficult. He was allowed temporary bail during the worst periods of his chemotherapy, but otherwise he was unacceptably incarcerated along with the rest of us.

In the spirit of frankness with which Ha and I have approached writing this book, we have to confess to some relatively minor tensions with some of the other accused – or, more to the point, their lawyers. These concerned strategic court delays – quite apart from illnesses and other problems. Put simply, our objective was to get through the trial as quickly as possible. Recognising that the legal processes were no more than a fiction, and the findings pre-ordained, we wanted to get to the point at which politics and diplomacy could work away: which was after the judgment was delivered. The objective of some of the others, understandably, was to string the trial out as long as possible – to remain an 'accused' rather than a convicted prisoner.

In the end, the difference – which had once been meaningful in terms of conditions – withered away. If anything, our detention on remand in Naypyitaw placed us in conditions significantly worse than those of convicted prisoners we had witnessed in Insein.

Accordingly, Ha instructed my lawyers to do nothing but push to a conclusion: to not call any witnesses on my behalf, to not ask too many questions to any other witnesses, to not join in any recall of prosecution witnesses for further cross-examination, to increase the tempo of hearings – to twice or even three times a week – and to do anything else possible to wrap matters up. In principle, my co-defendants by then were in agreement on the wisdom of all of this – Daw Suu and her lawyers strongly so. Somehow, the case had its own momentum and did not appreciably speed up, notwithstanding that U Nu followed Ha's instructions.

On these legal strategies more broadly, I found myself little more than a passenger. The difficulties – near impossibility – of me engaging in any serious and prolonged discussion of my case with Ha or anyone else, including my lawyer, meant that I literally had no idea what was the best way to proceed, or even that there were choices in the matter. Looking back, I suspect there were not, and the trial took the only course possible – of being a means to the junta's ends of punishing and eliminating people it regarded as enemies.

In the court itself, and in terms of routine questioning and other procedures, meaningful or otherwise, U Nu and Daw Suu's lawyer were by far the most effective. I cannot write much more about them here alas, for fear of inadvertently drawing unwanted attention to them. Suffice to say, they earned the respect of all concerned, including the prosecutors.

I hated having to participate in the sham – standing up for the judge and behaving as if it were a proper court. Nevertheless, I went along with the nonsense to the extent I thought I had to – that is, to avoid making mine and the lot of others worse than it already was.

Some funny moments occurred in the court with the handling of the 'case file'. This gargantuan document – full of much legal guff, copies of every paper supposedly proof of my espionage, and the verbose reports of police and prosecutors – strained the arms of the young women clerks who had to constantly pass it around as it was examined and quoted. Every now and again, the case file crashed to the ground from its unstable perch atop a partition, causing much mirth – and adding in its own way an articulate statement on proceedings.

I was never allowed to read the case file, even though I was this mega-novel sized document's 'main character'.

Back in the real world of that trial, something that stood out was Daw Suu's engagement with all of us collectively and her consistent, concerted efforts to keep everyone's spirits up. Demonstrating a remarkable ability to rise above her own suffering – four out of five days in a court, listening for up to eight hours at a time to the most errant nonsense conjured up by Myanmar's knavish junta – she managed to give us a lift. It was more than a boost in the broadest sense, it occurred to me. Daw Suu was attuned to the particular anxiety we felt as a result of the whole 'criminal justice' framing of everything. For her co-accused, being charged with a crime and placed in a jail was a most unlikely, horrific and – in the back of most of our minds, I think – shameful thing. She cut through this decisively – urging us not to get caught up in this faux-legal process, and to understand that all around us was nothing but the expression of raw and brutal power. Of a particularly ugly form of politics. And, yes, that our tormenters beyond the court were the true criminals, and the people of Myanmar the true victims.

Daw Suu was unfailingly courteous to the functionaries of the court, the police, the prison guards, the prosecution team and the pumped-up, pompous judges. Her compassion, wisdom, and sheer moral authority reasserted itself in the most trying and character-testing of circumstances.

A constant in my weekly conversations with Daw Suu was her pride in the Myanmar people's response to the coup, especially considering their brief experience of freedom and (imperfect) democracy. World affairs were a feature. As per above, I was sometimes her only source of information – on Ukraine, on the death of the Queen of England, on Afghanistan, on Biden, Xi and Trump. Boris Johnson's travails – she had met him, and liked him as an entertaining dinner companion – provided comic relief.

There were other perennials, too. Above all, our talk was of books and authors – particularly the titles that I was able to smuggle to her in the prison: Isaiah Berlin (and his two concepts of freedom), Edmund Burke (and his 'Great Melody' of campaigns against tyranny), novels by Julian Barnes and Ian McEwan, and a biography of J. R. R. Tolkien. Daw Suu was a big fan of Tolkien, and we discussed a great many things from his books – not least the immortal back and forth between Gandalf and Frodo in *Lord of the Rings*:

'I wish it need not have happened in my time,' said Frodo.

'So do I,' said Gandalf, 'and so do all who live to see such times. But that is not for them to decide. All we have to decide is what to do with the time that is given us.'

To Daw Suu I brought all manner of questions prompted by my own reading. In the absence of Google, I regularly asked her to draw on her phenomenal memory and skills as a polymath. Remembering well her proficiency across multiple languages – while heading the government, one of the few indulgences she allowed herself was to read French detective novels – I asked if she could explain *pied noir*. The way it was used, the author clearly intended to convey particular meaning beyond simple translation. Daw Suu picked up both the translation and deeper meaning straightaway. 'Sean, it means black feet. But it's more than that. The author is indicating someone who is French, but born in Algeria. The phrase comes from the black boots worn by French soldiers there.'

Court days were beyond dull. Because the proceedings were in highly formal Burmese and quickly exceeded my understanding,

I spent much of the time daydreaming. As in The Box, my thoughts ranged far and wide, from ruminations on economics and similar topics, to the profound silliness central to my make-up. I especially liked to fantasise about the superyacht I might own. A big one that could accommodate all my friends and family, and in which we could sail the world. I developed detailed itineraries, and made rough estimates of sailing distances and times, and how much fuel we might need. It kept me focused for hours across many weeks working all this out.

A distraction to the daydreaming, as well as the proceedings themselves, came via the presence of a mirror in the courthouse bathroom. It had been so long since I had come across a mirror. Prior to examining my reflection, I knew I had lost weight, had broken more of my teeth, bore the marks of exposure to the elements, had tattier clothes – and was a year older. In short, I didn't expect an oil painting to be staring back at me, and in this I was not disappointed. Nevertheless, it was an effort to stop gazing at myself. Not in the way of Narcissus, but in the manner of the vision Orwell paints of the broken Winston Smith in *1984*. Unlike Orwell's creation, however, I was not completely defeated by my awful doppelganger. Not yet.

But I was on edge. There was no longer the slightest doubt that I would be found guilty and sentenced. That meant I would be forced to don the dreaded blue prison garb. To prepare myself psychologically, I started wearing blue clothes well before the end of our trial. My reasoning was that this way, I could 'own' the wearing of such a colour and thus remove the sting from being forced to adopt it. After a few weeks, I abandoned the practice. Somehow the 'ownership' didn't convey as much comfort as I had hoped.

For me, fear of the unknown loomed large. My future now depended on diplomacy.

15

Judgement Day

Fitfully, inexorably, the case drew to a close. As August rolled into September of 2022 it was clear the case had only a few more weeks.

Throughout the trial I had been forbidden to speak in my own defence. Now, in the last week, I would get to make a statement. First, a reiteration of my plea. Then, a full three minutes to put my case.

Three minutes in 13 months; 180 seconds to get to the heart of the argument. All the arguments. Determined not to squander a single second, I prepared my statement, and memorised it.

At the court, the judge told me to stand, and swear on . . . nothing, actually. There was no Bible, and I was not offered the standard Buddhist script upon which to place my right hand. Was I trusted to tell the truth, the whole truth, or nothing but the truth? Or, as a foreign devil and accused enemy of the State, just assumed to be a liar?

I got to say, 'Not guilty.'

Then I got to leave the dock, and stand in the centre of the room.

'Shaun Tunna, do you have a statement?'

'Yes.'

'Please give it now.'

And so I began:

I am not a Myanmar citizen nor have I ever been a formal employee of the Myanmar State. As such, the OSA does not apply to me. But, even if it did, I would never breach Myanmar law. I came to Myanmar to help in its reform program and everything I have done has been to advance the interests of its people. My whole professional life is invested in Myanmar, a country I have grown to love. My work on Myanmar, of 30 years standing, is . . .

And that was it. I didn't get even my three minutes. U Win Tint, looking distracted and uninterested in what I had to say, cut me off.

'Yes, yes, yes,' he said in Burmese. 'Please sit down.'

I started to object. Actually, I started to shout, 'This is not right! You told me I had three minutes. I have not finished my statement.'

I looked around at everyone else. Daw Suu and her lawyer began to object, but they, too, were cut off. A hullaballoo rose up. The judge called for order. A police officer came over, placed his hand on my shoulder and arm, and pushed me back to the dock.

'This is bullshit,' I said, and thus ended, I guess, my last public statement in Myanmar.

Luckily, although none of it mattered anyway, my lawyers still had their concluding statement – submitted on paper, and briefly summarised to the court. And, as my lawyers put it in their arguments – which I learnt by heart, as I wasn't allowed to take any paper into the court – this was why I was not guilty of breaching Myanmar's Official Secrets Act:

1. Professor Turnell is not a 'citizen of the Union' nor a 'servant of the Government' – therefore, the Official Secrets Act does not apply to Professor Turnell.
2. The prosecution has not shown by evidence or testimony that the documents received and/or communicated by Professor Turnell were prejudicial to the safety or interests of the State.
3. The prosecution has not shown by evidence or testimony that the documents found on Professor Turnell's devices were actually 'secret' and/or protected as being 'secret' under the laws of Myanmar.
4. The prosecution has not shown by evidence or testimony that the documents found on Professor Turnell's devices were calculated to be or might be or is intended to be, directly or indirectly, useful to an enemy, and Myanmar has no 'enemies'. [This last point used an interview of junta leader Min Aung Hlaing when he declared Myanmar 'has no enemies'. If so, of course, this alone would cause the case against me to collapse!]
5. Professor Turnell has and had lawful authority to have received and/or communicated the documents found on his devices. Therefore, the prosecution has ignored section 3(2) of the Official Secrets Act that clearly provides that

if a document is obtained or communicated by 'a person acting under lawful authority', then that person should not be presumed to have communicated documents for a purpose prejudicial to the safety or interests of the State.

Thus:

As the Official Secrets Act does not apply to Professor Turnell and Professor Turnell has not breached the Official Secrets Act, then Professor Turnell should be found not guilty and released immediately and permitted to return to his family in Australia.

With regard to the immigration case against me, the defence was simple:

If Professor Turnell is not guilty of the charges under the OSA, he has not breached Myanmar law and cannot be guilty of the charges under the Immigration Act.

My fellow defendants all offered similarly watertight defences against the OSA charges and, having seen my efforts cut short, made brief but effective statements of their own against the charges.

All of this was well and good, and it would have been 'game, set, match' to the defendants in any country in which the rule of law truly prevailed. Myanmar was not such a country. What I had to do then was to come back to the court one more time for the judge's verdict. A gap of two weeks was needed for the sentencing hearing. It was unclear why. How long does it take to read something scrawled by the generals of the junta on the back of an envelope?

Ha was nervous in that last interval before verdict and sentencing. The day before my final court appearance she wrote to DFAT, 'I am getting more anxious as D-Day approaches, and try to console myself by thinking that our situation has to get worse before it can get better.'

On our call that week, we both consoled each other similarly. This was going to be a bad moment, but it was a necessary milestone on the way to my freedom, however long away this might be. It was, therefore, progress of a sort.

The afternoon before Verdict Day, Winston, U Kyaw Win and I were ordered to pack our things. As mentioned, the NDC was only for detainees on remand and, since it was a foregone conclusion that we would be found guilty the next day, we would henceforth be convicted felons. We would be fully and formally prisoners and, therefore, inappropriate residents for the NDC.

I hated the NDC, I hated the cell. I want to say that, even so, I felt a developing nostalgia. Just because it sounds more poetic. But I didn't feel remotely nostalgic for the place. I wanted out of it, out of everything.

So, pack we did, and the next morning – which was Thursday, 29 September 2022 – waited in freshly cleaned-out cells for that last trip to the court. All was familiar, but between us there was that feeling you get . . . well, I had never faced a situation like this before, so I could only liken it to that feeling between students, as you mill around an exam room ahead of the assessment. Nervous, silly jokes; an occasional breaking into uncomfortable reality as we speculated where we might go next.

Finally came the verdict.

I was asked to stand. Daw Suu and my fellow defendants were asked to stand.

Judge U Win Tint began to speak.

And boy, did he speak. Rapid fire and staccato, at breakneck speed that seemed almost an exercise in self-parody. Within a couple minutes he was done. Nodded at us. And walked out the door.

That's it? I turned to Winston: 'What just happened?' The ever-reliable Winston told me the verdict: I, we, had been found guilty and sentenced to the maximum jail term available of three years. With labour.

Later I was able to see the written verdict, and what was purported to be the reasoning behind it. Our/my main argument – that, under the law, the OSA did not apply to me as a foreigner – was given short shrift. According to the judgement:

> In construing the law, [we must] not just determine the letter of law, the spirit of law must also be determined ... Therefore, the allegation of Mr. Sean Ramon Turnell is not acceptable.

Fascinating that in post-coup Myanmar, a judge could write without terrible irony about the 'spirit of the law'.

Having thus rejected our major point of law, the verdict then found in favour of the facts of my espionage, and in my co-accuseds' facilitation of this:

The accused, Mr. Sean Ramon Turnell, son of Mr. Ramon Peter Turnell, is found guilty for the offence punishable under section 3(1)(c) of the Myanmar Official Secrets Act and hereby sentence him to imprisonment with labour for a period of 3 (three) years.

The accused, Daw Aung San Suu Kyi, daughter of U Aung San; U Kyaw Win, son of U Pwa Kyi; U Soe Win, son of U Tin Maung; U Set Aung, son of U Set Maung are found guilty for the offence punishable under section 3(1)(c)(9) of the Myanmar Official Secrets Act and hereby sentenced to imprisonment with labour for a period of 3 (three) years.

For the rest of us, the time already served in detention would count towards the sentence. For Daw Suu, the three years were added on to her already impressive collective tally of 20 years, with no offset (her collective sentence would ultimately grow to 33 years).

On the immigration charge, I received another three-year sentence, again with labour. Since time served counted against the OSA charge, not this one, no offset was given to me for this sentence. But it would be served 'concurrently' with the OSA incarceration.

All of my electronic devices were now officially 'confiscated by the State', while my other possessions, including my book on the Royal Navy (that telling piece of 'evidence'), 'shall be destroyed'.

Part 5
Insein, Free, Home

16

Back to Insein, Solitary and Death Row

While the verdict in my case was no mystery, considerable uncertainty existed as to what would happen next.

If the past was any guide, as a prominent foreigner, immediate deportation would quickly follow sentencing. For a brief moment, it seemed this might have been happening for me, too. Straight after the verdict, and as the four of us were being assembled to be driven back to the NDC, a group of immigration officials pulled me aside. With a fast-beating heart I did as asked, which was to sit at a desk and fill in forms that seemed to be scarcely more than an ID check. My now fellow *convicted* colleagues looked on expectantly, too. Alas, it was nothing but a bureaucratic procedure that transferred the possession of my passport from the court and the prosecutors to the Prisons Department.

An odd moment, a very Myanmar cameo had preceded this crushing little anti-climax. This came in the form of a question put to me by the immigration official.

'Please give us your passport,' he demanded.

My passport? Did he seriously think I had been allowed to keep it? What next – the key to my prison cell and the executive lounge? What on earth could make him think I still had my passport? I struggled not to sound agitated.

Eventually I stammered out, 'I think *you* have it. It was taken away the minute I was arrested. I have not seen it for more than 18 months. I'm sure if you ask your colleagues, they will be able to give you my passport. I hope you haven't lost it.'

That last comment of mine expressed genuine worry. The idea I might be swiftly deported was fast receding, but I would need my passport for *that* day, as long away as I now feared it to be.

A parting conversation with Daw Suu, who had yet more charges to face. She was completely calm. For her, getting three more years added to her sentence was practically another day at the office, really. She told us she was proud of us, proud of everyone who was standing up to the junta, and to have hope. We were doing the right thing. Above all, to keep thinking, planning, to be prepared for the day when once again we would have to put our shoulder to the wheel. The junta could not, would not, last.

The others made a gesture of respect in the form of a *kadaw*.

For me, Daw Suu had some last suggestions – strongly felt ones: to tell my story, our story, warts and all. She added a final 'thank you' for me to pass on to Ha, to Phuong, to my dad, to my sister Lisa. No time for awkward formalities, I gave her a hug.

Back to the NDC it was then. Daw Suu to her sealed-off cabin; the rest of us to the cells we had cleaned out. The verdict had been so concise that it was only mid-morning.

No instructions arrived, so we just hung about. Chatted with our fellow prisoners, who congratulated us on our sentence: at

An Unlikely Prisoner

least it wasn't 14 years. All of them concurred: an appeal was pointless. To me they said, 'Sean – soon you will be released.'

Night fell; still no movement. Bonus extra time in our Naypyitaw resort. Perhaps it was about the loyalty points.

The call came the next morning. It was time to go for me, Winston, U Kyaw Win. Minister U Soe Win, too. For the last few months he had been on bail in order to receive chemotherapy, but after the verdict this mercy was withdrawn.

The destination was Yamethin Prison, an hour north by car from Naypyitaw in the Mandalay Region. Yamethin was the junta's destination of choice for most of the senior political prisoners after sentencing. Its proximity to Naypyitaw and the tight control of the region by the *Tatmadaw* was likely the decisive factor in its selection. Probably, too, its remoteness was a consideration: Myanmar has a long history of sending political prisoners to out of-the-way locations. For an extra dimension of psychological retribution, and bonus punishment for families by making prisoner support more difficult and costly.

Our transport was a small minivan. For once, the security around us was light. Just a couple of armed guards, no handcuffs, and a relatively casual feel.

But casual was not how I felt. It's difficult for me to nominate the worst times of my imprisonment, but this trip was right up there. Uncertainty is never a friend when you are stripped of any control over your fate, but what worried me most was what my presence on this trip signified. We were geographically moving further away from any location that would suggest I might be deported. Even on that last morning in Naypyitaw, I hoped I might be sent on to Insein – a senior prison official had even told me this would happen as we stood around waiting to depart. Instead, and with each passing moment, I moved deeper into the junta's dystopia. Further away not just from home and loved ones, but stretching still more my supply lines of food, books and connection to the world.

The view from the van's windows would have once delighted me. I would have been all eyes and ears, analysing what I saw – how did the local economy seem as revealed before me? What were people doing to make ends meet? What government services appeared to be available, electricity, running water, infrastructure? What's more, it was an area I'd never been to before. Well, I couldn't have cared less right then.

I was completely absorbed in my troubles. What sort of cell would I get, would they put me among ordinary criminals? Would I be attacked by 'patriots' eager to take it to a foreign spy? Would I be allowed to keep the ten (the maximum I was allowed to carry) books I had with me? Could I really survive if, as all seemed to indicate, I was going to serve out my sentence in full?

We reached Yamethin, a largish and not unattractive town whose plentiful trees stood out against the dry plains that surrounded it. Golden pagodas shone here and there, and tea-shops, schools, and small monasteries offered signs of life. The jail was near the centre of town. In contrast, though, it was a thoroughly miserable-looking place. Yet another colonial structure, its ancient buildings and barbed wire–topped brick walls gave off that feeling of brooding horror achieved by Insein.

Some family members of my companions were waiting for us outside the jail. Humanity poked its head into proceedings: the guards allowed greetings, the exchange of food and essentials, even hugs. I had nobody, but for this I was glad. Exposing Ha or any of my loved ones to this wretched place was not something I wished for. Yet I felt the tears coming as I watched U Soe Win with his wife of 50 years and the son I had met once, at a conference. Winston with his indefatigable wife, who had got safely out of Myanmar but then came back to be closer to him. U Kyaw Win with his grandchildren. *I will bury this experience in the deepest part of my psyche*, I vowed to myself. *Never to be uncovered. Repression is not always a bad thing*, I thought – and still do. Then again, what am I doing now, but writing about it?

Next came the processing – *Always process before entering these places!* But then something happened to derail it: we were tested for COVID; I tested positive, and so did Winston. This was no surprise. For me it was Infection No.5 – like the French perfume minus the glamour. But the ramifications were no joke: now *none* of us could be admitted to the main jail.

The superintendent of Yamethin Prison, together with the camp doctor – both professional, reasonable – had a solution. In nearby fields, outside the walls of the main prison but within its secured boundaries of barbed wire, were some new open-plan cells. They were not occupied, and had never been. Meant to hold about 50 prisoners, they would be used for us four. Alone. As quarantine, for two weeks.

So that's where we were moved. Our stuff was duly carried over and set up: as elsewhere, the fetching and carrying was the work of Class C prisoners.

Our new space had the virtue of being clean, and we had affable neighbours in the form of grazing buffalo. The place had no solid walls. Just iron bars, so it looked like an enclosure at the zoo. This was helpful in keeping claustrophobia at bay, but not at keeping the mosquitos out. For the two weeks we would spend there, we needed a plan to keep sane. Ha had got a new book to me – about US Federal Reserve monetary policy in the 21st century – and we decided we would take turns reading aloud to each other from it. The others had their meditation practice, too. I watched them do it. Marvelled. And declared it beyond my ability to replicate.

Went the night. The only drama was figuring out how to go to the toilet without waking the others up.

Came the next morning.

And the doctor arrived. 'Professor Turnell,' – Winston interpreted for me – 'please pack up your things, you are going to Insein Prison in Yangon. Please, today.'

I was not free, not remotely. But this was surely a good sign. Had it taken place a day before, I would have been near euphoric. Now I was measured, cautious.

Not least of the reasons for this was, regardless of what was ahead of me, I now had to say goodbye to three people with whom I had gone to hell and back. And back again. As I have noted in these pages, there were times when I had faltered. Times when I lost my capacity to think, lost my ability to act in my own interests. I had observed no such failure in them. I also knew they had sheltered me, borne realities of our situation that they kept from me for my own psychological good. And then there were the practicalities. The extra workload and diligence imposed on them by someone who, through language and other deficiencies, was the weakest of the pack.

I couldn't thank them enough then, and I can't now. On that day when I left I did manage to gift each of them books. To dear Winston, among the most capable human beings I have ever met and with a mind fairly exploding in ideas, I gave the best economics books I had: 'Winston, one day you will put these in action. Again.'

The light-touch security arrangements of the move the previous day were not repeated for my singular journey today to Insein. My first indication of this came when I was, finally and horribly, handed the dreaded bright blue uniform to wear, as befitted a convict in transit. A coarse, roughly made shirt with a matching *longyi*. The latter is secured in the middle to stop it falling down. My Myanmar friends are incredibly skilful in tying this knot, and in discreetly positioning the *longyi*. I can barely do up my shoelaces, so I found it something of a challenge. I ended up tying two knots. A little tight, but better than an altogether new avenue for humiliation.

Wearing prisoner blue was confronting, but that turned out to be just for starters. Out came the handcuffs. I had expected this, but not to be shackled to a police officer, which came next. It was a reminder that personal space was not something I had anymore. And then, out came the leg-irons! At this point, I rounded on the plain-clothes officer who was clearly in charge of my move. I believe he was from Special Branch: he's going to appear often in the remainder of this chapter, so let's call him SB. 'You know you don't have to do this,' I remonstrated.

'I'm a 58-year-old professor. I'm not a threat to you. I'm not Jason Bourne.'

SB was having nothing of this. He spoke perfect English and had a nous about him that suggested he knew how the world worked beyond Myanmar. 'I understand your objections,' he said, and added that he was 'just following orders'.

'I never expected in my lifetime to hear the Nuremburg defence uttered in seriousness by anyone,' I shot back. SB didn't reply, but I knew he understood what I meant. He looked away.

He also looked away as the manacles were applied. Presumably they were made of steel, but somehow the word 'iron' better describes what they looked and felt like. A manacle was attached to each of my legs, just above the ankle. Connecting them was a solid iron rod. The effect of this was that it was extremely difficult to walk, which I guess was precisely the purpose. I had to waddle like a duck, and the pressure this put on my hip joints rapidly turned into a painful throb. It was going to be hard to go up and down steps or to climb into the waiting vehicle!

But I was getting ahead of myself because while all that was going through my mind, one last item was produced: a bulletproof vest. As a kid I had regarded these as most exciting items of apparel, but I do not recall ever thinking I might wear one.

'It's for your protection. Police vehicles are sometimes ambushed on the road to Yangon,' said SB, as the vest was strapped to my torso. It was heavy and stiff. Velcro on one side secured it in place. It was too big for me: the plate at the front extended all the way to my chin.

I could not resist retorting to SB, 'If we are attacked, I cannot imagine that I would be the target.' I could see he got my point.

Before we got on our way, anticipating that going to the toilet would be tricky, I raised the issue with SB. He told me the trip would take five hours at high speed and there could be no stopping. I reiterated that I was a 58-year-old guy and it was quite likely we would need to stop. 'No stopping. Go now.'

Well, okay then.

That taken care of, I was assisted out to the waiting minivan, and beheld a full carnival around me. This was to be a motorcade once more. Travelling in front was one of those police crew-cab SUVs. On the back platform were four police sharpshooters. All dressed 'commando-style': helmet, balaclava, bulletproof vests, gloves, and each holding what looked like (a copy of?) an American M-16 rifle. It started raining as we loaded up, so some of them wore plastic ponchos, too. The crew cab of the truck had two more police.

Next came the minivan, in which I was accompanied by SB; two plain-clothes 'others' (one seemed to be police, the other possibly military intelligence); my police-minder, to whom I was chained throughout; two prison guards; and the driver.

Bringing up the rear was another police SUV – carrying the same number of personnel as the one in front. So, all up, 19 people were watching over me, at least 12 of whom were heavily armed.

Thus assembled, our motorcade sped south to Yangon, slicing through a steady curtain of rain. As we traversed Naypyitaw, I looked left and right with genuine wistfulness. This place, my home for three or so years, had been the location of my greatest hopes and labours, and I would never see it again. Then we were on the highway. Cars hastened out of our path. If they didn't, the leading SUV would put its siren and lights on, and any recalcitrant vehicle would smartly change lanes.

It rained pretty much the whole journey. I tried to think happy thoughts. This was all just something I had to undergo on the way to my release. It was another milestone to mark off. Meanwhile, the leg manacles chafed.

From time to time, my eyelids would start to close and my head would feel heavy, and here the oversized bulletproof vest assisted by supporting my neck, allowing me to drift off briefly. After a while, however, I started to get that feeling: I needed to go. This was about three hours in. *Can I last? Sure*, I kidded myself. *Think happy thoughts. Actually, think any thoughts.*

No, I needed to go.

SB was sitting in the front passenger seat. I called out to him. 'I need to go.'

'No,' he said, firmly. 'I told you before. We cannot stop.'

I held on.

Okay, now I really need to go. 'I'm sorry, but I need to go now. I know you said we can't stop, but I'm telling you I have no option. It's your choice.'

SB made an exasperated sound, but then made a call on his phone. Then another. Then he picked up a walkie-talkie, and clearly spoke to the escort vehicles. 'We are stopping.'

He told me, 'This is authorised from the very top. You are being treated very well. Very special.'

I guessed where we'd stop. We were not far from the '115 Mile Rest-Centre' facility, named for the distance from Yangon. I had been to this place dozens of times. It was like any of those giant bus/car/truck stops you see the world over, but what was notable here was the profusion of casual restaurants it housed. It had always been a happily anticipated place for me.

But it was a wholly different experience this day. Alerted I suppose by the calls, by the time we arrived at 115 Miles, both sides of the highway were blocked by police. This allowed our motorcade to do a U-turn across six lanes then pull into the driveway of a police station tucked in between the restaurants and gas stations. I watched through the van window as we passed in front of the blocked-off traffic. So many halted vehicles, so many people wondering what was going on and whether the fuss was for a junta VVIP (as goes the exaggerated acronym in Myanmar).

No, it was just me. A man with an urgent need to go to the loo.

I was helped out of the van, and I sighed with relief when SB removed my leg manacles. He also put a coat over my handcuffs, though did not remove them. I surmised that he was ashamed that the assembled local police – highway patrol officers as far as I could tell – would see how I was treated.

This little drama out of the way – I did notice the sharpshooters used the stop for a quick cigarette and tea break – we continued south. It was still raining, but soon the familiar shapes of Yangon emerged out of the gloom. The army cantonments in the north of the city, the lovely Rangoon War Cemetery on the Pyay Road, the giant bus interchange station through which so many of the city's workers passed each day. Past the airport – so longingly did I gaze at it – and into the city's busy thoroughfares. But not so busy as before. As in Naypyitaw, more than a year-and-a-half on from the coup Yangon had the appearance of a city under siege. Major intersections ringed with barbed wire, armed soldiers at critical junctions. Sandbags and pillboxes dotted around. And the people? Maybe it was merely a reflection of my own mood, but the gaiety of the place seemed to be well and truly gone.

Soon we were into the dusty and crowded roads of Insein Township, and suddenly there were the gates of the prison guard house. The Gates of Mordor they had appeared to me before. Now they were part of my landscape, pillars of my everyday.

As I went to step out of the minivan I took a tumble. Between the leg manacles, the iron bar that kept my ankles apart and cramp from the trip, I had even less dexterity than normal. I fell flat on my face, and the front of my vest, shirt and *longyi* were smeared in dirt and dust. To their credit, the receiving prison officers at Insein were horrified at my condition, and urged the police to remove my shackles. The police rapidly did so – for the second time that day, they seemed embarrassed to have their treatment of me on display.

I must admit that, despite my terrible immediate situation and truly awful place of arrival, deep down I still had the idea that all of what had taken place this day was a plus. Yes, the trip had been horrible, and here I was back in one of Asia's most notorious hellholes – but surely, this was merely an interim step and I was about to be released and deported? Thanks to this mindset, I interpreted events around me as somewhat hopeful. For example, I noted that my 'check-in' to Insein this time around was quite perfunctory. No questions, not many documents exchanged, no search of my bags or seizure of books and so on. Perhaps I should have considered that, not having been outside the most maximum security detention these last days, there was no need for any of this.

An Unlikely Prisoner

My police custodians left. One of them, who I won't identify here, leaned close and whispered that he hoped things would go well for me, and thanked me for my work in Myanmar. SB gave only a curt nod.

The guards, only two of them with me now, indicated that we needed to head to my allocated cell. We set off along the walled alleyway towards the panopticon tower. When we got to the base of it, would we turn left to where my old cell was, to where I presumed Jacoob and my friends were? Or would we take a sharp right, into the compound where the VIP prisoners were held, the place of the wooden shacks and trees? Solitary confinement, but nicer views.

It turned out to be the latter, and I felt my heart lighten. Being placed in the VIP compound seemed yet more confirmation that I might soon be out. We meandered through the trees. I'd lost so much stuff in my moves – many items confiscated, others I had just given away, that I was travelling quite lightly and my breathing seemed easier than it had been in days. As we walked, I glanced around, hoping to catch sight of familiar faces. It dawned on me that the old cohort of remand detainees were gone. In their place were other prisoners. Younger. Kept in the concrete cells that were also part of this compound. There were quite a few prison uniforms hanging out to dry. The shirts and *longyi* were all orange.

And then it clicked. Orange uniforms were what prisoners on death row wore. What had been the VIP section of Insein was now death row, and that's where the junta had decided to house me. I have no doubt my placement here was deliberate – yet another effort to intimidate and punish, but in a way that would go unnoticed.

Death row, and the sentence at the end of it, was an acutely frightening thing at this time. Two months earlier, in contrast to previous military regimes in Myanmar (for decades the country had not carried out 'judicial' executions) the junta had administered the death penalty to four political prisoners. Executed were two prominent activists – the writer and 1988 democracy uprising veteran Ko Jimmy, and the former NLD member of parliament, Phyo Zayar Thaw, whom I had met a few times at Daw Suu's house – and two younger activists, who had been outspoken in their opposition to this latest coup – Aung Thura Zaw and Hla Myo Aung. All four were hanged. The executions had taken place inside Insein on newly constructed gallows.

As I digested this horror, we arrived at a wooden shack-on-stilts. I realised it was next door to the one I had stayed in a year ago; essentially a twin of the earlier cell.

Then I was introduced to the guards of the compound. Actually, I should say re-introduced, since some had been here last time, too. Most were decent young men in impossible circumstances. Any detailed praise I offer them here will not be helpful to them, though. I'll simply say that their behaviour to me was professional, and not without compassion.

From that point on in Insein, time just seemed to drift. Days passed, then weeks, then a month. I despaired anew. Kept isolated with no-one to talk to most days – except for very brief exchanges with the guards bringing me food – I found it difficult to stay optimistic that any chance of release might come.

An Unlikely Prisoner

After a couple of weeks my phone calls with Ha and the Embassy resumed. Also, Ha's letters once more reached me. From them I learned that the Embassy's consul, the very able and diligent Wes Knight, had made enquiries with the Prisons Department as to what 'with labour' meant according to my sentences. What work would I have to do? He was told that foreigners were not actually assigned work. On that score at least, I experienced some relief!

Ha also told me of the reaction at home to my sentence. That it had made the news, and that when I did eventually get home, I would have no problem in finding someone to buy me a beer. Australia's Foreign Minister, Penny Wong, had condemned the verdict, declaring that the Australian Government rejected the ruling, that I had been unjustly detained throughout and called for my 'immediate release'. Ha said she had spoken to her straight after the verdict, as well as before. It reassured me to know that the Foreign Minister was making herself available to Ha. It helped.

In her first letter to me following the verdict, Ha also disclosed her own feelings about the outcome, and my unexpected transfer to Yamethin. Her strength, compassion and love for me – all this was apparent – as well as my struggles sometimes with the practical world. I wasn't precisely the stereotype of the absent-minded professor, but the analogy wasn't entirely inaccurate:

> I was hoping, but not really expecting, that you would be allowed to return to Australia. I heard that you were calm and strong through the court yesterday. I am so proud of you, my sweetheart.

> I learnt that you had been moved to a new place together with the others. Although it was not unexpected, part of the process, and another step closer to returning home, it still hurt. Then a slew of thoughts arrived: would you be able to sleep OK this evening at a new place, do you get to bring the things you packed with you, books, food; would the guards there be nice to you, and then the thought of you wearing the 'uniform' – it is just a façade, and you should just wear your own clothes inside. I imagined that you may struggle with putting the *longyi* on, the tie-strings and all that. I imagine your frustrated moments. Having said that, it is OK, my dear, to feel frustrated, just let it out, don't keep it inside. Don't you ever forget that whatever you feel, that would be mine too . . .

With wonderful chutzpah, in an effort to improve my life in jail, Ha launched a campaign that I be allowed a radio ('with a big antenna'), and perhaps a TV. The Embassy enquired of the prison – who replied such items were strictly prohibited.

My book supply had dried up and my store severely reduced, but as I fell back into a routine in Insein, luckily new books started to arrive. By now Curtis Slover had at last, reluctantly, gone home.

Shortly before my verdict I had received news that Vicky Bowman, a former British Ambassador to Myanmar who had subsequently stayed on to establish the Myanmar Centre for Responsible Business, had been arrested, charged and convicted on absurd charges that amounted to little more than the crime of visiting her home in Kalaw, a lovely 'hill station' town not far from Naypyitaw. Vicky was – and is – a friend. She is also sharp, urbane, immensely experienced and about as 'Myanmar-wise' as it's possible to be. I was alarmed to hear then of what had happened to her, but what it signalled was chilling. Anyone, any foreigner, no matter how resourceful and brave, was vulnerable.

That meant Curtis was unsafe. Although he had all the virtues, in the final analysis, he was a foreigner with no diplomatic protection or anything like it. He was not only a friend of mine, but most demonstrably my key ally in Myanmar. He was way too exposed for his own good.

'Please thank him from the bottom of my heart,' I said to Ha, 'but tell him it's time to escape.'

His last day in Myanmar was on 11 September, 2022.

It was now nearly two years since the coup. After spending 12 months away from Insein, I was able to notice a drop in the quantity of food delivered to prisoners. In terms of variety and quality it was just the same, but the quantity available was diminished. There were supply and distribution problems both inside and outside of the prison. Some days, I went without. Had I not had my deliveries from outside, life would have been grim.

And indeed it did become grim after 19 October, when a bomb went off inside a parcel delivered to the prison. Eight people were killed: three prison staff and five visitors dropping off parcels to loved ones. Some died because of the bomb that went off; some died because prison guards had fired indiscriminately into the panicking crowd. I heard the explosion and what

I thought might have been guns firing. But such sounds had become common enough in Yangon, as protests rolled on and the military continued its ruthless repression of them. In short, I paid the sounds no heed.

The parcel-bombing, tragic in so many ways, also temporarily halted deliveries of food or anything else to prisoners. The shutdown lasted three weeks, during which I lost five kilograms – the amount of weight I had managed to slowly put back on in the last few months in Naypyitaw. Once again, I was back to around 45 kilograms.

The food shortages prompted yet another show of the astonishing generosity and giant spirit of the political prisoners with whom I was living. In the middle of the shutdown, for instance, I suddenly found that my food ration included extra hunks of bread. I asked the guard delivering the meals where the bread came from.

'They are a gift for you, Sean, from your neighbours on death row.' I conveyed my thanks, and later was able to reciprocate, using Ha's cookies. But how can one adequately respond to such boundless humanity? I had no answer then or now. All I can do is to tell this small but revealing part of their story.

My phone calls also stopped as the prison authorities hit the panic button with respect to anything from outside. Thereafter, time crawled. Between the torpor and the lack of any indication that release for me might be imminent, I experienced some of my worst moments in captivity. There was no sense of any forward momentum. However awful the trial was, at least the journey to its absurdist destination had a sense of direction.

I immersed myself ever deeper in my books, selecting titles on the basis of their time-consuming capacity. The stand-out was a street-by-street history of London. I used to dream I was there. But then that chilling old dream came back – the one that had me always returning to prison in chains.

And then I heard something that took me into graver depths. Insein had a team of inmate interpreters, one of whom I got to know well. He had been in the prison for over a decade, and knew close to everything that went down there. He was also a good man, notwithstanding his (acknowledged) criminal past – as a counterfeiter. I liked him and wish I could name and thank him in these pages.

But that's all by way of introduction to the source. The story came to me via the interpreter about a month into my return to Insein:

'Sean, I've been waiting to tell you that Jacoob did not make it. He's left us already.'

Now, that is literally what he said – I will never forget the words – so perhaps you can see that I was initially confused about where my dear friend and saviour Jacoob was. 'You mean he's been transferred? Released.'

'No, Sean, I mean he's dead. He was killed. He was murdered a month after you were transferred to Naypyitaw. He intervened to stop a fight between a junta supporter and another supposed political prisoner. But it was all fake, a set-up. As soon as he tried to intervene, both of the fighters turned on him. Then some guards appeared from another part of the jail and started to kick and beat him. They didn't stop.'

Jacoob survived for a few more hours. Taken to the prison hospital, he died the following morning.

I buried this news deep. I mentioned it to some of the guards, who confirmed the story, but were obviously disturbed that I knew it. After that I kept it to myself.

To keep my spirits up, I started to engage in small acts of rebellion. It sounds petty now, but one of these was to ensure that when I was forced to put the *longyi* on I did it incorrectly. I would just tie it around my waist in any old way, and wear trousers underneath. The guards and other prisoners would laugh when they saw me – usually while on my way to and from the phone calls – but they got the message, too. From the prisoners would come thumbs-up and the three-finger salute, sometimes a cheer.

I also grew a beard. I had begun this in Naypyitaw as a deliberate effort to make sure the physical manifestations of my imprisonment were visible. Further, I had not wanted to play the game of looking neat to the 'court'. I had no respect for it, for any of the process, and I rebelled against looking respectable for it. Of course, there was a counterargument that in doing so, I was disrespecting, even disempowering, myself. In the end, the lack of a razor (seized in the move back to Insein) decided matters, and by November 2022 I very much looked the vagabond.

Daw Suu, who saw the beginnings of the beard in the last days of the trial, quipped, 'Who is this wild man?'

The phone calls resumed in early November, but my mood remained dark and down. I tried not to think about the possibility of any sort of amnesty, even as I could contemplate almost nothing else. I walked faster, read harder.

On 16 November I had a routine call with the Embassy and Ha. It was our wedding anniversary. The second in captivity. As usual, Ha and I talked each other up, but most of the conversation was spent ruminating that I would likely be spending another Christmas as a prisoner.

17

Liberation, Homecoming and a Final Twist

Across the room and back again. Ten paces each way. Twelve thousand steps by 10 am.

That was my usual goal. I'd got 7240 steps under my belt on the morning of 17 November 2022, my 650th day in captivity, when a prison guard suddenly cranked open my door.

'Good news, Sean. You're going home.'

I stopped. It couldn't be: 4 January 2023, the 75th anniversary of Myanmar's independence, was the next likely date. Failing that, it might coincide with the Thingyan festival in April. Ha and I had spoken only the day before. We both acknowledged I would not be home for Christmas.

But *could* it be?

Myanmar has numerous public holidays, and 17 November 2022 was Myanmar National Day. An annual holiday held on the tenth day after the full moon of the month of *Tazaungmone*, it commemorates the beginnings of student-led protests against

British rule in Myanmar in 1920. The anniversary must have slipped my mind.

'You are going home. Please pack. You have ten minutes.'

I stared at him. The moment I'd ached for had arrived but I couldn't comprehend it. Time seemed to stop. Then I felt rising excitement. Joy? Apprehension. Yes, this in lock step. With a tremor in my voice I said: 'Please, please tell me you are not joking.'

When I look back on this now, it's like watching a surreal movie. At first I move slowly, wasting precious minutes trying to figure out what to do. I'm not ready.

More guards appear. Mostly they are the young guys in their Premier League jerseys. They have friendly smiles. They stand around. But apparently I have to rush.

I move towards some of my tote bags. I lovingly pick up books only to put them down again. *Ha's asked me to bring nothing home*, I remember. But these books are old friends by now. Can I leave them behind? Won't I need them? What if this is all false, and I am just being moved to another part of the prison, maybe a different prison entirely? Maybe I'm going to be sent to Cambodia, and into the hands of my erstwhile liberator, Hun Sen? What if he won't give me anything to read?

The fog in my brain somehow clears and I know I have to leave them – all of my stuff, in fact. I pick up speed and begin organising. The books could form the core of what might be a revitalised prison library: the guards promise they will do this. The other things, well, they could be divided up among other prisoners, hopefully most will go to the guys on death row . . .

One thing I do not distribute, since I have none, is my shoes. But they are on my mind. *Can I get on a plane, if that's what I do today, in flip-flops?*

While I was almost the last person to know I was going to be released this day, one of the first to know was Ha. At 2 am Australian time (9.30 pm the previous day Myanmar time) she received a call from someone in 'our' law firm in Yangon telling her that I was about to be deported.

For a few seconds Ha held her breath. But she dared not let her hopes rise. She'd been here too many times before. 'How do you know? What is the source?'

The answer, this time, was a good one. 'Ministry of Home Affairs, very senior. Source is very reliable. But they are not supposed to tell us. Please don't go public yet.'

Somewhat assured, nervous, tense, Ha did not even try to go back to sleep. She turned to the great clearing house of information regarding Myanmar: Facebook.

And there it was. Rumours circulating all over the place. Sean would be released tomorrow (Myanmar time), for the holiday. What holiday was it? Ha googled, and this anniversary – obscure anywhere except Myanmar – was revealed.

A box ticked then – there might just be something behind the rumours.

Then she had to sit there. Think.

Check flights out of Yangon. What was the earliest one out? Time to enact the plans long in preparation. Singapore was the safest transit. Bangkok second. Absolutely not anywhere in China, the junta's ally and protector.

Check the news. Check again. Refresh the site. Do it again. She woke up Phuong.

Still too early to call anyone.

At last, the clock showed 5 am. Ha rang Janelle Saffin. Janelle had heard nothing certain. She happened to be in Sydney that day, for a sitting of the New South Wales Parliament. Ha made her way to Janelle's hotel in the dawning light and together they took a long walk along Sydney's waterfront. And talked through next steps.

By then, Ha had also contacted Ian Gerard of the consular section of DFAT to see what they knew. An email at 2.54 am, a phone conversation at dawn. DFAT could not confirm, but would check with the Embassy.

More hours passed. Screenshots of a news broadcast in Myanmar announcing my release were proliferating on Facebook. Dear friends in Myanmar started flooding Ha with messages: Sean was definitely coming home.

At 12.30 pm DFAT confirmed. It was 8 am in Yangon. I knew nothing.

As the afternoon rolled on, the Embassy was told by Myanmar's Ministry of Foreign Affairs that a seat for me had been booked to Bangkok. The Embassy was asked to pay for it. It was then up to DFAT to get me back to Australia from there.

Every flight out was booked. Strings were pulled, favours called in. Two seats to Melbourne were found. Home was Sydney, but the feeling of the Australian Government was to get me back to Oz as soon as possible.

*

Meanwhile, back in Insein and ignorant of all of this, I finished packing. A bag with one change of clothes. Three books. One of Ha's cookies. And my elephant. The latter was the sole item I really wanted to bring home, made out of used coffee sachets by a prisoner in Naypyitaw, and given to me as a gift. It was precious, and the only souvenir of my time in prison.

In those last few minutes in my cell, I started to pack one of my blue prison shirts. I was told to unpack it. Prison property.

We set off. My legs felt wobbly and my mind was racing. I thought about taking mental photographs of these too familiar but receding surrounds. Such sensory input was not successful and my mind was in overload. Through the VIP compound to the waves and cheers of my death-row friends. Out onto the roundabout beneath the panopticon. Wave to other prisoners. V for victory signs now. As well as the three fingers. Down the long concrete ally to the guard house. And into the room that had been the location for my phone calls.

And there I discovered I was not alone. Over 5000 prisoners would be released that day (most of whom were no more guilty of anything than I was), but in this room were about a dozen. Political prisoners, all. Four were foreigners – me, Vicky Bowman, my dear friend Kyaw Htay Oo (the Myanmar-born US citizen who I had last seen about six months earlier in Naypyitaw), and Toru Kubota, a Japanese documentary-filmmaker arrested in July 2022 for recording a protest against the junta.

We foreigners were being released under a 'pardon order' of the State Administration Council (the official name of the ruling junta) that also commanded our deportation. Apart from being a 'gesture' to mark the holiday, according to the junta's official proclamation, the order was based 'on humanitarian grounds', and made in the spirit of 'better bilateral diplomatic relations and friendship between their respective countries'. A condition of the order was that 'if they commit another offence, they will continue to serve the remainder of [their] sentences'. The order was signed by Lieutenant-General Aung Lin Dwe, Secretary of the Council.

In the room we greeted each other – foreigners and Myanmar prisoners alike – with joy. Swapped stories. Tried to remember what we knew of each other. 'Vicky, remember the last time we met at the Embassy?' Worried. The sentiment came from the shared concern that something would go wrong. Especially, as often happened, new charges and re-arrest might take place as we stepped out through the prison door.

And we waited. And waited. Three hours went by. We'd pretty much exhausted the happy talk, and a sort of anxious silence descended. It was broken as each of us – almost in turn – tried to lighten the mood with stories of what our first meal outside would be. I said, 'What I most want is a glass of red wine with Ha. And an ice cream.'

The delay turned into slow process. Any money or precious items that had been taken away from us when first imprisoned was returned. I got back many hundreds of thousands of kyat – alas, merely hundreds of dollars – all of which I managed to surreptitiously pass on to a prisoner friend standing nearby. Most importantly, I got back my wedding ring. I had objected to its original confiscation most vigorously. With it safely on my finger once more, the healing could begin.

Process came to an end, and it was time to join several hundred other soon-to-be former prisoners in a nearby hall to hear a speech from a senior official of the Prisons Department. The event was broadcast on Myanmar television. I think the speech was mostly about being a good and law-abiding citizen. I thanked the Lord I could understand very little of it.

Soon after, we four foreigners were put in a bus for the short drive to the airport. It was late afternoon by now, raining and dim. The mood inside the bus, however, was getting lighter by the second. This was happening! Yangon International loomed ahead. I had been here so many times, but never before had my heart leaped at the sight of it. The bus did not stop at the main entrance but pulled up by some unmarked doors at the side. It was the entrance to the VIP part of the terminal.

And there they all were. So many of the people who had helped me, sustained me inside Myanmar during my incarceration; the people in whom I had invested such hope. Angela Corcoran, the Australian Chargé d'Affaires, was the first person I saw, and from me she got a big hug. Or was it that she hugged me? Unsure. Didn't matter, since soon there were hugs all over the place. As I leaned in to hug Tony Egan, Australia's military attaché, I towered just about to his knee. Physically, this was somewhat awkward as my belt was long gone and I was holding up my trousers because I had lost so much weight. Tony promptly came to my sartorial rescue. In an act of gallantry, he removed the belt from his dress uniform and gave it to me. I have it still – a wonderfully quirky token of the day.

Because my newly freed colleagues and I were from different countries – the UK, US, Japan and Australia – the place was heaving with diplomats, as well as numerous senior officials of the junta, and hangers-on more broadly. Three people who stood out for me, not least since I knew they had stood up for me, were the US Ambassador to Myanmar, Tom Vajda; the UK's Myanmar aid chief, Rurik Marsden; and Japan's Ambassador to Myanmar, Mr Ichiro Maruyama. It was an especially poignant reunion with Ambassador Vajda – the last time I'd seen him was the afternoon before my arrest.

I had not met Angela Corcoran in person up to that point, but in the flesh she was every bit as gutsy and straightforward as she had been on the phone. She had, in fact, barely one day earlier left Yangon for a planned meet-up with her daughter in Singapore. Upon hearing of the possibility of my release, and with her daughter's kind forbearance, she had abandoned this and high-tailed it back to Yangon – just in time for my arrival at the terminal. The Australian team had a range of things for me beyond Tony's belt – from snacks, to clothes, to a new mobile phone. The latter I didn't really use. I used Angela's phone to make some critical calls, and I had forgotten not only phone numbers, but how to even use a mobile phone. I know this sounds bizarre, but about a year into my imprisonment I tried to remember how to use 'apps' and the like, but couldn't really recall how these worked.

Naturally, those critical calls I made were to Ha and Phuong, my dad, Lisa, and my nephews Tim and Mitch. The calls were brief, full of joy, and the sort of talk you engage in on these extreme situations when you cannot remember even the last word you said. Emotional noises, really. But no less meaningful for that.

Angela also sent the first pictures of my now-free self to Ha. Of course, I was still Mr Beard, under 50 kilos and appearing something of a wreck. Ha texted Ian that I looked 'like a jungle man'. She told him how happy she was, but also felt 'devastated at seeing him like that. What have they done to him!?'

Meanwhile in this VIP terminal it was all chaos. There were junta-linked journalists and a blizzard of photos were taken while TV cameras trailed around. A few exceedingly awkward conversations took place. For me, this was with officials from Myanmar's Ministry of Foreign Affairs and from Immigration. Some of them were trying to be nice, even praising my 'dedication' to Myanmar and wishing that I might one day return. The handshakes were over-firm and prolonged and, together with the look in their eyes, these were people who wanted to express something they could not say.

But we were not at the airport for a diplomatic reception. We were there to get on planes. So finally the hullabaloo came to an end and we were escorted to our respective departure gates. For me, Kyaw Htay Oo, and Toru, it was a Myanmar National Airways flight to Bangkok. The other passengers tried not to look too hard (such things being impermissible in the new Myanmar). Angela was beside me and would come with me all the way back to Australia. As we got to the airbridge, however, there was a final formal matter. An immigration official came up to us, and read a stern proclamation of my misdeeds, ending in a statement that I would 'never be allowed back to Myanmar except with the explicit approval of the President'. I met this last sudden chill with a reassurance that, unfortunately, I could never see myself ever coming back to Myanmar.

And then this same official softened, and in a different voice said, 'Please don't hate Myanmar.'

I was surprised only for a moment, before replying, 'I could never hate the people of Myanmar. I love Myanmar and always will.'

He gave me a nod, I gave him a nod, and it was onto the plane for us emancipated ones.

Business class! Truly it was a day from the ridiculous to the sublime. The seats were booked by Myanmar's Ministry of Foreign Affairs. I guess they did this to keep us away from the majority of the passengers. Angela sat beside me, Kyaw Htay Oo and Toru across the aisle. In a wonderful moment we looked at each other and laughed at the absurdity of it all. Three men in flip-flops amid suits.

As the plane ascended I took in some long last looks as Yangon slipped away below us. How often had I seen this view? A hundred, two hundred times? Would I ever return to this place that meant so much to me, that defined my professional life and then some? The golden glow of the Shwedagon Pagoda pierced the enveloping clouds, the old colonial buildings at the riverfront came into view, the parks, the lakes, the markets. I just caught the edge of Insein before we crossed the river, arched over the paddy-fields of the delta, turned east over Thanlyin. The mud-brown of land-sea indeterminacy that was Myanmar's border with the world disappeared from sight.

We still could not yet feel completely free. We were on the State flag-carrier, and thus technically under the control of the Myanmar authorities. So, alas, I cannot report cheers at wheels up, or even recall the moment we left Myanmar airspace. What if the plane turned around?

After an hour we started our descent, and I anxiously looked at the farmland below. Long, thin narrow strips. Mechanised.

Yes, this was Thailand. Then came the bright lights of Bangkok. Lights much brighter than could be managed by poor electricity-deprived Yangon. The wheels touched the tarmac, and in orderly fashion we filed off with everyone else from the plane. Deliverance.

More diplomats and staff from our respective countries were there to greet us. Amid the exchanges and the need for us to go to different flights at different times at different gates, we got separated. We'd given each other hugs on the plane, but that was it. We were each to our own homelands now.

For me there was a two-hour gap, and a team from the Australian Embassy in Bangkok was there to pamper me, basically. I was whisked off to a very flashy VIP lounge (we were the only ones in it), where I had my first hot shower in almost two years. A new shirt, trousers. No shoes, though – nobody knew my size. So the flip-flops stayed on, but with socks as a flourish. Ha had ordered (yes, it was as strong as that) that the beard 'must go' before entering Australian airspace. Alas, even her powers were not sufficient to circumvent Suvarnabhumi airport's security screening, which did not allow the delivery of a capable razor to do the deed. So, the beard stayed on.

As the plane was taxiing in Bangkok, Angela had got a message asking whether I was okay to speak to Australia's Prime Minister, Anthony Albanese, and Foreign Minister, Penny Wong. This was very okay. And so I did. They could not have been nicer, nor more heartfelt in welcoming my freedom. I told them both about the way I put my Embassy tote bags (with the Australian coat of arms emblazoned on them) at the front of my cell with the message (at least in my own head) that you don't mess with the emu or the kangaroo. I know it all sounds a bit cheesy now, but it seemed the right thing to do, and then say at the time! I also told Albanese that for much of my adult life I had lived in his Sydney electorate, but had to apologise for not voting for him at the Australian federal elections just a few months earlier. I was otherwise detained, I said. Australia has a system of compulsory voting where one is fined for a non-appearance at the voting booth. A notice fining me had duly arrived. The Prime Minister promised the penalty would be waived.

In a press conference soon after our conversation in Bangkok, the Prime Minister made an emotional statement:

> Occasionally in this job you have a big moment, and I've just spoken to Sean Turnell, who has been released from 650 days of unfair, unjust imprisonment in Myanmar and he has now landed and is well in Bangkok.

A sign of things to come, as we made our way around the terminal, was the amount of people taking photographs of us. The Thai Embassy team tried to keep us out of sight, but the images quickly emerged on Facebook. Also going viral at this time was the photo of my bearded self with Angela, sent to Ha, DFAT and then just about everywhere. From Ha came a 'family statement', circulated throughout the media by DFAT:

I am overwhelmed with joy at the news that my beloved husband, Sean, is coming home. I would like to take this opportunity to thank all those who have strongly advocated for and assisted to secure his release. I specially thank the Australian Government, in particular DFAT, the Foreign Minister and her office, the Embassy in Yangon for their persistent efforts and support. After nearly 22 months apart, our priority right now is to spend time together as a family.

It was a holiday maker–filled Jetstar 787 that took Angela and me on to Melbourne. After both of us attempted perfunctory efforts to sleep, Angela was game to be peppered with my questions. I had a barrage of them, some about what had happened this day, others about the backstory behind my arrest and incarceration. What *didn't* I know about? (Quite a lot, it turned out!) What were the major Australian and world stories that I had missed? The Queen was gone, Ukraine was bravely resisting the Russians, Max Verstappen seemed on track to win Formula 1 – but what else was there?

For a moment or two I tried to watch a movie: *Star Wars – The Rise of Skywalker*. I couldn't do anything more subtle, anything that would tax my hunting mind. Skywalker was too convoluted as well. Really, the Emperor was still alive!?

I tried listening to some music, the great missing element in my life. Nothing too slow. I settled for the Eurythmics, 'Would I Lie to You?' *I could have used that with the judge in Naypyitaw,* I thought.

A very nice surprise was that the pilot came down to see me halfway through the flight. He welcomed me aboard, told me how he had been following my plight. Warned me there might just be a bit of media interest when we arrived in Melbourne.

While I was in the air and transitioning to a world that had digital as well as analogue realms, Ha was on her way from Sydney to Melbourne on an early morning flight arranged by DFAT. There she was joined by DFAT's Ian Gerard and Andrew Cumpston. They had a couple of hours to hang about in a special reception area before my silver and orange plane dropped in.

From above, as the cabin was prepared for landing, I caught glimpses of Melbourne's fast-growing skyline. The last announcement from the captain told the passengers which luggage belt their bags would appear on, before signing off with a 'Welcome home, Sean'. More singular treatment was to come when the plane landed, and everyone got up in that barely civilised scramble to disembark. The flight attendants kindly asked for everyone to step back to let some 'special passengers' off. As we made our way past the rows of frequent-flyer status people, I could hear whispers of both recognition and mystification. 'Oh, that's him'; 'Who is that scruffy guy, and why does he get to get off first?'

Through customs and immigration. I was being escorted by Ian Gerard and some other officers of both DFAT and Border Force, but I still had to present my passport and make the usual customs declarations about not being in possession of items detrimental to Australia's biosecurity. Since I was carrying more or less nothing except a couple of books, all of this was rather easy.

I had to say goodbye to Angela at this point, though, since she was due back in Canberra to begin the briefings of these recent events.

I knew that in moments I would see Ha (Angela's phone having offered a barrage of updates after we'd touched down). I'd thought about our reunion for so long. Dreamed about it endlessly, craved it constantly. Now the moment had arrived. Would it be awkward? What on earth to say? Something funny, pithy? A gentle enquiry into her health, on what she had been up to lately?

Of course, I should not poke fun, since it was a lovely moment and not even slightly awkward. I recall hugging her, kissing her, squeezing her, smelling her fragrance, and saying whatever came into my head. Any planned words were abandoned in a more fundamental embrace of souls that should never have been separated.

We didn't hang around the reception area because within a few minutes it was time to finally board a flight home to Sydney. I must reveal, however, that this was no normal plane we'd be flying, since the Prime Minister had arranged for us one of the air force's VIP jets, a Dassault Falcon 7X. Something of a Ferrari in the rarefied air of private jets, its nickname (so the pilots told me) was 'The Shark'. At the risk of outraging the Australian taxpayer, the plane was beautifully appointed. The cabin staff were superb and very friendly, the pilots professional but approachable – being plane-geeks, both Ha and I had lots of questions – and the food, well, excellent. We were given a copy of the *Australian* newspaper that had our photo on the front. We posed for a picture in the cabin, with the newspaper as proof of life, despite my terrible beard suggesting survival might have been a day-by-day proposition.

We landed in Sydney and a Commonwealth car drove us home. There, I was finally reunited with Phuong, my dad, my sister Lisa, my brother-in-law, Michael and nephews, Timothy and Mitchell. More reunions would take place through the day, and in the weeks to follow. For the moment, though, I was finally able to use the words I'd always wanted to say – to quote Sam Gamgee: 'Well, I'm back.'

Health issues – physical, psychological – were the most immediate and straightforward things to grapple with on my return. DFAT provided me with an all-over health check the day after I arrived home. Since I'd been in an extremely unhealthy environment for so long, there were many diseases to check for. Thankfully, the tests revealed I had none. There were chronic ailments from my imprisonment – damage to my feet, skin issues, some skeletal problems from living on a concrete floor. Above all were my teeth – damaged and broken from food impurities and a long period of inattention. It was also confirmed that I had to put on weight: I was about 20 per cent below where I needed to be. Luckily, on this front I had, in Ha, the best physician imaginable. Fattening me up became her crusade, and 'upsize me' the command. I cannot imagine a better problem to have, really.

Sleep (that is, the lack thereof) has been one of my biggest health problems since my release. One of the first things I had to do was to try to relearn sleeping in the dark. The lights of my cells (electricity permitting!) had been on 24 hours a day.

Throughout much of my imprisonment I'd worn eye-masks of the sort you get on a plane, and I'd got used to the gentle pressure they applied to your eyelids. It probably sounds odd – but as a result I became troubled by both the lack of light, and the absence of the device to keep light from me. Of course, I also had to reacquaint myself with soft mattresses, clean sheets and comfy doonas.

Closely aligned with sleep problems was the return of a recurrent dream. As noted earlier, in prison this consisted of a narrative that had me home, but in which something (details varied ever so slightly) compelled me to go back to my cell by sundown. Since my return from Myanmar the story is almost a mirror of its predecessor. Now I am in the prison, holding a piece of paper that authorises my release. I approach the guard house with this, only to be turned back because the form I'm holding does not have the right stamp on it, or a critical signature. So I'm returned to my cell, and within the dream my rescue – this book – is the unreal story. I wake up with my heart beating, after which further sleep is usually impossible.

But disturbed sleep and bad dreams are a torment for lots of people, and in truth my psychological coping mechanisms have been doing fine. The care I draw upon constantly from Ha, Phuong, and all my family and friends makes it so much easier for me. I cannot imagine how my recovery might have gone without it.

In her book about her experiences as a prisoner in Iran, our friend and supporter Kylie Moore-Gilbert wrote, 'I remain in awe at the human brain's powers of adaptation and survival.' I can only wholeheartedly agree with this. That power of adaptation, the fantasy world I shielded myself with via the books, the love of Ha and my family, the knowledge that I had friends rooting for me – allowed me to survive in Myanmar's prisons, and all protect me still.

Ever present in my mind was to do what I regard as my sacred responsibility to my colleagues still in prison in Myanmar, as well as to use my freedom to highlight the plight of the Myanmar people more broadly. It was easier said than done this time around, though, since the stakes were now very high. Not perhaps for me personally but for the possible repercussions of my actions upon my imprisoned colleagues, not least my fellow defendants. The decisive factor was that they had urged me to speak out, fully understanding this may have an impact on them. So, I felt 'authorised', if you like, but the idea that others would continue to bear some of the costs of my actions weighs heavy upon me.

Another self-appointed responsibility was to find out as much as I could about the murder of Khin Maung Shwe (always Jacoob to me) in Insein, and to commemorate this extraordinarily brave and compassionate man. His death had been covered up in Myanmar, and had not come to any international attention. Of course, one terrible reason for that is because his death was just one of at least 4000 other killings made by Myanmar's junta since the coup.

Within a few days of getting back I tapped my network of Myanmar friends to try to find out the truth of what happened to Jacoob. I cannot name them, but people close to my dear friend were able to supply me with the terrible details of his death. These I published in social media, together with some photos of Jacoob. The latter mostly taken before prison, but there was one especially good one of him after he had been taken into custody. By 'good one', I mean that it captured so well his defiant dignity. The upshot of all of this was a huge and international reaction that paid tribute to my friend (I discovered that my assessment of Jacoob was shared by so many others), but also seriously irritated Myanmar's ruling junta. This would have pleased him mightily.

It hardly needs saying that social media is a powerful beast, but certainly I (sometimes accidentally) used it to great effect beyond highlighting Jacoob's murder. As I am sure everyone reading will agree, social media is very hard to get right. In my situation, any situation, it's there as a valve (and escalator) for your anger, fear, anxiety and all sorts of other emotions often best not shared. Sometimes out of anger I would bash out a post (usually triggered by news about the situation of an old friend in Myanmar, or generally due to the junta's wanton cruelty and destruction), allow it to circulate for a few minutes, then delete it. Others I just tapped out with me as the only audience. Other, more deliberative but still angry missives I left out there, including one in which I called Myanmar's junta 'knaves and fools'. I only mention this last one because I later heard definitively that it got under the skin of Min Aung Hlaing personally.

The Jetstar pilot's warning that there would be a good deal of press interest in my return to Australia proved more than correct.

Apparently, some of the TV channels in Australia even filmed the plane as it began its descent into Melbourne.

Once back in Sydney, the requests for interviews and the like numbered in the hundreds. How to handle, how to prioritise these? How to do it effectively – in ways that got an important message across, not only about mine and Ha's experiences, but that would have the most impact on those suffering in Myanmar? How best to convey the thanks that I owed the people of Australia, to my friends and supporters all over the world? How to avoid getting caught up in some pathetic celebrity vortex at the cost of affecting family, and my own integrity?

Obviously, there was no easy solution to any of this, so we just winged it; Ha had better intuition in these matters than I did, and it was fine initially. After a while, we tried to pare things back to an essential core. I ended up doing probably about a dozen interviews, but knocked back – with apologies – a hundred or more others.

Two particular sets of interviews that we did do stood out, and we were satisfied that they would remain our most comprehensive records on events for the time being. One of these formed the basis of a series of articles with Amanda Hodge of the *Australian* newspaper, a national broadsheet. The other was a lengthy television interview with Sarah Ferguson of the Australian Broadcasting Corporation's *7.30*. For any reader overseas, the ABC is Australia's equivalent of the BBC, and *7.30* our most prominent current-affairs program. We were not paid for any of these interviews.

After that we largely eschewed the media – not for any ideological reasons or anything like that, but simply to repair our home life, reacquaint with family and friends and, well, write this book.

It must be said, though, that while media was something that needed to be carefully managed, before setting it aside in order to 'move on', Ha and I got a lot out of it. Interactions with interested people – of all sorts, but united in the fact that we didn't know them before all this and they didn't know us – was (and still is) an absolute delight. Neither of us had experienced any kind of celebrity before, but we appreciated being allowed a glimpse into the emotions our story seemed to stir in others.

When people welcomed me home and praised Ha for her courage and steadfastness, we kept sensing this desire to connect with us that seemed to come from the heart rather than as a product of, say, political sympathy or a concern for the rights or wrongs of what was happening in Myanmar. My plight seemed to have struck a more subterranean core – maybe simply it was a near classical story of fall and redemption, of loss and homecoming? I'm sure Ha's resolute determination to protect her mate, so transparently on display, had something to do with it. Whatever the reasons, I can scarcely recall an encounter – especially in the early days of my return – where the greeting to us was not made amid tears and choking voices. Inevitably, we in turn were moved that other people were so moved. It was all extraordinarily life-affirming, and filled me with a profound gratitude that, even now, I find difficult to put into words.

Some of the most emotionally affecting encounters I had were with people from Myanmar. One in a pharmacy with a Burmese-Australian mother and her two teenage daughters.

She greeted us in tears, which had her daughters in tears, which then brought us to tears. I don't think a coherent word was spoken by any of us. Nevertheless, meaning, in all its complexities, was unmistakable.

I will never forget coming across some young Myanmar migrants working on Sydney's rail system: they were simply raucous in their joy. And the beaming faces of a Myanmar family, newly arrived in Australia, who asked Ha and me to pose with them in front of the Christmas tree in Sydney's Martin Place.

Meanwhile the local Burmese community, among whom we already had longstanding and loyal friends, organised a reception one Saturday morning at a community centre in Sydney's west. It was poignant to learn that since the coup, they have been meeting there every weekend to raise money for their brothers and sisters in Myanmar and their great struggle for freedom. They do this mostly by selling wonderfully delicious Burmese food and sweets to each other. In essence, they have been taxing themselves in the broader cause.

The Burmese community in Australia is neither large nor rich. But, like their family and friends in Myanmar, they are among the best and bravest people I know.

I had been away from Australia nearly two years, and I had missed the drama of the most extreme COVID lockdowns. I was surprised by all sorts of things I encountered in these first few weeks back. I guess what leaped out at me most was how prosperous everyone seemed to be. This is not to deny many inequalities, of course, and my gaze was necessarily limited. Nevertheless, this sure looked like a healthy and wealthy country, and one fantastic place to live.

I caught up on all the events I'd missed, which was in itself an intense experience. On the personal front, this included discovering that my dear Uncle Billy Turnell had died, as had two of my economist heroes, emeritus professors both: Geoff Harcourt and Ronald Findlay. As a current affairs junkie, I had kept up as best I could through Naypyitaw's BBC Wall Service, so I was across big news stories such as the death of Queen Elizabeth II, the Australian federal election and, just to keep it real, the slapping incident at the 2022 Oscars ceremony: oh, dear, Will Smith. Keen to catch up on the Australian stories I had missed, I spent hours scanning a backlog of headlines and clicking on articles every now and again. The story that rocked me most, I think, was the death of Shane Warne. For anyone unfamiliar with the shared sporting obsessions of Australia, the UK and South Asian countries, there is only one game – and it defines true civilisation – cricket. Warne was a high-profile practitioner of that game.

Two weeks after my return, Ha and I went to Canberra for what I guess could be called 'official' meetings. All were immensely pleasurable.

The first of these was with DFAT. There was still some work to do, debriefings to undertake – but also some big thank yous to extend. The size of the team in DFAT that was rounded into helping me took me aback. There were lots of hugs and tears, and – from me – expressions of heartfelt, if inadequate, thanks.

Similar briefings took place with other agencies concerned with foreign relations at the pointy end. One thing I was able to clarify was that no 'deal' had been done to secure my release. No payments and no favours were given to Myanmar's junta to get me back to Australia.

At Parliament House, Ha and I had meetings with the Prime Minister, Anthony Albanese, and Foreign Minister Penny Wong. From the Opposition, we spoke with the shadow Foreign Affairs spokesperson Simon Birmingham, and former Foreign Minister Marise Payne. These meetings were memorable, warm occasions. Albanese was as informal, funny and emotionally expressive as he had been on the phone. Ha got on especially well with Penny Wong, who observed that, 'while not wanting to rework old stereotypes', Ha did not contradict Wong's experience of 'the powerful women who somehow emerge from Vietnam'. Marise Payne was exceedingly kind, and we reminisced fondly about a dinner we'd had together while she was the Minister and on an official visit to Naypyitaw, where at that time I was still roaming free! Simon Birmingham was extremely well-informed on everything to do with our case and voiced much concern about Myanmar's trajectory. This is not fashionable to say, I'm sure, but I came away impressed by all of them.

From the Prime Minister's office we made our way to the House of Representatives, where we were ushered into seats on the floor of the chamber itself. There, we received a standing ovation from the members, and some exceedingly flattering speeches.

In his address, the Prime Minister spoke of the days I had spent in detention and described it as:

something no human being should have to endure and yet he has done it with grace and even in inhumane conditions with profound humanity.

We are so glad, as you've seen from the response across the chamber here, to have you back.

Peter Dutton delivered a no less eloquent speech. Our ordeal, he said, 'went on for way too long . . . against a very significant adversary'.

Both leaders drew accompanying 'hear hears' from all the other MPs. It's hard to adequately respond to such a situation, which so far exceeds the dreams of your life that it is impossible to convey. At a practical level, as the nation's leaders are gazing at you and clapping, it's hard to know where to look. Or what to do. Smile certainly, bow slightly, put a hand over your heart, look a little silly. Ha, with her customary aplomb, pulled it off magnificently, and simply looked elegant and dignified. I looked more like a butler being praised for my shoe-shining prowess.

We went on to the Senate, to another standing ovation, and kind words from Penny Wong and Simon Birmingham.

Heartwarming encounters with friends and strangers alike in Canberra capped off and brought to an end what Ha and I regarded as our official homecoming. It would have also been a natural end to the chronological narrative of this book, too.

Alas, Myanmar's junta had other plans.

18

The Junta Strikes Back

Like one of those horror films in which the seemingly vanquished villain leaps back to life, so – a few days before Christmas – did Myanmar's junta come back to disturb our idyll.

Junta leader Min Aung Hlaing was annoyed with me. I'd been ungrateful for his mercy. Unappreciative of his hospitality. Impolite to his dignity. Face needed to be saved. I had made some online posts, and appeared on TV. He was not going to take it anymore.

Consequently, a little more than a month after my return, my world once again came under threat.

My amnesty, the thing I had longed for each of the 650 days in captivity – was officially revoked.

It was DFAT that notified me. An afternoon phone call from Ian Gerard, passing on the news from Angela and the Embassy in Yangon. A wax-sealed official document had arrived at the Embassy from Myanmar's Ministry of Foreign Affairs, declaring that – to not waste its mix of pompous, yet not quite eloquently expressed umbrage – Sean Turnell:

... was guilty of breaking the rules specified by ... his amnesty decree by sharing misinformation about Myanmar in some social media ... and in interviews with some news media before completion of the remaining punishment term ...

Therefore the amnesty decree for Mr SEAN TURNELL, an Australian citizen, issued by the State Administration Council with Order No.74/2022 is annulled ...

The decree made a point of saying that my original amnesty had been a decision of the Chairman of the State Administration Council himself.

Two days later, another decree was issued, demanding that I appear at Pyinmana District Court on 21 December 2022 to answer for these breaches under the Code of Criminal Procedure, Section 401, Sub-Section (3). Failure to appear would see the original sentence apply once more, and a warrant issued for my arrest.

To highlight the nuttiness of all this, let me tell you that these letters were issued on 6 and 8 December respectively, officially translated on 11 December – but not actually delivered to the Australian Embassy until 20 December! This was one day before I was supposed to appear in Pyinmana Court. Had I been mad enough to want to present myself at the court, it would not have been physically possible: no flights would have got me there in time. Pyinmana is right near Naypyitaw, so even with the best flight connections, it is at least 24 hours away from Sydney.

There was also the fact that I had been deported from Myanmar and ordered never to return ...

Initially, I was inclined to laugh it off. This was so patently absurd, the junta so devoid of legitimacy and international standing that this was all impotent sound and fury, signifying nothing, surely? Indeed, if I'd pissed off Min Aung Hlaing, then wasn't this a good thing? The man had unjustly locked me up for almost two years, tormented my family and friends. He was a murderer and usurper. A man responsible for mass rape and genocide. In speaking out against the treatment he had meted out to me – and far worse to others – I was only doing my duty to truth and (real) justice. To do anything else, to stay silent, was not possible for anyone with any sense of decency. Wasn't it so?

Well, yes, but none of this was to deny that this reach-out from the junta did us harm. DFAT took the decree extremely seriously, and told us that should the junta take the matter to Interpol, it could lead to a Red Notice being issued against me, which would allow other jurisdictions to arrest and deport me back to Myanmar. They acknowledged it was a long shot – and that most countries would dismiss out of hand a request from the junta, even if Interpol itself agreed to accept it.

I was aghast at this – surely Interpol would not accept such a thing? It turned out, however, that while Interpol usually issued Red Notices for the likes of Osama Bin Laden, Al-Saadi Gaddafi, drug cartel chiefs and assorted Russian gangsters, on occasion they have also issued them for political activists who are not criminals but are branded as such by authoritarian rogue regimes.

The outcome was a severe up-ending of our short-term travel plans, at least. Most egregious was that it knocked out our eagerly anticipated – many times the topic of the prison phone calls between Ha and me – return to Vietnam: Ha's birthplace, home to her mum and dad, and a whole cast of beloved family and friends. Visits to the US and UK also had to be postponed. In the scheme of things, it was minor stuff, but it mattered to us.

Probably more wounding was the psychological effect. What had been demonstrated in all of this was that Myanmar's blood-drenched junta could still reach out to me. Still determine the parameters of my freedom. Still be the arbiter of my freedom of speech. And there would be no end to it.

News of the junta's decision to revoke my amnesty and seek my re-arrest did not take off in Australia until an article by Amanda Hodge appeared in the *Australian* newspaper on 26 January, after which it 'went viral'. Prompted by Hodge's and other reports, a DFAT spokesman responded that:

> The government is deeply concerned that Myanmar authorities have annulled Professor Turnell's amnesty and issued a subpoena for him to appear in a Myanmar court. The Australian Government never accepted the basis of Professor Turnell's detention, nor the charges against him, and we are disappointed that he is now being asked to answer for an undefined offence following his release . . .

On our behalf, Janelle Saffin issued a statement rebutting root and branch the junta's actions. Her opening comments captured the matter succinctly, we thought: 'This is all complete legal nonsense . . .'

Of course, it was a truth that also summed up all of the experiences of the 22 months I had been detained. Finally, a verdict to agree on.

Some Final Thoughts and Acknowledgements

The junta's vengeful actions towards me have clipped my wings a little, but fundamentally I am today a free man.

The same cannot be said for the nearly 55 million people of Myanmar. Since my release, the brutality of the ruling junta there has only increased in scale and intensity. The death toll mounts, the torture continues, the economy reaches new lows – war and pestilence literally stalk the land.

Whatever its original objectives, Min Aung Hlaing's coup has obviously failed. Yet, the military remains in charge, adrift in atrocity, seemingly devoid of ideas beyond their own worst instincts.

Inspired by renowned Russian writer and dissident Aleksandr Solzhenitsyn, throughout my time in detention the image that Myanmar had come to resemble an archipelago of prisons was often on my mind. Now the situation is worse. Less a nation of prison 'islands', the mainland state of Myanmar has become one giant prison that ensnares just about the whole of its population.

On every indicator available, Myanmar continues its slide towards a failed state.

For Ha and me, away from all of this at home in Australia, things have turned a corner. The traumatic events recalled in these pages have left their legacy, but with each passing day we grow stronger, and life becomes more meaningful. We do most of the things we promised we would do during our calls and letters. Not quite all. Life is messy. Those marathon walks we were going to do? Well, the couch is so comfortable, and streaming TV shows so seductive.

The ongoing despair for us then remains the situation facing our friends in Myanmar. Most of my fellow prisoners languish in the country's dreadful prisons, and as I return to the daily enjoyments of my life in a free and prosperous democracy, my mind wanders incessantly to what they face.

Throughout my time in Myanmar's prisons, I imagined writing this book. The thought of that gave me purpose and pleasure. Much of this pleasure, however, came from the extra thought that by writing a book, I would get to thank the people who gave so much to me, often at immense cost to themselves.

Consequently, this must be a longer set of acknowledgements than might be typical. I don't want to just thank people who helped me write this book. I want to thank people – and there are so many of you – who helped save my life.

Let me begin by thanking my co-accused: Daw Aung San Suu Kyi; U Winston Set Aung; U Soe Win; U Kyaw Win. All are patriots. All are courageous and deeply moral people who did their best to create the peace and prosperity in Myanmar that its people deserve. I admire them unreservedly. Their imprisonment is a monstrous injustice, and I crave the day they are unconditionally free.

I owe so much to other political prisoners I met in Myanmar's jails. In more ways than I have been able to describe in these pages, these brave people rescued and protected me. Some I have been able to mention – Paing Ye Thu, Ye Min Oo, U Min Thu, Jacoob. Others I did not even know by name. Many more I dare not name here for fear my praise could deliver to them further retribution. My dear friends and saviours: for the moment, I can only say thank you.

Similarly unnamed must be the wonderful young people with whom I worked at various policy and research institutions in Myanmar. They are the country's future, scattered all over the world though they are now. Hopefully soon, a fairer wind might bring them back home. There and then to begin the task of rebuilding.

Beyond the people of Myanmar are people from all over the place who went the distance for me.

At the 'official' level, let me begin here by thanking the folks from the Australian Embassy in Yangon, and the people back home in Australia's Department of Foreign Affairs and Trade. Some of them have appeared in the text above already, so to simplify matters here – and to avoid terrible mistakes – let me name them in alphabetical order, and without rank or precise affiliation: Paul Bruce, Nicholas Coppel, Angela Corcoran, Nicholas and Andrew Cumpston, Tony Egan, Andrea Faulkner, Ian Gerard, Julie Heckscher, Vanessa Hegarty, Jeremy Kruse, Kim Lamb, Kate Logan, Tricia Martino, Dylan Roux, Fabia Shah, Jeff Turner, Tim Vistarini, and Victoria Wheeler. Thank you to Vice Admiral David Johnston, and the many men and women of the Australian Defence Forces for their unobtrusive efforts on my behalf.

Australian politicians of all stripes have been helpful and generous to me. Special thanks to Australia's Prime Minister Anthony Albanese; Foreign Minister Penny Wong; senators Simon Birmingham and Marise Payne; MPs Andrew Charlton, Anoulack Chanthivong (and his adviser, Aaron Rule); Jim Chalmers; Mike Freelander; Andrew Leigh; Jamie Parker; and Alicia Payne. As told in this book, former Australian Prime Minister Kevin Rudd volunteered to be an envoy to Myanmar's junta on my behalf. No small thing this, and I thank him for it.

Janelle Saffin is a politician, too, and used all her political wiles to try to secure my release. Even more importantly, perhaps, she deployed her compassion and endless energy in assisting Ha and my entire family in getting through it all. I have written of Janelle in the text. In this spot, however, let me just say, Janelle, you were a marvel.

With fellow Aussie Leigh Mitchell I shared many a Myanmar moment, and an ever-growing mutual love for the place. Thank you, Leigh.

I was lucky enough to have some loyal and powerful friends in and around the US Government, working both in Myanmar and in Washington. Ha contacted them within a few days of my arrest. This reach-out was enormously important in protecting me in the early days of my incarceration, a time when my treatment swung between caution on behalf of the junta and a desire to make an example of me. The US State Department became the 'front door', through which Ha found her way to the US

Treasury, and to the offices of Senate Minority Leader (and longtime supporter of the people of Myanmar) Mitch McConnell. Among the specific individuals from the above agencies, and more besides, it gives me considerable pleasure to thank: Alex Albertine (already mentioned in this story as a virtuous book trafficker), Derek Chollet, Robert Kaproth, Scott Kofmehl (likewise already mentioned as a book man), Scot Marciel, Teresa McGhie, Mike Martin, Derek Mitchell, Steve Parker, Jennifer Petersen, Paul Pleva, Lynn Salinger, Thomas Vajda. In Senator McConnell's office, present and past, I would like to give special tribute to Robert Karam and to Paul Grove – when Ha told me they had been in contact with her I rejoiced.

Scarcely behind the US in its energetic attempt to alleviate my situation was the government – and authorities more broadly – of the United Kingdom. Special thanks here to Dan Chugg, Joe Fisher, Rurik Marsden, Ed Miles, Andrew Patrick, Joanne Raisin and to the indefatigable Tom Coward. Tom was one of my principal suppliers of books, and scoured regional bookstores as well as his own shelves in keeping up the flow. King Charles III was a constant champion of my cause, and in his quiet and unobtrusive way was a great support for Ha. I found out about his concerns for me even as I languished in Insein, and the knowledge helped sustain me. After my release, Ha and I met the King at Windsor Castle, days before his coronation. A meeting, a gesture, that will stay with us.

Michael Marett-Crosby is from the UK, but his presence in my story defies easy categorisation, least of all geographical. One day, perhaps his good works might become publicly known. In the meantime, my dear friend and brother-in-arms, thank you.

At one with Michael in endeavours on our behalf has been Mathea Falco, my sage friend from the city by the Bay. It could be said of both me and Myanmar that we have no better friend. James McTaggart, our friend in the Highlands of Scotland, thank you, dear sir.

The labour movement in Australia was wholeheartedly supportive of me, as they have always been supportive of democracy in Myanmar across the decades. Special thanks to president Alison Barnes of the National Tertiary Education Union, and old friend Kate Lee of Union Aid Abroad-APHEDA. Equally, on the capital side, my thanks especially go to the Australian Chamber of Commerce in Myanmar (AustCham), whose members collectively and individually did all sorts of things behind the scenes. Special thanks here to Chris Hughes and Bec Mohr, as well as Brad Jones, Kevin Murphy, Gill Pattinson, Eugene Quah and Chit Su Win Htein.

Accion International and its CEO Michael Schlein have been extraordinarily kind to Ha and me. Similarly big hearted have been George and Alex Soros, and the Asia teams more broadly at Open Society Foundations. Our recovery would have been considerably more uphill without their generosity.

My case was taken up by a great many diplomats in Yangon representing a host of countries. Apart from the ambassadors of the US and the UK already noted I want to particularly thank Japan's Ambassador, Ichiro Maruyama; Singapore Ambassador Vanessa Chan; Denmark's John Nielsen; and Italy's Alessandra Schiavo.

My university, Macquarie, was fantastic. Vice Chancellor Bruce Dowton was in touch with DFAT on a weekly basis, and mobilised the university's own communications and marketing unit to press my case. The Department of Economics at Macquarie, led by its head, Lisa Magnani, supported Ha throughout.

Professors Wylie Bradford and Tim Harcourt have been with us through thick and thin, and took on many burdens that my situation imposed. Big brains, bigger hearts. Wylie – straight over the top, I think!

Tinzar Lwin and Alison Vicary – there at the start of all of this for me, and there throughout.

Academics from around the world reacted with alacrity and empathy to my situation. As noted in the book, a vast range of actions were put in place, from petitions to protests. I'm especially thankful to David Throsby, Peter McCawley, Melissa Crouch, Charlotte Galloway, Nicholas Cheesman, Monique Skidmore, Jonathan Liljeblad, Hal Hill, Martin Krygier, Choi Shing Kwok and Moe Thuzar (and everyone at the Institute of Southeast Asian Studies, Singapore), Peter Warr, Susan Banki, Andrew Selth, Lindsay Stubbs, Htwe Htwe Thein, Chris Lamb, Peter Drysdale, and Nicholas Farelly.

Powerful, principled, and purposeful women are a constant in my life. They appear through this book. Maureen Aung-Thwin and Priscilla Clapp are two of them, and personify all that I like best about New York and Washington respectively. In these two cities they are surely the centre of all things Myanmar in the USA. Leanne Ussher, while in New York, led from there the campaign for my release, applying her boundless imagination and compassion to the task. Leanne and Heinz (Jufer): I knew you would, but thank you, my dear friends!

Zali Win – banker, philanthropist, wise counsel, friend – greatly in your debt, mate. To dear friend and colleague Bob Conrad, with whom I was often 'in the trenches' in Myanmar, thanks of equal magnitude are happily due. Matt Hamilton was usually alongside Bob and me, the personification of the engaged scholar. Matthew Arnold – much obliged too, mate.

Friends old and new rallied to our cause. Among the former were the crew from James Meehan High School: Karen Newman, Elizabeth Campbell, Melinda Coenen-Eyre, John Eccleston, Steve Golding, Gabi Haiden, James Hansen, Kim Hogan, Linda McDermott, Greg Reid, Tony van der Ark.

Friends, colleagues, campaigners for Myanmar, journalists and more – thank you: Kim Aris, Mia Astari, Daw Zin Mar Aung, Sean Aylmer, Fahmid Bhuiya, Igor Blazevic, John Brandon, Ross and Maureen Brown, Victoria Bruce, John Buchanan, Steve Cima, Catherine Condon, Kelley Currie, Neville Daw, Michael Dobbie, Paul Donowitz, Ben Dunant, Ross Dunkley, Ali Fowle, Sarah Ferguson, Kyaw Saw Han, Joan Harcourt (all the Harcourts!), Amanda Hodge, Paul Hutton, Larry Jagan, Tom Kean, Jeremy Kloiser-Jones, Herve Lemahieu, Kaye Lin, Nyantha Maw Lin, Joanne Lindsay, Bertil Lintner, Mark McDowell, Craig and Hester Macmillan, Poppy McPherson, Dave Mathieson, Mary Miller, Tocher Mitchell, Jack Myint, Maung Maung Myint, Moe Zaw Oo, Frank Perez, Thi Thi Power, John Reed, Gwen Robinson, Ben Rogers, Jeff Stein, David Steinberg, Ian Storkey, Debbie Stothard, Alison Tate, Phil and Kanchana Thornton, Show Ei Ei Tun, Dr Kyaw Moe Tun, Zaw Zaw Tuseng, Liz Tydeman, Steve Ujvarosy, Victoria White, David Wolfberg, Yadanar, U Soe Win, Chosein Yamahata, Aung Zaw, Thant Zin.

Three sheilas and a bloke (their label to confuse the prison guards) – Lyndal Barry, Sophie Butcher, Jo Daniels, Clay O'Brien – thank you!

To Matthew Lee and Lu Ha. Just how many times do you have to come to the rescue of your neighbour? Thank you for being there for us, going above and beyond.

Instrumental in my recovery at home has been the kindness extended to me by Kylie Moore-Gilbert and Peter Greste, both of whom preceded me in that category of Australians unjustly detained abroad – a sadly large and growing list. I have noted already how Kylie's book was of great assistance to me. I am pleased to say that the courage and compassion of the author herself matches the virtues of her book.

My imprisonment cost my extended family much stress and anxiety. Apologies for this, but thank you for your efforts on my behalf, and your love beyond it all. My cousin Blake Turnell, greatly known to the world as the musician Chillinit, rallied his many fans (I believe tens of thousands responded) to campaign for my release.

Glenn Worley. My closest friend for over 50 years. Thank you, mate. We've just about done all we planned in Year 6 I reckon. London's Elysian fields only now await. And if they're full, the Fountains Abbey will do nicely.

And then there are the people who guided me through this book! Could not possibly have done it without my literary agent, Margaret Gee. Margaret has her own family connection to Myanmar but is, by popular consensus, the superstar in her field. Certainly that has been our experience, but on top of this she is super nice. Sophie Ambrose from Penguin has been a visionary and inspiration for this book. Simply, I wouldn't have written it without her. Anne Reilly has been a superb editor. She would disclaim it, I'm sure, but on so many occasions she has turned sow ears into silk purses. Precisely the same applies to my copy-editor and photograph producer, Kalhari Jayaweera. I cannot write highly enough of this team of bibliophile wordsmiths. Of course, any remaining oddities of 'voice' in this book reflect the underlying oddity of the author himself.

Among all my debts, the last are both the heaviest but also the most joyful to record. My dad, Peter Turnell, is the most decent and genuinely moral man I have ever encountered. To the extent that I have any virtues at all, they stem from his lived example and that of my dear late mother, Diana Turnell. The home they created was a place of profound love. My sister, Lisa Brandt; brother-in-law, Michael, and nephews, Timothy and Mitchell Brandt, I put through hell and back. As always, they rallied with love and a practical just-get-it-done philosophy, which they have often had to leverage to help their sometimes hapless brother and uncle. Tim and Mitch – Australia's future is assured if you are representative of our young men. To my Vietnamese mum and dad, Vu Huu Nam and Ung Thi Thu, thank you for your love and manifest kindnesses. I crave being back with you, and all of our extended family, in our second home of Hanoi.

Our daughter, Phuong Pham. Seeing you emerge to be the wonderful person you are has made everything worthwhile. You rose to the occasion magnificently dear P, and my pride in all that you do is boundless.

Curtis Slover. How do you thank someone who puts their own life and safety on the line for you – and does it day after day for nearly two years? You cannot fully, of course. But to you, sir, the embodiment of the very creed of the Great Republic, thank you. To Curtis's wife, Jill Bradshaw – thank you for your own great efforts for us, and for letting Curtis venture ever more into the breach.

Finally, to my wife, Ha Vu. There is not the space here to write of the debt I owe you, or the love I have for you. Instead then, let me devote all of the words in this book to you. In so many ways, this story is yours.

Notes

p. ix   'We are vanquished, for a moment . . .' Marc Bloch, dedication to fellow historian Lucien Febvre in Bloch's *The Historian's Craft* (first published in 1949 as *Apologie pour l'histoire*), Manchester University Press, Manchester 1992. The last great work of Bloch, *The Historian's Craft* was written while France was under Nazi occupation, during which time Bloch suffered greatly as a consequence of his principled role in the resistance. Bloch was executed by the Nazis in 1944.

p. x   'For the missing names . . .' Reflecting most common usage, throughout this book I use the name of Myanmar for the country also widely known (and officially known before 1989) as Burma. This choice is not meant to convey any judgement on my part as to the appropriateness of this name (the arguments in favour of Burma are well understood by me – indeed, depending on context, I have often used the name Burma myself), but simply the fact that 'Myanmar' was the name overwhelmingly employed with respect to the events described in this book. However, the label 'Burmese' continues to be the common adjective used for the collective peoples of the country.

p. 32   'Meanwhile, as a consequence of my disrupted interview with the BBC. . .' See, for instance, this report in the *Guardian* newspaper on the day of my arrest, 'Myanmar: Australian adviser to Aung San Suu Kyi, Sean Turnell, "being detained"', *Guardian*, 6 February 2021.

p. 33 'The statement concluded by saying that Ha and the family...' Anthony Galloway, '"He brought jobs, investment and hope": Family calls for release of Australian academic held in Myanmar', *Sydney Morning Herald*, 9 February 2021.

p. 41 'On her release, Christa Avery herself voiced support for Ha's suggestion...' '"Incredibly relieved": Australian couple freed from house arrest in Myanmar', *Guardian*, 5 April 2021.

p. 42 'According to the transcript of the call provided to Ha...' Vice Admiral Johnston would have another go a few months after this first effort. Alas for me, and for the theory that Myanmar's junta were responsive to foreign military outreach, this would have no more success. Soe Win's response was privately communicated to Ha.

p. 51 'It was after reading this book...' Interview transcript, Christiane Amanpour with Aung San Suu Kyi, CNN, December 24, 2012; edition.cnn.com/TRANSCRIPTS/1212/24/ampr.01.html?nav-edition=on

p. 52 'Likewise valuable were the recollections of Louis Walinsky...', Louis Walinsky, *Economic Development in Burma 1951–1960*, The Twentieth Century Fund, New York, 1962.

p. 58 'In the words of fashionable-once-more American...' Hamilton cited in Ron Chernow, *Alexander Hamilton*, Penguin Press, New York, 2004, p. 156.

p. 87 'The only treatment these wounds received was a purple powder...' The purple powder was, I believe, gentian violet, derived from a widely used medicinal plant in Myanmar.

p. 100 'Even more effective in this context...' Robert D. Kaplan, *Imperial Grunts: On the Ground with the American Military, from Mongolia to the Philippines to Iraq and Beyond*, Vintage Books, New York, 2006.

p. 108 'Ross told Australian reporters on getting home...' Chris Barrett, '"People were out to get me": Australian publisher speaks out after release from Myanmar jail', *Sydney Morning Herald*, 2 May 2021.

p. 123 '[I]f the rule of law were applied...' This quote, and all subsequent quotes from my legal team, comes from the weekly summaries of my legal proceedings provided by our law firm in Yangon, and privately communicated to Ha. These summaries include information that could endanger friends and colleagues in Myanmar, and thus are not in the public domain. Bold emphasis is in the original.

p. 165 'I can be confident in this assessment...' Sean Turnell, *Fiery Dragons: Banks, Moneylenders and Microfinance in Myanmar*, NIAS Press, Copenhagen, 2009.

p. 170 'One of these included Daw Suu's female bodyguard...' 'Ex-Bodyguard of Myanmar's Suu Kyi Given Two More Years in Prison', *Irrawaddy*, 31 March 2022, irrawaddy.com/news/burma/ex-bodyguard-of-myanmars-suu-kyi-given-two-more-years-in-prison.html

p. 180 'Indeed, I think if I was, we really would have something to worry about...' This is word-for-word as I recall it – I remember the conversation and the question well, so often did I tell the story later.

p. 185 'Friends also actively marked the anniversary by submitting a formal petition to the Australian parliament...' 'Appoint Envoy to get Sean Turnell out of Myanmar jail', Parliamentary petition, March 2022, aph.gov.au/e-petitions/petition/EN3917

p. 186 'Rudd was up for the gig. He wrote to the Myanmar Ambassador...' Kevin Rudd's letter offering his assistance was sent to Myanmar's Ambassador to Australia on 20 December 2021. Ha was copied in on the letter, which is in her possession.

p. 187 'US Secretary of State Antony Blinken called for my release...' 'Joint statement on Australia-US Ministerial Consultations (AUSMIN) 2021', 16 September 2021, state.gov/joint-statement-on-australia-u-s-ministerial-consultations-ausmin-2021/. The second statement at a meeting of the Quad (11 February 2022) demanding my release: 'Secretary Antony J. Blinken And Australian Foreign Minister Marise Payne, Indian External Affairs Minister Dr. Subrahmanyam Jaishankar, and Japanese Foreign Minister Yoshimasa Hayashi At a Joint Press Availability', 11 February 2022, state.gov/secretary-antony-j-blinken-and-australian-foreign-minister-marise-payne-indian-external-affairs-minister-dr-subrahmanyam-jaishankar-and-japanese-foreign-minister-yoshim/

p. 188 'He even started assigning the congratulations...' 'Myanmar Releases the Detained Australian Professor as per PM Hun Sen's Request', Fresh News, 7 February 2022, freshnewsasia.com/index.php/en/localnews/27271-2022-02-07-06-27-28.html

p. 189 'He "would like to ask for understanding..."' 'Cambodian prime minister admits "mistake", says Australian economist Sean Turnell still detained in Myanmar', *ABC News*, 8 February 2022.

p. 199 'The prosecution strategy was essentially to set out a narrative...' I have made some corrections here to the grammar of the English translation of the official charge.

p. 203 'One document, for instance, was about the memorandum...' This document is discussed in Part 1 of this book, on page 26.

p. 205 'It led to the issuing of a statement...' 'Professor Sean Turnell Trial', Media Release, 10 June 2022, Foreign Minister of Australia, Senator Penny Wong, foreignminister.gov.au/minister/penny-wong/media-release/professor-sean-turnell-trial

p. 215 'This last point used an interview of junta leader...' This statement of Min Aung Hlaing was widely reported in the Myanmar press, and reached us (with much incredulity) in the prison. I have not been able to find any reference to the claim in the international press, or that part of the Myanmar press searchable online.

p. 237 'Australia's Foreign Minister, Penny Wong...' 'Sentencing of Professor Sean Turnell', Statement, Minister for Foreign Affairs, Penny Wong, 29 September 2022, foreignminister.gov.au/minister/penny-wong/media-release/sentencing-professor-sean-turnell

p. 239 'Some died because of the bomb...' Han Thit, 'Bomb blasts, gunfire at Myanmar's biggest prison kills eight, including guards', *Myanmar Now*, 19 October 2022, myanmar-now.org/en/news/bomb-blasts-gunfire-at-myanmars-biggest-prison-kills-eight-including-guards?page=1

p. 240 'I had no answer then or now...' I did not know the names of these wonderful individuals, and I probably could not name them even if I did. No further prisoners have been formally executed at the time of writing. However, it must also be pointed out that, according to one reliable source, over 1000 prisoners have been killed by their captors in Myanmar's jails since the coup. Assistance Association for Political Prisoners (Burma), *Daily Briefing Since Coup*, continuing series: aappb.org/wp-content/uploads/2023/03/English_-Deaths-in-Junta-Detainment-27-March

p. 253 'So, alas, I cannot report cheers...' I regretted this, since I'd recalled well the excitement of this moment as related by Kylie Moore-Gilbert, *The Unchained Sky*, Ultimo Press, Sydney, 2022, p. 400.

p. 255 '**Occasionally in this job you have a big moment . . .**' Anthony Albanese cited in Katherine Murphy, '"A remarkable man": Anthony Albanese confirms release of Sean Turnell from Myanmar jail', =*Guardian*, 18 November 2022.

p. 256 '**I am overwhelmed with joy at the news . . .**' Ha's statement cited by Penny Wong, Minister for Foreign Affairs, Press Conference, Adelaide, 18 November 2022, foreignminister.gov.au/minister/penny-wong/transcript/press-conference-adelaide-1

p. 267 '**In his address, the Prime Minister spoke of the days . . .**' Our reception in the parliament was widely reported, but for a taste and the comments of Anthony Albanese, see Joseph Huitson, 'Australian economist Sean Turnell given standing ovation in Parliament after being released from prison in Myanmar', SkyNews.com.au, 1 December 2022.

p. 269 '**A wax-sealed official document had arrived at the Embassy. . .**' Extract from document privately supplied to me from inside Myanmar, 20 December 2022.

p. 272 '**The government is deeply concerned that Myanmar authorities have annulled . . .**' The revocation of my amnesty was widely reported, but for an accessible taste, see Erin Handley, 'Australian government "deeply concerned" after Myanmar military junta revokes Sean Turnell's prison amnesty', *ABC News*, 26 January 2023.

Discover a new favourite

Visit **penguin.com.au/readmore**